Igor Zabel
Contemporary Art Theory

AF395560

JRP|RINGIER & LES PRESSES DU RÉEL

Igor Zabel
*Contemporary
Art Theory*

Igor Španjol [ed.]

Table of Contents

Foreword

Translated from Slovenian by Sunčan Stone.

Unfortunately, the lives of people and what they leave behind is usually evaluated in its entirety and given full meaning only once they have departed. The work of Igor Zabel was marked by his broad horizon, which was always noticeable, no matter whether he was studying comparative literature, history of art and philosophy, or, later on, researching 20th century art, writing on contemporary art, performing curatorial work (at his base, the Moderna galerija in Ljubljana, or outside of it), writing short prose, literary or art criticism or translating literary and scientific works. The years that Igor Zabel lived fully and creatively in numerous fields were truly cut too short; the traces that remain behind him, luckily, preserve not only his vast, insightful and in-depth knowledge on various aspects of art and broader cultural creativity, but also present an inspiring source for future research in modern and contemporary art—from socialist realism, high modernism and conceptual art to postmodernism and contextual art—particularly in Central, Eastern and South Eastern Europe.

To shed light upon and evaluate the importance of Igor Zabel's work, especially in the field of visual arts, and at the same time keep his heritage in dialogue with contemporary theoretical and curatorial practices is one of the key goals of the Igor Zabel Association for Culture and Theory. ERSTE Foundation co-founded the Association together with the Zabel family in 2008 to promote knowledge sharing and networking in contemporary visual arts and culture as well as to encourage cultural dialogue in the Central and South Eastern European region and beyond.

Following the established and prestigious Igor Zabel Award for Culture and Theory, which is awarded biennially for theoretical, curatorial and scientific achievements in the field of visual culture related to Central and South Eastern Europe, we now present this collection of Igor Zabel's texts on modern and contemporary art to the scientific public as well as the broader audience. These texts were all published in various catalogues, magazines and books during his lifetime, but now they have been compiled into a single publication and translated into English for the very first time.

The structure of this book, which has been worked on with great patience and diligence for a long period of time, was originated by two close colleagues of Igor Zabel, Barbara Borčić, director of the SCCA-Center for Contemporary Art in Ljubljana, and Zoja Skušek, his longtime publisher in Slovenia, who came up with the first selection of texts. Unfortunately, not all of the texts could be included, and so, during the preparation of this book, we once again realized just how vast an opus Igor Zabel left behind.

We would like to thank Moderna galerija Ljubljana, and especially its director Zdenka Badovinac, for all the support they offered in the production of this book, and most certainly Igor Španjol for his dedicated editorial work. Our thanks go also to Katja Kranjc, Sabina Povšič and Dejan Habicht from Moderna galerija for their most kind support. Further, we would like to thank Rawley Grau for his excellent and accurate translations into English, and Zoja Skušek and Jana Intihar Ferjan for giving us the permission to use the bibliography. Our thanks also go to Dunja Kukovec, who helped this project almost to its completion. This book would not have emerged without the initial encouragement given by Josef Dabernig, and we wholeheartedly thank him for this.

Mateja Kos Zabel and Urška Jurman,
Igor Zabel Association for Culture and Theory

Christine Böhler and Christiane Erharter,
ERSTE Foundation

Theory as Poetry

Translated from Slovenian by Sunčan Stone.

"If you feel like working on the exhibition, it would be cool if we got together next week and came up with the plan for the outline for the proposal for the main action plan, whadaya think?" This is how collaborations with Igor Zabel usually kicked off and how he, in his characteristically humorous style, functioned in the numerous cooperative projects he worked on and how he reacted to them. He approached large and demanding specialist tasks as well as complex art and current cultural concepts with humor and in a playful manner, with an ironic distance and critical skepticism. He looked upon his own work in the light of almost all of the Eastern European sins, as shown and synthesized in the exhibition *Seven Sins*,[1] i.e., collectivism, utopism, masochism, cynicism, laziness, unprofessionalism and love of the West. It seems that, with his way of working, he gave the best example of what he defended as important in his texts:

critical, even though often ironic and playful, cautious reactions to all of the contradictions in the ideological, social and cultural discourses that surrounded him. The analysis and reflection of his everyday circumstances thus coincided with his research on the broader and more complex structures that defined these intimate and banal marginal experiences, these ephemeral, yet charming events.

In his everyday operative work,[2] albeit demanding and strenuous, he saw the profession of a curator predominantly as intellectual pleasure and as an opportunity to foster an art discourse and theoretical studies based on the deconstruction of the traditional art history logic of linear development that is built upon an a priori value system, arrogant confidence, ignorance and simplification of terms. The Slovenian painter Sergej Kapus ascertained that in Zabel's expanded understanding of art, "the recognition that the subject's position cannot be presented as a relation between consistency and the focus of the artwork and a context that would remain outside of it as a frame or a background"[3] was of key importance.

Regardless of his incredible erudition, penetrating thought and enviable intellectual constitution, he was too busy as a curator in the full meaning of the word to have time to write books—"As soon as this exhibition ends, I will start searching through my computer and start on a book…"[4] —thus almost his entire priceless legacy can be found in the vast collection of individual essays and articles written after lectures. So this book is truly the least we owe him. He elegantly set one of the first volumes of his collected essays on its way with a modest commentary that we can borrow on this occasion as well: "It is easy to ascertain that the emergence of these texts was decisively connected to my work in the Moderna galerija in Ljubljana. By this I do not have in mind merely individual exhibition projects, but all of the multidimensional and lively events that take place within it. The personal meetings with numerous artists, critics, curators and others were of great importance for the texts that are collected here. The debates with certain artists that I write about here were much more than courteous conversations or additional information on their work, for they influenced my understanding of art and time and thus my writing."[5]

The texts in this book emerged during a period of extremely intense development in contemporary art and some of them are more than ten years old, yet they have an obvious dimension of duration, even though Zabel was well aware of how contemporary art is constantly changing and ages quickly, in the same way that the artworks he wrote about do. Even more, the development of events in international art scenes and in the local cultural and political scene once again proves their freshness, relevance and great importance. Therefore we did not deal with his texts as a legacy and with nostalgia, but as a live language and material of valuable potential from which we can learn and on which we have to build upon in the future.

Of course, in cases like this, we have to ask ourselves how the author would attempt to deal with the translation of his essays. Zoja Skušek, the editor of Zabel's books that were published in the Slovene language, and her collaborator Barbara Borčić prepared the first selection of texts for this book and divided them into four chapters. The first, *East, West, and Between*, is dedicated to geopolitical issues: the dialogue between (the former) West and East and their perception of the other in the context of the complex relations that followed the fall of the Berlin Wall. The second chapter, *Strategies and Spaces of Art*, covers the issue of the art system: the strategies of exhibiting, the roles of the curator and the institutional frame of art production. The third chapter, *Ad Personam*, presents Zabel's discussion of individual artistic opuses and thematic complexes, in which he develops a new understanding of the art tradition in Slovenia, founded on avant-garde practices. The chapter *Extras* is a selection of more personal columns that will bring his authentic views on life and work closer, especially to those who did not know Igor Zabel personally.

"It was only during my last visit to Slovenia that I realised to what extent learning about Slovenian art was truly connected to reading Igor's texts and trying to understand his special way of looking at things," Brian Holmes told Zdenka Badovinac.[6] When discussing phenomena and trends of Slovenian art in the 20th and 21st century, from impressionism and social realism to conceptual art and the most recent contemporary practices,[7] as represented in the chapter *Ad Personam*, Igor Zabel disputed the narrow definitions and borders of art and always asked himself how any individual term should be understood first. He thought everything out precisely before he attempted to deal with the canonically defined modernistic art traditions. In most cases, he discovered that a certain art term is applied to a more complex part of culture, and he ascertained that individual practices, such as for instance avant-garde art and politics, can't be divided from each other. This is why some of the best works of art often move away from the established principles and dominant patterns or belong to a sort of intermediary field.

He attentively (re)systematized the complex and heterogeneous art production in the Slovenian space, provided the necessary theoretical referential frame and —taking the global paradigmatic changes into account— initiated a new interpretation tradition in which he did not overlook its complexity and constitutive contradictions. To this, his precise understanding of the often neglected problem of the context in which a certain art practice emerges and through which it obtains its specific function, value (understanding its goals and evaluating how successfully they have been fulfilled) and meaning was of great importance. He was aware that in a world that had experienced a deep social, economic and political transformation and was defined by the processes of integration as well as differentiation, there was a need for a new definition of the position of art and other fields linked to these changes. At the same time, he patiently explained what these re-evaluations really meant and why were they necessary: in short, we could summarize, in order to disable the establishment and preservation of the dominant model of control over cultural production, the model that is based on processing art tradition into mythology and nation-constituting unambiguity, on excluding and marginalizing all "phony" art approaches, on ideologizing culture, reticence and the isolation of the national space.

His professional work in the international context, which also strongly marked the tactical starting points of the activities of the Ljubljana Moderna galerija and thus almost the entire Slovenian cultural space in the 1990s, also emerged from his critical awareness: "… the possibility of an author, institution or cultural space establishing itself as a more or less relevant factor in the international world of art is based on the fact that they can respond to the events in this world from their own, unique standpoint. Of course, this is not an appearance in an ethnologically characteristic costume, but a standpoint that can enable a new view in the international network or a new perspective on it."[8] This view was, of course, critical towards the systems of differentiation and exclusion, new divisions and strategies of the strong Western countries in preserving their dominant position in the global culture, and especially towards the growing role of multinational global capital, new structures of nobility and their exploitation of critical art.

When cooperating internationally, he systematically and with great affection took into account the possibility of the productive exploitation of those multilayered and complex conditions and circumstances of his operation that were traditionally understood as an obstacle. Honestly, and sometimes even over-naively, he enjoyed the fact that he lived in a period in which Slovenian and "Eastern European" artists in general were becoming increasingly established in the international system and that he was also contributing to the fact that the former Yugoslav art scene was developing and becoming recognizable and seriously considered in closer connection with international artists, institutions, curators and others who operate in this field, including the art market. He showed that the international art system was slowly and gradually changing in its interaction with local systems, and he drew attention to the idea that these unavoidable globalization processes might have a positive side.

He considered critical or political art—again in the light of his personal work—in a way that revealed the inner contradictions of the world of contemporary art and the reciprocal relation between the concepts of "political" and "autonomous" art, due to which it is impossible to consider "engaged" art as a single unambiguous response to the complex questions on the relation between art and society. "These are not merely academic questions. They are very practical, real issues that must be addressed by any artist, curator or critic who wishes to reflect on their position and work. Anyone who wants to be sure that what they do is meaningful must confront these dilemmas and work out an answer to them, at least provisionally."[9]

He was aware of the gap between the western and eastern experience following the end of the Cold War, which was impossible to simply overcome or understand as something static, for this was a constantly changing complex relation. In critical discussions of this issue, collected in the chapter *East, West, and Between*, he opposed the dominating concepts of understanding our time, Fukuyama's end of history and Huntington's clash of civilisations:

"What seems more productive to me (and perhaps not totally utopian) is an attempt to reformulate European identity in a way that would connect elements of both western and eastern social and cultural systems into a new unity. Unavoidably, such new unity will be highly complex and heterogeneous, and not without contradictions, struggles, and conflicts. Also, such an identity would necessarily be understood as something variable and changeable, and without definite outer limits."[10]

From this, we can also discern Zabel's characteristic realization that no knowledge is self-sufficient and that every thought emerges through a conversation that is based on a vast number of responses, or, as his long-term debater Zdenka Badovinac, the director of the Moderna galerija, said: "Igor knew that no definition is final, but that it merely deals with a more appropriate relation with the other. He was in constant dialogue with cultural history, history of art, the ideas of the current moment, with the people that surrounded him. It is not a coincidence that one of his key texts, in which he analyses the relation between Eastern European art and the western art system, is entitled *Dialogue*. Even though Igor always opted for the brighter side of truth, he was—notwithstanding his mild and fair character—a strict analyst and critic of the power games that dominate any dialogue."[11]

He also emphasized the importance of dialogue within the role of the curator as a selector, author of exhibitions, interpreter and co-creator of the exhibition context. He saw the eminently personal nature of the work of a curator for modern and contemporary art as an opportunity to deconstruct the position of power, and explained: "Speaking about 'deconstruction,' I am not trying to say that curators can eliminate their role as the instance of power in the institutional system of the world of art, but rather that they reveal this role clearly and no longer present it as something 'objective' or 'natural'."[12] At the same time, for a more precise understanding of this deconstruction or demystification one has to know that "... a curator never works in a clear and neutral space; his or her activity is therefore a response to particular determining conditions. For example, as somebody coming from the area of so-called Eastern Europe, I experience how the work of artists, critics, and curators from this area is a priori caught in a specific system of assumptions (of cultural difference, etc.) and how we are often expected to 'represent' a particular 'identity,' etc. It therefore seems almost unavoidable to reflect these ideas and to build an effective strategy to deal with them."[13] However, the limitations of such a strategy are soon revealed: "... the critic and interpreter can be aware of their particularities. They can try to include this into their work strategy. However, the following will remain an illusion: the point from which we observe and speak will never become transparent and we will not be able to uncon-ditionally understand the social role of our own behavior, especially in light of the historic development of society."[14]

On the other hand, he saw the spatial and cultural definition of this "visible field," captured in the institutional and production machinery of the art system, as well as all restrictions and necessities in general, as an opportunity and an advantage, to be approached with constructive irony and by mock-staging a sort of soc-artistic mythologization of his own position within the art system. "Individual as well as national identities are internally heterogeneous and often contradictory, fluid and changeable and in a constant process of being established,"[15] he liked to emphasize. In a most general way, his curatorial strategy, defined in greater detail in the chapter *Strategies and Spaces of Art*, could be summed up as a conscious operation to make the circumstances of art practice visible, revealing and (self)criticising their contradictory position within the system. Through his work, he ascertained that certain coincidental or personal decisions and circumstances can be of great importance for an exhibition concept. On the other hand, he also observed how important the critical self-reflection of the protagonists' life circumstances is for art and cultural production and how working as a professional in the field of art can decisively mark our lives.

When somebody who is close to us—as a friend and colleague—passes away, we inadvertently "discover" signs from the past that supposedly predicted his death. We blame ourselves for not recognizing them. We think that if we had noticed them in time we would have been able to prevent his death. In this sense, it is hard to avoid the thought that his last two projects, *Towards Zero Gravity* and *Another Speedy Day*, announced the events to come. Who knows whether he suspected that the titles of these projects predicted his fate? In the essay on the first project, he used examples from Slovenian 20th century art to discuss the tension between the concepts of gravity, body, materiality, and limitations, on the one hand, and weightlessness, mentality, spirit, and limitlessness on the other. In his text for Vadim Fiškin's exhibition *Another Speedy Day*, he discussed the transience of the work of art, its momentariness and constant escaping and disappearing into nothing while breaking free from the force of gravity and physical captivity. However, Igor Zabel did not experience this universal and unavoidable temporariness as something tragic. He managed to capture it in a balanced and elegant way with a grasp that kindly and understandingly merged both: poetry and theory. When he wrote about the liberation from the limitations of the physical body, he discussed the liberation from the physical entrapment in spatial and temporal parameters. It is only the liberation from physicality that enables the flight through time and our greatest utopia, i.e. that it is possible to totally abolish the limitations of our ephemeral existence.

It seems that he not only grasped his fate, but also precisely described it, perhaps even predicted it, as early as 1998, when he wrote for the catalogue for the Zagreb Salon, at which he was a visiting selector:

"The city is par excellence the environment for the body. It seems that our corporal activity naturally belongs to the urban space. The open landscape seems to be forgotten; it is now strange to us, a space we often feel to be uncomfortable (think of Asimov again). The city basically involves bodily experience: we walk, on crowded buses and trams we are surrounded by other people, we jog, we are threatened by crime. But, in spite of this physical presence, a flaneur is somehow disappearing in the spectacle that surrounds him. He, with his own body, is dispersed all over the city space.

When artists in the 1960s started to use their own bodies as a medium, they also discovered the city as an open, free space. Actions in the city have put forward a liberated body, moving freely through physical and social environments, playing, experimenting, 'expressing' itself. They made possible ecstatic actions in which the body transcended its limitations and merged with the universe. Today, however, the body seems to disappear in the game of visual spectacles, in the game of real and virtual spaces, in new technological possibilities approaching the ideal of the 'real time,' an absolute transgression of temporal and spatial distances. On the other hand, however, the bodily experience becomes stronger, more radical and extremely real (or, possibly, caught in a desperate effort to reach the real). The city, the 'natural environment' of our bodies, is certainly not a peaceful, neutral, and safe space. It is saturated by a constant treat: viruses, accidents, and violence are all permanent possibilities there. The cosmic body, so it seems, has now become an illusion. Today, both our body and mind are programmed, determined by arrangements of strings of information."[16]

Igor Španjol

[1] *Seven Sins: Ljubljana–Moscow, Arteast exhibition*, Moderna galerija, Ljubljana, 20. 12. 2005–28. 2. 2006. Curated by Zdenka Badovinac, Viktor Misiano and Igor Zabel.

[2] On the contradictions of professional everyday life, see the columns "The Soil in Which Art Grows" and "Professionals, Dilettantes, and Amateurs," both reprinted in the chapter *Extras*.

[3] Sergej Kapus, "Zabelova koncepcija zgodovine," *Zbornik za umetnostno zgodovino*, XLI, Slovensko umetnostnozgodovinsko društvo, Ljubljana, 2005, p. 280.

[4] Zoja Skušek, "Eleganca in erudicija," *ibid.*, p. 285.

[5] Igor Zabel, "Introductory Note," *Speculationes*, ISH–Fakulteta za podiplomski humanistični študij, Ljubljana, 1997, pp. 6–7.

[6] Zdenka Badovinac, "Nerazložljiva navzočnost," *Delo*, 27. 7. 2005, p. 8.

[7] Even in this evasive field, he opposed tendentious unambiguous generalisations: "Much recent art has been described in a very general way as conceptual or post-conceptual. I believe that it is this complexity of relations [between the visual and non-visual — comment by Igor Španjol], rather than any direct reference to the actual practice of the conceptual artists of the 1960s, that influenced the nature of this art." Igor Zabel, "Art at the Limits of the Visible," *Primerjalna književnosti*, vol. 27, special issue, 2004, p. 141.

[8] Igor Zabel, "Teritoriji," *Razširjeni prostori umetnosti. Slovenska umetnost 1985–1995*, Moderna galerija, Ljubljana, 2004, p. 199.

[9] Igor Zabel, "Commitment," p. 68.

[10] Igor Zabel, "Haven't We Had Enough?," p. 110.

[11] Zdenka Badovinac, from her eulogy speech for Zabel, 28. 7. 2005, typescript.

[12] Igor Zabel, "Exhibition Strategies in the 1990s: A Few Examples From Slovenia," p. 126.

[13] Igor Zabel, "Making Art Visible," p. 154.

[14] Igor Zabel, "Umetnost in kvaliteta," *PlatformaSCCA*, no. 3, January 2002, SCCA-Ljubljana, p. 52.

[15] Igor Zabel, "O jerhastih hlačah," *Delo*, 31. 12. 2003, p. 14.

[16] Igor Zabel, "Gradski krajolik," 33. *katalog razstave zagrebački salon*, MGC Klovićevi dvori, Zagreb, 1998, pp. 12–13.

I. EAST, WEST, AND BETWEEN

Dialogue

First published in *Art Press*, no. 226, Paris, July–August 1997, pp. 37–42.

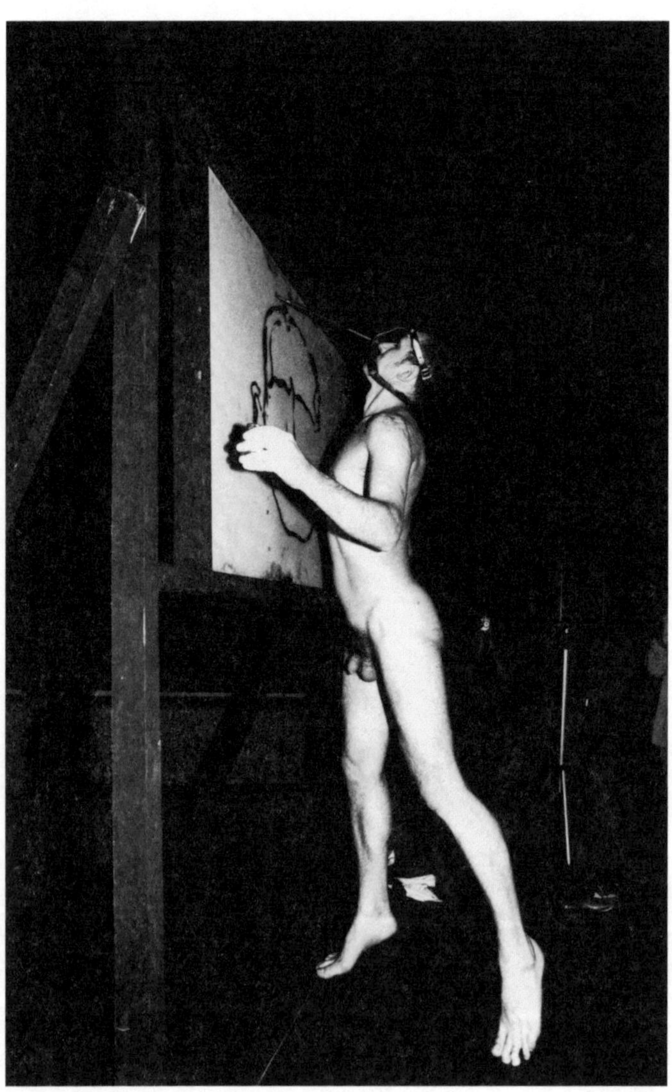

Oleg Kulik, *Two Kuliks*, 1998
Performance accompanying the exhibition *Body and the East*, Moderna galerija, Ljubljana, 1998

In September 1994, the Russian
artist Ilya Kabakov spoke at the
AICA Congress in Stockholm.
He was describing his experience
of a "culturally relocated person."
One of the aspects of western
culture he was interested in was the
permanent tendency to criticize,
provoke and even destroy within
this culture. He compared his
experience of this tendency to the
experience of an orphan living in
a children's home who is visiting
the family of his friend. This friend
is sick of his home and his behavior
is aggressive and insulting, while
the visitor himself sees a totally
different picture: a nice home and
kind, intelligent parents. But there
is another essential aspect, the
friend's family is strong enough
not to be threatened by the boy's
outbursts. The same is true of
the western culture, says Kabakov,
and continues:

> "Western culture is so vital, so
> stable, its roots are so deep and

so alive, it is so productive that speaking in the language of it, the parable above absorbs, recasts and dissolves in itself all destructive actions by its own 'children,' and as many believe, it sees in these actions its very own development—what is elegantly referred to here as 'permanent criticism.' But I would like to add a footnote here: this criticism, like the destruction itself, is permitted, if it can be so expressed, only from its own children. That same mom described above would have behaved quite differently if I had started to act up at the table the same way as her son. Most likely she would have called the police."[1]

It did not take too long, less than a year and a half, for the event Kabakov was somehow predicting to actually happen. It took place during the opening of an exhibition called *Interpol* in the Färgfabriken Contemporary Art Center in Stockholm; an exhibition trying to establish "a global network" between Stockholm and Moscow. One of the participants, the Russian performance artist Alexander Brener, destroyed a work of another participant, the Chinese-American artist Wenda Gu; another Russian artist, Oleg Kulik, who appeared on the show as a dangerous dog on a chain and actually bit some people, was attacked by the audience and was later taken away by the police.

There have been a lot of discussions (and even more rumors and gossip) about the *Interpol* scandal. I believe that the affair is so attractive because it is not just another scandal in the art world. It implies an extremely serious question: the relationship between East and West, and it indicates that this relationship is far from being idyllic. I believe that it was not the intervention of the police which had made this tension explicit (after all, one should expect such intervention) but *An Open Letter to the Art World*,[2] signed by a group of artists and other participants of the show (all from the West) and broadly distributed. What is surprising is the fact that the letter was written and signed by artists and critics whose position is essentially based on the tradition of "permanent criticism," referred to by Kabakov. Of course, they were not necessarily expected to agree with Kulik's and Brener's actions, but one would at least think they would be more careful in the way they criticize them, since the tradition of 20th century art offers a number of examples of aggressive, destructive, and subversive actions which have, by now, attained a status of historical or even canonical fact. Some examples of destroying other artists' works are now considered to be major points in the development of modern art. (Immediately I can think of at least two examples; the best known is, perhaps, Rauschenberg's *Erased de Kooning*. Another is the so-called Wolfsburg Affair from October 1961: "at the opening of the exhibition *Junge Stadt sieht junge Kunst* Arnulf Rainer paints over the etching *Mond und Figuren II* by Helga Pape, which had won second prize, with black paint and attaches a label with the inscription: 'Painted over by Arnulf Rainer.' Rainer is arrested and sentenced to a fine for willfully damaging a work of art.")[3] The *Open Letter*, however, is not simply a protest against the two Russian artists and their actions; it attacks them, as well as the Russian curator Viktor Misiano, with direct but, at the same time, very general and imprecise *political* accusations: "a new form of totalitarian ideology," "hooliganism and skinhead ideology," "a direct attack against art, democracy, and the freedom of expression," "speculative and populist attitude," "classical model of imperialistic behavior," "attitude that excludes female artists." In short, the *Open Letter* treats the destructive actions of both Russian artists as being eminently political rather than artistic statements.

One could easily dismiss the *Open Letter* as ridiculous and reactionary since it lacks any precise analysis and reflection and because its criticism (as well as the position and the values this criticism implies) is just a set of phrases. I believe, however, that we have to understand this letter as a kind of "slip," i.e. that we have to recognize its symptomatic value; and it is this value that makes it so very interesting. One has to ask: what made a group of artists and critics who (at least some of them) ascribe to a line of critical and subversive art to write a letter (and distribute it all over the world) in such a style which could easily be used by a representative of any conservative or totalitarian system? What made them blind to the style and form of their own writing? What made them directly and roughly denunciate the artists (as well as the curator who was trying to understand the destructive actions as artistic statements) as being politically incorrect and against art, democracy, freedom of expression, and women—only because they did something which is well established in the tradition of 20th century art as a legitimate means of artistic expression, however radical and problematic?[4]

I do not believe that those who have signed the letter consider Rauschenberg and Rainer to be "hooligans," "skinheads," and "enemies of art, democracy and freedom of expression." We must, therefore, conclude that Brener's action must be seen in an important aspect different from, say, Rainer's. And since they have done exactly the same thing: destroying the work of a fellow artist at the opening of a group show, the difference has to lie elsewhere. I believe that Kabakov, with his "footnote" indicates the correct answer to this question: the Russians do not belong to the "family." Rainer's action is included in a certain code where it has a precisely determined meaning and value; on the other hand, the position of Brener's action seems to be at the point where two codes clash. Thus, his action could not be legitimized by the code which it was actually questioning and attacking.

There are two sentences in the *Open Letter* that I find essential: "This attitude denies every possibility of a dialogue between the (former) East and the West. It is a speculative and populist attitude that cannot be accepted as the basis of a dialogue." Something has been made very clear here. Brener and Kulik are not two individual artists, they are not even Russians, they represent "the East"—politically correct called "the (former) East." The *Open Letter* makes clear that the problematic point of the *Interpol* scandal is not the behavior of individual artists. Brener, Kulik, and Misiano only represent an "attitude," which actually is the "attitude" of the East. This coincides with the fact reported by Misiano, that only western artists were invited to sign the letter:

> "Nobody asked other Russian artists to sign this letter, though most of them do not identify with the destructive gestures of Kulik and Brener. What's more, the Slovenian artists Irwin were also excluded. Ridiculous. Ljubljana is the West for Russians, but the logic of confrontation has stated the western sanction: Ljubljana is the East."[5]

Interpol was obviously more than just a group show. Its main
problem was not a network between different artists and
different artistic attitudes and practices. The show was about
the West-East dialogue. And actually, the result of the
"scandal" at the opening was a sharp division and confrontation between the eastern and the western artists. The show,
says Misiano in the same text, "was to be a metaphor of the
new Europe and post-ideological order (where there is
no more East and West)." Nevertheless, the confrontation
remains. The East is still the East, although it is now
called "the (former) East." (Does anybody speak about "the
former West"?) The idea of a global network in the post-
ideological new Europe, a model (presumably) replacing
the topography of the East-West division, proved to be a veil
covering the actual conflicts and confrontations. Even more,
such rhetoric can actually serve as a means in this conflict.
A conflict, that is, which is essentially based on the will
to establish a dominant position in the discourse and thus
in the practice itself.

A dialogue is only possible on a certain common basis
that both parties in the dialogue accept. For example, if
I want to discuss with somebody, the meanings of the words
we use have to be established and clear to both of us. The
quoted sentences from the *Open Letter* make clear that it was
exactly on this level of accepting a common basis that
the West-East dialogue had failed. The Easterners did not
accept the terms of the dialogue that were supposed to be
"natural" for the Westerners. By not accepting these terms,
Brener, Kulik, and Misiano (representing the East) "deny
every possibility of a dialogue between the (former) East
and the West," since their own attitude "cannot be accepted
as the basis of a dialogue." I believe that one of the
best descriptions of these problems can be found in Lewis
Carroll's *Through the Looking-Glass*:

> "When *I* use a word," Humpty Dumpty said, in rather
> a scornful tone, "it means just what I choose it
> to mean—neither more nor less."
> "The question is," said Alice, "whether you *can* make
> words mean so many different things."
> "The question is," said Humpty Dumpty, "which is
> to be master—that's all."[6]

Thus, one could perhaps say that the struggle for a dialogue, or better, the struggle for the terms of a dialogue, represents the struggle for the position of the master.

The *Interpol* scandal demonstrated that the West-East division persists and that it was not surpassed with the fall of the communist regimes. Furthermore, this division is clearly not confined to the area of art. As the ideological oppositions between the capitalist and the socialist systems are no longer functional, it has been replaced, for example, with the idea of the "clash of civilizations." Again, I believe that at the basis of this "clash" lies the struggle over the most basic, "human" and "natural" issues which themselves correspond to a certain power structure. For example, Samuel P. Huntington,[7] who has introduced the idea of the "clash of civilizations," also describes how the West ensures its domination by presenting its interests as the interests of the "world community" and how it presents its own fundamental values as universal, while in fact they are not valid within most other civilizations. Of course, one may assume that the concept of a world consisting of basically different (and often hostile) civilizations also corresponds to a certain strategy of power and control. The idea of the "clash of civilizations" is actually much more than just an attempt of a neutral scientific description of the contemporary world. It introduces a certain system of interpretation and representation that is directly applicable in international politics. One could, for example, notice how important American specialists in foreign affairs started to use Huntington's terms in describing conflict areas such as Bosnia.

The East-West "conflict," as far as art is concerned, develops in an essential aspect on the level of the fight for codification of the field and thus for its domination. It is this codification that determines the terms of the dialogue or, as Humpty Dumpty has said, which chooses their meaning.

The sharp political division between the East and the West during the Cold War period also implied a confrontation of two artistic models: the modernist art in the West and the socialist realism in the East. Western art has presented itself as the "natural" development of genuine art as opposed to the politically suppressed art of socialist realism and its derived forms, which was not regarded as genuine art, but simply as political propaganda. In the light of this understanding, eastern artists have been seen as a kind of underdeveloped and suppressed western artists, and it was supposed that they would immediately join the general developments in the West if they were free to do so.

The identification of western art of the 20th century with modern art as such (this identification is actually a part of the "Western universalism," as it is described by Huntington) introduced a subtle dialectic of domination. The essential success of this dialectic lies in the fact that to a great extent, eastern artists had accepted it themselves. Modern art was thus located in the West. But, as western art is deemed universal, eastern artists also belong to the same idiom; however, they form only its periphery. All the constitutive structures, institutional, conceptual and commercial, are located in the West, thus they are controlled by it. The East more or less accepts (with some delay) and repeats the main currents of western art. (I remember a participant at the CIMAM Congress in Dubrovnik in 1987, who expressly said that *all* the important modern art was produced in the West and none in the East.) Thus the function of eastern modernism, inside this constellation, was often not to represent an autonomous statement and position, but to serve as a confirmation of the original western artist or particular movement. In her article *Abstract Expressionism, Weapon of the Cold War*, Eva Cockcroft describes an example of using innovative eastern art for strengthening the position of the West, regardless of the actual role and meaning of this art inside its original context:

> "During the post-Stalin era in 1956, when the Polish government under Gomulka became more liberal, Tadeusz Kantor, an artist from Cracow, impressed by the work of Pollock and other abstractionists which he had seen during an earlier trip to Paris, began to lead the movement away from socialist realism in Poland. Irrespective of the role of this art movement within the internal artistic evolution of Polish art, this kind of development was seen as a triumph for 'our side.' In 1961, Kantor and 14 other nonobjective Polish painters were given an exhibition at the MoMA.

> Examples like this one reflect the success of the
> political aims of the international programs of
> MoMA."[8]

Such a constellation permits a very limited acceptance of
eastern artists into the central area of art. An average
eastern artist has, in his effort to produce modern art,
remained a kind of "incompletely realized western artist,"
and thus, a second class artist. (It is, of course, only natural
that the "Second World" produces second-rate art.)
Most often, the eastern artists who have succeeded in the
West are those who have actually moved there and became
its integral part. Still, some eastern artists have reached
a certain international response, partly due to their quality
and the genuine interest of some western critics and
curators, but also because they could serve as evidence for
the universal value of modern art and, as mentioned above,
as an affirmation of the western artists and artistic
developments. Nevertheless, the codification of the field
and the construction of its history and tradition resulted in
a marginalization or total ignorance of important eastern
phenomena. For example, eastern avant-garde artists of the
1960s and early 1970s simply do not exist in historical
surveys of art of this time, except those who have moved
to the West.

Establishing itself as the center, the West has also
installed itself as a general reference point. East-East
communication, insofar as it has existed at all, has been
running via the West. This was even present in the recent
project, the *Europa-Europa* exhibition at the Bundeskunsthalle
in Bonn. I found this show very important for presenting a
number of lesser known or unknown artists and works.
(Among others, it made us aware of the fact that certain
important achievements of, say, Carl Andre, Barnett Newman
and others were preceded for more than half a century
by the works of artists like Alexander Rodchenko, Olga
Rozanova and others.) Still, the selection criteria for the
contemporary section seemed to depend, to a great extent,
on the artists' international reputation (which actually
means, their reputation in the West).

I believe that we are witnessing a somehow different
situation now, i.e. a change from the eastern artist as an

"incompletely-developed-Westerner" to the eastern artist as a representative of a different and exotic culture. In the above-mentioned speech about the "relocated person," Ilya Kabakov also describes how an artist who is coming from the East or from the Third World is, in advance, committed to represent his origins:

> "Belonging to some 'school' now—be it Russian or Mexican, French, or Czech—is perceived as a negative ethnographic factor, hindering the artist to a certain degree from entering into the western artistic community on an equal footing. However, the artist who has arrived from these places often himself doesn't know about this circumstance, this 'hump' on his back appears only in the new place upon crossing the border, and as Boris Groys wrote, like a growth on his back, it is visible to everyone except the owner of that back. This is precisely the same thing as when a critic in an offhanded manner writes 'the young artist from India,' or 'the famous Mexican painter'—everyone silently understands what this epithet means."[9]

I believe that this change demonstrates an important modification in the field of East-West relationship, a shift which is connected to the *détente* process and the eventual collapse of the socialist regimes. During the time of the Cold War, in a situation where the political and ideological confrontations ensured a firm, bi-polar structure and therefore balance and control, Western modern art easily claimed to be universal. The post-Cold-War era does not supply such controlling mechanisms anymore. The necessary result is that the situation of art (as well as that of other related fields) has to be redefined. The freedom of traveling, for example, could be a universal value and a proclaimed right only as long as the bi-polar system made it impossible for a large majority of (eastern) people to travel freely. As soon as these limitations disappeared, the right of free travel had to be reduced by the West.

As opposed to the proclamation of the universal value of western modern art during the Cold War period, post-Cold-War ideology stresses the differences. (On a more global level, a similar development can be observed in the discourse of so-called multiculturalism.) As the ideological and political differences disappeared, the East is now established through "cultural" and "civilizational" differences, which are by themselves a starting point of conflicts, of the "clash of civilizations." (In his description of the *Interpol* incident, Wenda Gu, the artist whose work was destroyed by Brener, spoke very openly about the "cultural war.")[10]

The idea of modern art originally did not need the idea of a "dialogue"; the "substance," so to speak, was common, the only question was to what extent and how it was realized. Through the idea of "civilizational differences," however, the Easterner is established as the "other," thus an inter-cultural and inter-civilization dialogue is necessary. An eastern artist now becomes attractive for the West not as somebody producing universal art, but exactly as somebody who reflects his particular condition. He is not only an artist, but particularly a Russian, Polish or Slovene artist, or simply an eastern artist.[11] This was clearly present in the *Interpol* incident. Renata Salecl, in her analysis of Kulik's actions, wrote about this question:

> "The paradox [...] is that Kulik was invited as a particularity—as a Russian dog. I am certain that if an American artist were to play a dog, he would be of much less interest for the international art scene than the Russian artist is. We all know that the majority of people in today's Russia live a dog-like life. And the first association a Westerner makes in regard to Kulik's performance is that he is representing this reality of contemporary Russia. Kulik-dog is therefore of interest for the western art world because of the fact that he is the Russian 'dog.' [...] And, in regard to Kulik's performance it can be said that the West finds an aesthetic pleasure in observing the Russian 'dog,' but only on condition that he does not behave in a truly dog-like manner. When Kulik ceased to be the decorative art-object—the eastern neighbour who represents the misery of the Russian dog-like life— and started to act in a way that surprised his admirers, he quickly became designated as the enemy."[12]

In short, the idea of the West-East dialogue could be understood as a way of reorganizing these relationships after the end of the Cold War era, i.e., as a way to deal with the "other." If earlier, the dominant position was achieved through the universal value of western modern art, it is now achieved through the definition of the "other" and, at the same time, through the definition of the basis of communication.[13] As Wenda Gu reports, Misiano said that "this incident creates an essential stage for a dialogue between Eastern and Western Europe."[14] But it seems clear that this "stage" includes a reorganization of the very field of dialogue and thus opens the question of "who is to be master." Unavoidably, the western pole of the "global network" could only see mere aggression, imperialism and destruction in this attempt.

[1] Ilya Kabakov, "A Story about a Culturally Relocated Person," Speech at the XXVIII AICA Congress, Stockholm, 22 September 1944, now reprinted in *M'ars* (Ljubljana), no. 3-4, 1996

[2] The letter was signed by Olivier Zahm, Elein Fleiss, Jan Aman, Catharina Ahlberg, Catti Lindahl, Thomas Lundh, Magnus af Petersens, Matthias Wagner K, Birgitta Muhr, Wenda Gu, Ioanna Theocaropoulou, Ulrika Karlsson, Dan Wolgers, Erns Billgren, Bigert & Bergström, Johannes Albers and Fredrik Wretman.

[3] Dieter Schwarz, "Chronology," *Wiener Aktionismus / Viennese Actionism*, Ritter Verlag, Klagenfurt, 1988, vol. 1, p. 168.

[4] Recently, Brener has caused another big scandal by attacking a painting by Malevich in the Stedelijk Museum in Amsterdam. This action again, and even more radically, opens up the question of artists attacking and destroying works of other artists. Personally, I think that such actions are highly problematic and not something one could easily agree with. Also, I believe that an artist who has destroyed such a work has to take full responsibility for his action. Attacking a work of art does not necessarily imply a relevant artistic position and statement, but sometimes it does. In such cases, the destructive and unlawful behaviour has a function and meaning, and we have to regard it as a relevant statement — like, I believe, in Brener's case. Personally, I do not agree with Brener's attacks on Wenda Gu's and Malevich's works (no more that I agree with the destruction of the works by de Kooning or Helga Pape), but, of course, these attacks were not meant to be agreed with. They are deliberate hooliganism, which, however, has a deep meaning in the context of Brener's artistic position. If those who have written the *Open Letter* would actually read Brener's text in the *Interpol* catalogue instead of just searching for politically incorrect and compromising quotations in it, they could perhaps understand it.

[5] Viktor Misiano, "The Response," *Flash Art International*, May-June 1996, p. 46. (The quotation discloses one of the reasons why I am so interested in this affair. As I am based in Ljubljana, my position is in advance determined by the discourse of the West-East dialogue.)

[6] Lewis Carroll, *Alice's Adventures in Wonderland & Through the Looking-Glass*, Bantam Books, Toronto, New York, London, Sydney, Auckland, 1981, p. 169.

[7] Samuel P. Huntington, "The Clash of Civilizations?," *Foreign Affairs*, no. 3, Summer 1993, pp. 22–49. Prof. Huntington has expanded and elaborated the questions dealt with in the article in his recent book, *The Clash of Civilizations and the Remaking of World Order*, Simon & Schuster, New York, 1996.

[8] Eva Cockcroft, "Abstract Expressionism, Weapon of the Cold War," *Pollock and After: The Critical Debate*, Francis Frascina (ed.), Harper and Row, London, 1985, p. 132.

[9] Ilya Kabakov, *op. cit.*

[10] Wenda Gu, "The Cultural War," *Flash Art International*, Summer 1996, pp. 102–103.

[11] In recent western discussions about contemporary Russian art, especially about artists like Brener and Kulik, such an attitude was often present. One can easily notice how these two artists came to represent the wild, aggressive, irrational, non-understandable, dangerous, animal-like essence of "Russia" (or, perhaps, the "East" in general), and how their actions are received with a mixture of fascination, admiration, fear, hatred and, of course, pleasure.

[12] Renata Salecl, "Love Me, Love My Dog," *Index. Contemporary Scandinavian Art and Culture*, no. 3–4, 1996, p. 117.

[13] It would be, perhaps, more accurate to say that this new strategy is still often combined with the idea of "universalism."

[14] Wenda Gu, "The Cultural War," *op. cit.*, p. 103.

"We" and the "Others"

First published in *Moscow Art Magazine*, no. 22, Moscow, 1998, pp. 27–35.

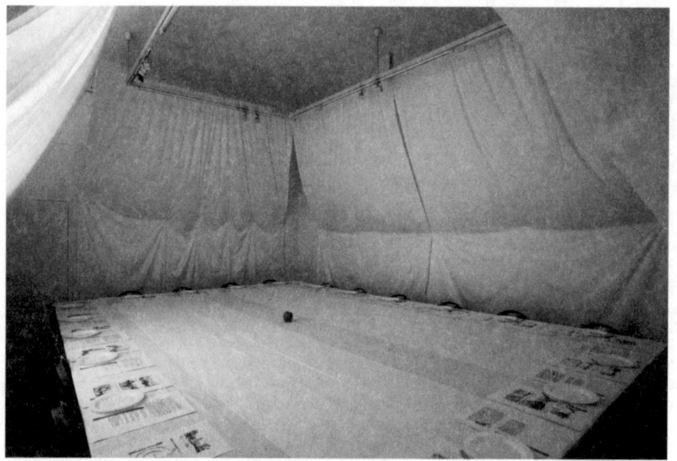

Ilya Kabakov, *Twenty ways to get an apple listening to the music of Mozart*, 1997
Arteast 2000+, Umetnostna galerija Maribor, 2008

Other's Other

As the starting point, I will simply use the title of the conference[1]: *We and the Others.*
The phrase seems to be simple and symmetrical, but as soon as one reads the subtitle (*Russian Artists in the West–Western Artists in Russia*), it becomes clear that the relationship between "us" and "the others" is far from being balanced and equivalent. The title indicates that the contemporary world is basically determined by the experience of "otherness"; in such a world, Russian art is confronted with many "others": for example, the art of the Far East (like China or Japan), of the Islamic world, of Latin America and Africa, to mention just a few areas where one can observe considerable artistic activity in recent years. However, the title does not refer to these "others," but to one and very special "Other": to the West, the western art world. But why is western art understood

not just as one of several, basically equivalent art idioms, but as the other, so to speak? The answer is obvious: within the global network of art, western art seems to hold the position of a "commanding point." Institutions, capital, markets and concepts are based in the western world or essentially connected with it. One could say without too much exaggeration that the West actually determines what art is and what is not. And even the much discussed "transcultural" processes cannot avoid this determinant; a certain regional art phenomenon or idiom is first appropriated by western interpretations, institutions and capital, and subsequently "re-localized" or "projected back" into its original context. This relationship, of course, gives a very different meaning to the notion of "otherness." It may be true that western art is "other" for us, but what really matters is that "we" are "others" for the West.

This relationship is global. South African and Japanese arts are perhaps little known each to the other, and difficult to understand, so one could describe their relationship with the notion of "otherness"; however, this is not really important. Much more important is to what extent they remain unknown, unintelligible and thus "other" for the West. The perversity of such a situation is that "we" in advance understand ourselves as being "others" for the West, that "we" look at ourselves through "the other's eyes," so to speak. This is, of course, a phantasmatic view; but through it, "we" understand ourselves as "the other's other."

Very similar issues are discussed, e.g., by Ekaterina Dyogot, who speaks about the problem of identity and representation in contemporary Russian art. She describes the situation in which from the outset, an artist is forced to function as a representative in the relationship Russia–the West: "In Russia, when one is speaking about representation, about the 'inward' and the 'external,' one is inevitably speaking about Russia as opposed to the West, the West being the only reference and place to be represented when the unrepresented is mentioned. When unrepresentable, the reference is unavoidably to Russia."[2] What Dyogot is describing is a world marked by otherness and demanding representation; but it is also a world determined by one special other, the West.

The Phantasmatic "Other"

Certainly, it is not only in art that we speak about a divided world, a world built of closed, mutually unintelligible units. As a matter of fact, this view corresponds exactly to the new paradigm in global politics, a model that is supposed to serve as the basis for establishing the "world order." These views are, for example, developed in *The Clash of Civilizations and the Remaking of World Order*, the much discussed book by Samuel P. Huntington;[3] and this book is certainly not presenting just a private speculation, but offers concepts for political interpretations and strategies. It is a paradigm that has replaced the modernist universalistic model. Huntington describes the world as a kind of patchwork of civilizations (based on ethnical, religious, cultural and other similarities). These civilizations are assumed to be in a conflictual relationship with other civilizations. This is essentially a post-Cold-War, but also a post-colonial model. The symmetry of political and ideological oppositions and the classical relationship between the colonial capital and colonies have disappeared; instead of this, we now have Huntington's paradigm which, in my opinion, tries to ensure the civilizational unity of the western world and, at the same time, to define and ensure its position in a world which cannot be directly controlled anymore in such a way that it is still possible for the West to secure its vital global interests.

Why do I think that one function of Huntington's paradigm is to secure western identity? We repeatedly speak about the West as a single and coherent unity, but in fact it is very heterogeneous: it has its own centers and peripheries, its own antagonisms and fights for the dominant position and hegemony (let us think only of the polyvalent relationship between European and American culture). The strong evocation of western identity can be further understood as a symptom, indicating the fact that this very identity cannot be taken for granted anymore. As a matter of fact, the western world is itself heterogeneous in the cultural and even civilizational sense, and therefore itself a potential (sometimes even actual) space of conflicts. The role of the multinational capital and development of the new "global cities," centers of the global economy networks, introduce important new factors, too.

The modernist ideology of the Cold War and the neo-colonial
era was based on the idea that modern western forms and
values are modern forms and values and therefore universally
valid. Certainly such an ideology can be understood as a tool
for dominance and control. As such, modernist universalism
was combined with a kind of ethnographic approach to
the "other," basically pre-modern, forms. The model of the
"clash of civilizations," on the other hand, corresponds to a
world where the West, with its will to power and control, is
challenged by emerging new centers of power. According to
this model, modern civilization is not necessarily western
and neither is western civilization necessarily modern.[4]
I believe that the intention of this theory is to safeguard the
essential interests of the West at a time when the West
cannot aim for universal dominance anymore. But there
may be another far-reaching aspect. Not only is power
re-distributed territorially, it is becoming de-territorialized,
global, fluid, and abstract. The strong evocation of identity
and differences can therefore also be understood as a reflex
of the very crisis and disappearance of such an identity.

All this indicates that "the West" itself, together with
its particular "western identity," is perhaps just a phantasm
—which is also "our" own phantasm, our own "other,"
the base on which "we" construct "our" own identity.
The paradigm of "the clash of civilizations," of the world
all split in differences and conflicts, in "other" civilizations
and cultures, is, in a certain sense, deeply occidocentric.
Its function is to ensure the civilizational unity of the West
and, at the same time, its political and cultural primacy.
The logic we can discover in Huntington's undertaking is, in
fact, very similar to the logic of the title of the conference.
In his approach, too, we first have a picture of the world as a
patchwork of different civilizations; but, actually, his book is
not only written from the position of a western observer but
also with the ambition to establish a system of explanation
through which the West will be able to deal with "others."

The relationship of the western world towards these
strange "other" civilizations and cultures is exactly the one
described by the title of the conference: "we and the others."
As "our" position is not universal anymore, it is necessary
to "understand" and "explain" other cultures. Very often,
these explanations follow the pattern critically analyzed by

Edward W. Saïd in his *Orientalism.*[5] Just as "Orient" and "Islam" (concepts discussed by Saïd), these "other" cultures appear as timeless phantasmatical entities, e.g. as "archaic," "irrational," "wild," "dangerous," etc.

From such a point of view, one would try to explain contemporary Russia and its contradictions not through an analysis of actual political and economical antagonisms, but through a phantasmatic "Russian essence." This eternal and unchangeable essence seems to be strange, dangerous and attractive at the same time, and it includes such issues as the Orthodox and mystic traditions, the emotional, irrational and poetic Russian soul, etc.; it can, for example, also imply the idea that Russians "by their nature" prefer strong, authoritarian political figures to a fully developed democratic system.

Western Curators in Africa

The world of "others," or rather, the world of The Other (the West) and (its) others therefore demands interpretation and explanation, and only these can be the basis for a possible "dialogue." This relationship implies a construction of a system of identities and representations; the "explanatory" relationship with "another" culture means that all the products of this culture have to be understood as representing it and its identity. In these inter-cultural relations, artists are, regardless of their own intentions, forced to function as "representatives" of their strange world. When "we" deal with artists from "other" cultures, "we" search for this "other" in their work; for example, how does a certain Russian artist (re)present the phantasmatical "Russian essence" in his work? This very "explanation" of the "essence" and "identity" which are "represented" in a, e.g., work of art, however, re-confirms our own "essence" and "identity."

If I return to the above-mentioned text by Dyogot, I might say that one of her main points is exactly the problem that a Russian artist cannot avoid being such a representative: The Russian artist perpetually finds him/herself between the Scylla and Charibdys of two representational mechanisms that are switched on automatically and ruthlessly. In Russia, being a "contemporary artist" means to represent western culture. In the West, on the other hand, a Russian artist must inevitably represent Russia.

We could certainly point to a number of examples where the reception (and sometimes also success) of Russian artists in the West was connected with the fact that they could be used as representatives of the Russian (and earlier also Soviet) essence. The position of Ilya Kabakov, for example, is very interesting in this respect, especially because he has, as a "re-located person," obsessively talked about his experiences in the Soviet Union for a long time, about reality, ideas, fantasies, etc.[6] In spite of this, he did not want to accept the role of somebody "typical," of a "representative"; but this was, to a great extent, exactly what was happening to him. His *public toilet/apartment* at the 1992 *Documenta*, for example, is certainly using elements taken from the Soviet reality, but it is actually a very personal, poetic and ironic construction, a network of meanings, of fragments of realities and, arguably, of references to personal experiences and obsessions. But of course, it could not avoid the equation: to live in the USSR is like living in a public toilet.

Perhaps it would also be possible to understand the extremely negative reactions to the recent "scandal" with Alexander Brener and Oleg Kulik in Stockholm (and to Brener's action with Malevich's painting in Amsterdam), as well as the incredibly quick subsequent integration of these two artists into the "business as usual" of the contemporary art world through these relations. The Stockholm project was (explicitly) about the East-West dialogue and (implicitly) about the dominant position in this dialogue. The *Open Letter to the Art World*, denouncing Kulik, Brener and Viktor Misiano as being against art, democracy and women (can a "politically correct" mind produce more terrible accusations?) because they did not take the proposed terms of the "dialogue" for granted, as "natural," was just a symptomatic "slip." Very quickly, both Brener and Kulik were re-codified and the role and meaning of their actions was determined. The art world found their place inside its normal discourse —exactly as representatives of "the other," in their case, of the wild, destructive, dangerous, naively critical, but also strangely attractive "Russian essence." Now they are supposed to behave aggressively, to break windows, etc. The paradox here is not only that by understanding them merely as representatives of the phantasmal "Russian essence," we overlook the very dimensions that make their art interesting as art,[7] but also the fact that two strategies we often meet in contemporary Russian art (violence on one side and a highly private, almost unintelligible language on the other) and which can be, among others, understood as an attempt to act against the system of representation/explanation,[8] are eventually appropriated by the very same system and acquire a "representative" value. But Dyogot also speaks about a contradictory double mechanism of representation: Russian artists are supposed to represent Russia for the West and, at the same time, the West for Russia. This insight turns our attention to the fact that there are other structures besides the game of representation active in the contemporary art world. One of them is the idea that western modern art is, in fact, *the* modern art, that modernization (in the visual arts as well as in other areas of cultural and social life) is westernization. Other social and cultural forms are assumed to be essentially pre-modern, and have primarily a folklorist value. So in the world of contemporary art we meet at least two systems. The older ("modernist") one claims that history and development of western modernist art has a universal value and is, as a matter of fact, the history and development of modern art as such; the more recent ("post-modernist") one admits that very different "modern" cultures exist in the contemporary world, that western forms are not universal and that cultural products, such as works of art, function as "representatives" of their respective cultures and civilizations.

Let me illustrate this very general issue with a small anecdote. In the mid-1980s, when not only Eastern European art, but also art from Africa and Latin America was becoming interesting for the West, a group of curators went to Africa to select some artists for an international show. After they had made the selection, however, they were surprised to hear from the local art experts that they had left all really important artists aside and selected only the most horrible "African" kitsch. How could this have happened? (After all, the curators were certainly professionals...) I believe that the explanation could be roughly this: in Africa, these curators encountered two kinds of art. One was the product of western-influenced intellectual elites (one often calls the "modernizers" or "westernizers"), who considered western forms to be universal not only in art but also in society and the economic sphere. The curators from the West, however, could hardly see "authentic" art in these works. Most probably, they understood them as provincial copies of western originals; but for them, they were non-authentic not only because they were copies, but also because they were signs of a loss of roots, traditions and thus identity itself. To put it simply, they were not "other" anymore, and this "other" and "different" was exactly what the curators were looking for. It is not surprising, then, that they preferred artists who were openly using the "indigenous" traditions; for them, this was the genuine, real African art. Local intellectuals ("westernizers") were, of course, shocked: for them, these works were extremely bad, non-authentic, folklorist art, a false, nostalgic image which does not correspond with the reality of the developing, modern Africa anymore.[9]

United Colors of Multiculturalism

I believe that this parallelism between the position of the Second and Third Worlds in their relationship with the First World is no coincidence. In both cases, basically the same strategy is active: "permitting" the "cultural differences" (based on the idea of a primacy of western cultural forms). In his criticism of the so-called multiculturalism, for example, Rasheed Araeen discovers exactly the same structure. The West, in his opinion, uses multiculturalism "as a cultural tool to ethnicize its non-white population in order to administer and control its aspirations for equality" as well as "a smokescreen to hide the contradictions of a white society unable or unwilling to relinquish its imperial legacies."[10] Araeen's description of the strategy of "cultural difference" corresponds almost literally to the problem of the "representational" role of the eastern (especially Russian) artists. "As for the dominant discourse, it is so obsessed with cultural difference and identity to the extent of suffering from an intellectual blockage, that it is unable to maintain its focus on the works of art themselves. [...] The obsession with cultural difference is now being institutionally legitimized through the construction of the 'postcolonial other,' who is allowed to express itself only so long as it speaks of its own otherness."[11]

Araeen concludes his analysis with an alternative vision: "The prevailing western notion of multiculturalism is the main hurdle we now face in our attempt to change the system and create an international paradigm in which what takes precedence is art work, with its own set of rules for production and legitimation in terms of aesthetics, historical formation, location and significance, rules not necessarily derived from any one or originary culture."[12]

Araeen's analysis introduces the very broad field of "multiculturalism," which, however, exactly corresponds to the system of representation/explanation I have discussed above. But, since his criticism also indicates the question of cultural imperialism, I will mention a different document here: the *Letter of Support for Alexander Brener*, written by Eda Čufer, Goran Eorevij and the Irwin group on the occasion of Brener's trial in Amsterdam.[13] Among other things, the letter connects Brener's action, and his activity in general, with criticism of the western strategy of "maintaining cultural, symbolical supremacy through the economical supremacy" by appropriations (in Brener's case, appropriation of the paintings Malevich left in Berlin after his exhibition in 1927); I believe that this "symbolical supremacy" is exactly the dimension which distinguishes the West from other "Others." The letter then asks: "Is it true that the global capitalism is a new definition of the cultural colonization of the western world of all the rest of the world?"

The systems of power and domination as seen by Araeen and by the writers of the letter, however, are not completely the same. Araeen's criticism describes multiculturalism as a tool of imperial ambitions which still exist but are not universal and open anymore. The question of global capitalism, however, indicates a different system of domination.

Here, I will refer to Slavoj Žižek, who has developed an interesting issue about multiculturalism and global capitalism.[14] For him, multiculturalism is "the ideal ideological form of the global capitalism." As the power of this global capitalism is not located in the colonial metropolis anymore, the difference between the colonial state and colonies has disappeared; capital now treats all states as regions that are to be colonized.

The ideal ideological form of this global capitalism is, of course, multiculturalism, an attitude which, from some kind of empty global position, treats every local culture the same way the colonizer treats the colonized nation—as "indigenous people" who need to be researched and "respected." In other words, the relationship between traditional imperialistic colonialism and global capitalist self-colonizing is exactly the same as the relationship between western cultural imperialism and multiculturalism: just as global capitalism includes the paradox of colonization without the colonizing state, so multiculturalism includes the Eurocentric distance and/or a paternalizing respect for local communities without being rooted in a particular culture.[15]

"Very often we meet the idea that multiculturalism is not neutral, that this neutrality is nothing but a mask of an Eurocentric and Occidocentric position," continues Žižek; this idea is, in a sense, true, but he offers an interesting explanation. For him, this "Eurocentrism" is just a kind of blind spot which hides the obvious truth: that there is no local position anymore, that the subject is abstract and universal: "The horror is not the (particular living) spirit inside the (dead universal) machine, but the (dead universal) machine in the very heart of each (particular living) spirit."[16]

Here, we are confronted with two opposite assumptions: that the West, through global capitalism, culturally colonizes the rest of the world, and that global capitalism as a completely de-localized system colonizes the whole world, including the West.

In the contemporary world, we do not meet a single system of power and domination, but different systems which can also be in conflict. These conflicts also take place on a symbolic level. The struggle against hegemony in terms of race, ethnicity, gender, etc. indicates a fight between an older, patriarchal and colonial system in which these differences were functional, and a more recent one in which the differences are not useful anymore and can even be an obstacle. We can also assume that this shift corresponds with the shift towards global, multi-national capitalism. Through this shift, we can understand the difference between multiculturalism as described by Araeen (a tool to ethnicize and a "smokescreen") and the one referred to by Žižek—i.e., a multiculturalism that indicates that all such differences are eventually inessential.

Benetton's famous slogan, "United Colors of Benetton," and its advertising campaigns are a clear example of this process: regardless of their haircut or the color of their skin or their sex (or the culture they belong to, one might add), all the different people on Benetton's poster are basically identical, the same. It is interesting to note how closely Benetton's advertising follows contemporary critical art, i.e., art that questions systems of dominance based on territorial, racial, cultural or gender differences. I believe that this connection is not purely accidental and that Benetton only offers an especially clear example of how new global structures of domination can even explore critical art in their struggle against those symbolic and ideological structures that are in their way.

But even the global structures of power are not completely deterritorialized, completely "virtual." It is especially relevant that one effect of globalization is the centralization of controlling and managing functions, and in this centralization, major cities in the highly developed countries (and their networks) gain a special importance.[17] Global power is thus not only connected to the West, but, through the importance of its major centers inside this global network, the West has redefined its crucial role inside the global power system. The new centers are certainly not just abstract points; being, as Sassen notes "command points in the organization of the world economy," they are connected to the economical, political and also symbolical structures. (Here, we could mention a very recent example of how corporate economic power succeeded to construct an important center of symbolic values using exactly the strategy of appropriation, as it was mentioned in the above-quoted Letter of Support; I am thinking of the new Getty Center near Los Angeles.)[18]

However, one could probably not say that the West is really the "subject" of global capitalism. Through new global centers, the deterritorialized and abstract global power is somehow "anchored" into territory, although not necessarily completely integrated into it.[19] Around these points (and perhaps also in connection with locally existing power structures) new cores of domination are coming into existence.

This vision of the impersonal global capital colonizing the whole world and collecting symbolic values in its "command points" sounds very pessimistic. Is it in any way possible to approach a new "international paradigm" in art, as indicated, e.g., by Araeen? We all secretly assume that the multicultural world of otherness is just a surface and that there is the Other that is different from others in the sense that we are all different from it. But is there a chance to stop understanding ourselves as "the Other's others" and to take the idea of globalism literally? Especially Russia, with its position, its political power and its artistic and intellectual potentials has perhaps a very real possibility of establishing a different, alternative international cultural network. But such an endeavor would demand a concentration of energies, and, in the first place, an escape from the game of representations, from the position of being the "Other's other."

[1] This text is the revised and partly extended version of the paper which I presented at the conference *We and the Others (Russian Artists in the West), the Others and We (Western Artists in Russia)*, organized in the context of the Moscow International Art Fair *ART MANEGE 97* on 6 and 7 December 1997.

[2] Ekaterina Dyogot, "The Revenge of the Background," *Zonen der Ver-Störung*, Silvia Eiblmayr (ed.), Steirischer Herbst, Graz, 1997, p. 44.

[3] Samuel P. Huntington, *The Clash of Civilizations and the Remaking of the World Order*, Simon & Schuster, New York, 1996.

[4] Huntington, *op. cit.*, p. 69.

[5] Edward W. Saïd, *Orientalism. Western Concepts of the Orient*, Penguin, London, 1995.

[6] Ilya Kabakov, XVIII congres de AICA a Stogolm (1994), "A Story about a Culturaly Relocated Person," *M'ars* (Ljubljana), no. 3–4, 1996, pp. 35–45.

[7] In his paper at the *We and the Others ...* conference, *We and the Different*, Alexander Jakimovich has indicated an approach to Kulik's work which is essentially more interesting than the stereotype of the "Russian dog"; he understands his actions as a part of the effort to reach not only beyond humanistic, but also human art.

[8] In his paper at the conference *Living with Genocide*, Ljubljana 1996, Viktor Misiano spoke about the two strategies (used by Alexander Brener and Yuri Leiderman, respectively) which are a response to the artists' position in Russia (the proceedings of the conference appeared in *Living With Genocide: Art and War in Bosnia*, special issue, *M'ars*, Ljubljana, vol. II, no. 1–2, 1999. See also Dyogot, *op. cit.*

[9] See also the reactions of the British reviewers to the Chinese avant-garde art, as decribed in: Hou Hanru, "Entropy; Chinese Artists, Western Art Institutions, A New Internationalism," Jean Fisher (ed.), *Global Visions. Towards a New Internationalism in the Visual Arts*, Kala Press, in association with The Institute of International Visual Arts, London, 1994, pp. 83–84.

[10] Rasheed Araeen, "New Internationalism, or the Multiculturalism of Global Bantustans," *Global Visions: Toward a New Internationalism in the Visual Arts*, Jean Fisher (ed.), Kala Press, London, 1994, p. 9.

[11] *Ibid.*, p. 9.

[12] *Ibid.*, p. 10.

[13] The letter is available on the Internet: http://www.heck.com/nsk/nsksupport.html

[14] Slavoj Žižek, *Kuga fantazem*, Društvo za teoretsko psihoanalizo, Ljubljana, 1997, also the article S. Žižek, "Multikulturalizem ali kulturna logika multinacionalnega kapitalizma" ("Multiculturalism, or The Cultural Logic of the Multinational Capitalism"), *Razpol* (Ljubljana), no. 10, 1997, pp. 95–123.

[15] Žižek, "Multikulturalizem...," *op. cit.*, p. 114.

[16] *Ibid.*, p. 116.

[17] Saskia Sassen, "The Topoi of E-Space: Global Cities and Global Value Chains," *Politics-Poetics. Documenta X–the book*, Cantz Verlag, Ostfildern-Ruit, 1997, pp. 736–745.

[18] Martin Filler, "The Big Rock Candy Mountain," *The New York Review of Books*, no. 20, December 18, 1997, p. 33.

[19] Sassen, *op. cit.*, also the article Peter Noller, Klaus Ronneberger, "Metropolis and Backcountry–The Formation of the Rhine-Main Region in the 1990s," *ibid.*, pp. 708–714.

The Strategy of History Writing

First published in *Celostna umetnina Stalin*, Založba /*cf.*, Ljubljana, 1999, pp. 147–159. Translated from Slovenian by Rawley Grau.

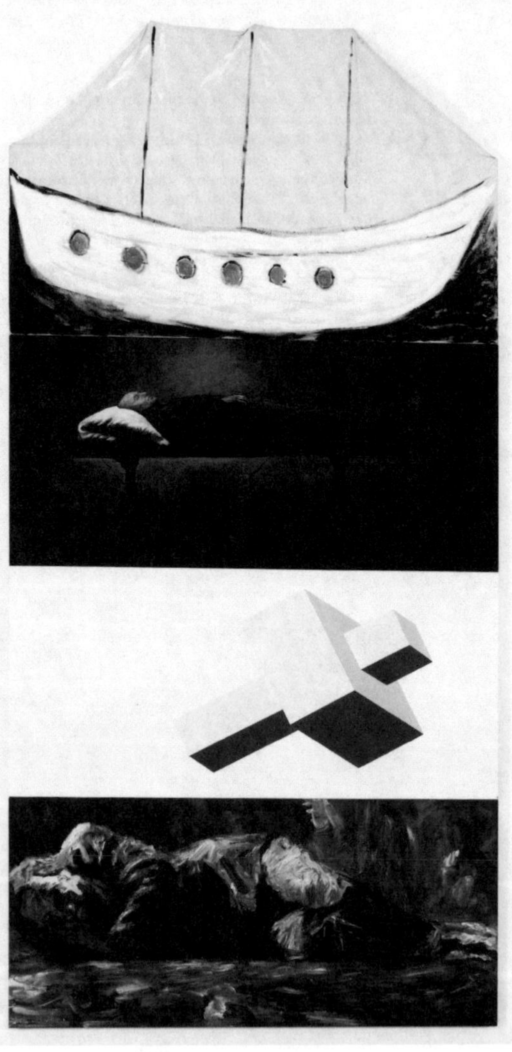

Komar & Melamid, *The Smooth Sailing with Lenin*, 1985

The writing of history is neither a neutral nor an objective under-taking. One might say it is always about the construction of an image for a given historical period or development. This construction will necessarily leave some things out and emphasize other things, while drawing connections and tracing lines of development between them. Today, if we open any book on "modern art" published around 1900 we will be astonished. We will not find any of the artists we think of today as the most important figures in the evolution of modern art but, rather, artists who are now viewed as second-or third-tier figures or who have been completely forgotten. We will discover, to our surprise, that the line of development we consider to be the history of modern art was in its own day something marginal, while today's view has pushed aside artists and movements that in their own day were consid-ered central.

Such a construction is not, of course, arbitrary; rather, it plays (more or less clearly) a specific role in symbolic and ideological systems—that is, the systems through which various power systems establish themselves in the social consciousness. The fields of art and culture and the history of art and culture reveal with particular clarity how power systems operate within symbolic systems; in other words, how the stories and developmental systems they construct are presented as "objective" facts, while perspectives that are incompatible with such constructions are covered up, marginalized, or excluded. When Boris Groys wrote *Gesamtkunstwerk Stalin*,[1] then, he was not entering a neutral field of study, but one that had already been constructed in a specific way. The book itself was also, in its own way, a strategic maneuver within this field.

Even a cursory examination of the book will show that Groys treats, in succession, three artistic phenomena, or rather, three essential periods, in the development of Soviet art: the avant-garde art of the revolutionary and post-revolutionary periods; Stalinism and the theory and practice of socialist realism that are associated with it; and Sots Art. This succession shows us that through his book he is attempting to establish an idea about a specific artistic and cultural tradition. Since traditions are usually established retroactively, we can also assume that this line of development has been established precisely because of Sots Art and that this contemporary phenomenon is what has forced Groys to redefine the historical phenomena. The language of Sots Art cannot be understood without first being familiar with the language and principles of socialist realism, while, conversely, Sots Art can shed new light on socialist realism and its connection with the Russian avant-garde.

This, in fact, is the most surprising and original thesis of Groys's book: namely, the assertion that we can trace a direct line of continuity between the ideas and practices of the Russian avant-garde and the ideology and practice of Stalinism (also including socialist realism). After all, we usually think of Stalinism (with socialist realism as its art system) and the avant-garde as two extremes in total opposition to each other. This is true not only in western thinking, where the dualism *the avant-garde vs. socialist realism* parallels the dualism *western democracy vs. eastern totalitarianism,* but also of the leftist interpretation that understands the Russian avant-garde as the true cultural expression of the pure Leninist phase of the revolution, while socialist realism is seen as the expression of Stalinist totalitarianism, which is itself viewed, in fact, as a betrayal of the revolution and a rejection of its ideals. According to Groys's provocative claims, there is, on the contrary, no such opposition between the avant-garde and Stalinism but rather an essential continuity in which Stalinism realizes the ideals of the avant-garde—something the avant-garde itself was incapable of doing because of its inner limitations and contradictions. Groys was undoubtedly aware that his new ideas turned the established thinking on its head; the points he emphasizes show clearly that his writing was aimed against conceptions we accept as self-evident—and it is precisely this "self-evident" quality that is the result of a specific construction of history or a specific cultural ideology.

It is interesting to reread Clement Greenberg's first important text, the essay *Avant-Garde and Kitsch* (1939) in the light of Groys's ideas.[2] Written in the context of American Trotskyist thinking, this essay may be considered one of the first, and also one of the clearest, formulations of the notion of modernism that would come to be closely connected with this critic's name. Many years later, Greenberg himself, looking back on the late 1930s, when he wrote the essay, defined the Trotskyism of this period—and his own work as well—in the light of the new context created by the Cold War. He writes: "[S]ome day it will have to be told how 'anti-Stalinism,' which started out more or less as 'Trotskyism,' turned into art for art's sake, and thereby cleared the way, heroically, for what was to come."[3]

In the very title of his 1939 essay, Greenberg sets up an opposition between two systems: *the avant-garde* and *kitsch*. The avant-garde is, as he shows, identical with modernism, while kitsch is a broad concept that includes not only the products of mass culture but also academic art and the art of totalitarian regimes. In general, one can say that the common feature of kitsch in art is the permeability of the medium, while modernism, on the contrary, emphasizes the resistance of the medium. The basic demand of modernism, which accords with the modernist principle of "art for art's sake" (as Greenberg himself says), or formalism, is the assertion that the work of art must be nothing other than what it is in itself. The painting as such is not the depicted reality, but rather the medium of this depiction, that is to say, paint applied to a canvas. Through the gradual elimination of apparent depth, modernism reduced the artwork solely to that which it is in itself (in other words, its medium) and its immanent qualities. Thus, the modernist artwork is, in Greenberg's words, "the imitation of imitating"; it presents nothing other than its own medium.[4] The modernist artwork is designed so that it is possible to see clearly how and from what it is made; this is also its core content. With kitsch, on the contrary, the medium disappears and the fictional reality pulls the viewer into itself.

Using the hypothetical (perhaps it would be better to say "phantasmatic") example of the "Russian peasant" who finds himself standing in front of two paintings, one by Picasso, the other by Repin, Greenberg points to the difference between the avant-garde and kitsch:

> "But the ultimate values which the cultivated spectator derives from Picasso are derived at a second remove, as the result of reflection upon the immediate impression left by the plastic values. It is only then that the recognizable, the miraculous and the sympathetic enter. They are not immediately or externally present in Picasso's painting, but must be projected into it by the spectator sensitive enough to react sufficiently to plastic qualities. They belong to the 'reflected' effect. In Repin, on the other hand, the 'reflected' effect has already been included in the picture, ready for the spectator's unreflective enjoyment. Where Picasso paints *cause*, Repin paints *effect*. Repin predigests art for the spectator and spares him effort, provides him with a short cut to the pleasure of art that detours what is necessarily difficult in genuine art. Repin, or kitsch, is synthetic art."[5]

Kitsch, then, is ideal for manipulating the spectator. One could say that Greenberg sees the manipulation point in the spectator's desire, which penetrates the painting and seeks pleasure in it. Modernism opposes this penetrating desire with the opacity of the medium, through which it suspends desire and achieves a reflective effect and, with it, pleasure on a higher level (the level of high culture), whereas kitsch, on the contrary, escapes this desire and promises it instant and direct gratification. Because kitsch, thanks to its synthetic nature and the immediacy of the pleasure it promises the spectator, is closer to the masses than the high art of modernism, totalitarian regimes have appropriated it for their art. In 1939, such were the regimes of German Nazism, Italian Fascism, and Soviet Stalinism (there is no contradiction whatsoever with Greenberg's declared leftism—as a Trotskyist he was, after all, also an anti-Stalinist).

In Greenberg's essay, then, the conceptual relationships that will later play such a key role in the Cold War period are already set forth. On one side is the avant-garde, that is, modernism, which largely belongs to the West (Greenberg draws particular attention to its origins in western bourgeois society, while never mentioning the Soviet avant-garde at all) although it is also the universal high culture of the modern era—and "international socialism" is necessary precisely in order to preserve high culture. On the other side is kitsch, a lower form of culture that belongs to the world of bourgeois mass production; in the totalitarian regimes, however, the social stratification that ensures the existence of a high culture has been eliminated (in the West it has been weakened but not eliminated) and kitsch has become the official and sole accepted art. Of the three regimes he mentions, only the Soviet regime was still in place after 1945, and from there it was a short step to the dualistic system that dominated the understanding of culture during the Cold War period.

Groys's book can be read as a response to Greenberg's ideas as well as to the later conceptual relations that were based on them and that defined the relationship between modernism and socialist realism. Groys underscores precisely those aspects of the avant-garde that diverge in essential ways from Greenberg's system.

Mainly, in the light of Groys's book, the avant-garde is far from being solely a western system. This does not mean, of course, that Groys's book opened up the Russian avant-garde for the West; the Russian avant-garde had long been known in the West, if too often marginalized. Camilla

Gray's book *The Great Experiment: Russian Art 1863–1922*, published in 1962, was relatively late in coming, but it nevertheless provided a very detailed survey of the history of the Russian avant-garde, which was later supplemented in the 1970s and 1980s by several major exhibitions. Groys's book, however, placed the avant-garde in a different context and in a different tradition. At the same time, it also expressed doubts about the self-evident nature of the assertion that socialist realism can be dismissed summarily as kitsch. And finally, it argued against the notion that the avant-garde and socialist realism represent two diametrically opposite poles. But what, in fact, do all these reassessments mean, and why are they necessary?

Greenberg, both in his essay on the avant-garde and kitsch and in later writings, stressed modernism's development toward purity and autonomy. (Let's recall that, two decades later, he understood Trotskyism, including his own, as the antecedent of an "art for art's sake" aesthetics.) Both critics and artists saw modernism as an essentially autonomous art production, which confined itself to intra-aesthetic problems. Greenberg, for instance, sees in the development of the avant-garde a tendency for social withdrawal and depolitization—an assertion that seems quite unusual, considering what we know about the tendencies of the historical avant-garde movements. The only way to understand his assertion (which overgeneralizes certain tendencies in art while simply ignoring other, very explicit avant-garde phenomena) is in the context of his vision of avant-garde art's development toward modernism as a pure and abstract artistic language. Later, he saw the paintings of Jackson Pollock and other representatives of American abstract expressionism as presenting the mature form of this tendency—which was the culmination of a consistent and uninterrupted development that began with impressionism.

The group of art critics who appeared on the scene in the 1970s, however, had their doubts about the absolute truth of these assertions, and about the established descriptions of abstract expressionism as an entirely free, individual, avant-garde, and autonomous form of art. Max Kozloff, in his 1973 article "American Painting during the Cold War," was the first to demand that we renounce our smug assertions about the triumph of abstract expressionism and ask ourselves, "[W]hat, after all, can be said of American painting since 1945 in the context of American political ideology, national self-images, and even the history of our country?"[6] Kozloff and other writers were convinced that it was necessary to revise the then-current understanding of abstract expressionist practice and, indeed, the entire history of post-1945 American art (hence the label "revisionists") and to locate this art in the social and political context of the period. More simply, this revision demonstrated that the United States had been directly exploiting abstract expressionism as a cultural weapon in the Cold War with the Soviet Union. The values attributed to abstract expressionism (individualism, experimentation, boldness, progressiveness) were expressly defined as American progressive values—in sharp contrast to the conservatism and ideological stamp of art in the Soviet Union. These analyses showed how American state structures, including the Central Intelligence Agency, supported institutions like the Museum of Modern Art in New York and promoted American art abroad, and also how they supported certain Eastern European artists who could be displayed as proof of the triumphant influence of American art and culture.[7] (An often-mentioned example of this is an exhibition at MoMA in 1961 that presented Polish modernist painters, including Tadeusz Kantor. "Irrespective of the role of this art movement within the internal artistic evolution of Polish art, this kind of development was seen as a triumph for 'our side.'"[8])

I should mention that later "revisionists of revisionism" showed that relations within the American cultural arena were somewhat more complicated. The cultural ideology of the West was not uniform and homogeneous; in the United States, for instance, there was opposition between the liberals, who supported abstract art, and the conservatives (such as the notorious Congressman George Dondero), who saw abstract art as an attempt to destroy traditional American values and a form of Soviet infiltration. These later analyses showed how the success of America's modernist artists abroad helped to solidify their position at home. This position was even more complicated, since not all political liberals supported abstract art while not all political conservatives opposed it. Also, the tension between

America and Western Europe was a further complication.
In addition, several of the leading modernist artists abandoned
their apolitical stance, at least on occasion, and expressed
clear political viewpoints. Some of the leading American
modernists exhibited doubts about the capitalist system and
sympathies for leftist politics, while Picasso—in direct
contrast to the thesis that great modernist painting must
necessarily be autonomous and apolitical—continued his
politically engaged art with the painting *Massacre in Korea*
(1951), an explicitly anti-American work that, in fact, had
much in common with socialist realism.

Nevertheless, we can say that the cultural ideology
of the West, which in essence took shape right at the time of
the Cold War, was successful: it developed simplified
concepts and conceptual oppositions that even today are
accepted as a natural and self-evident framework for
understanding the art of the second half of the 20th century.
On the one side (the western side), we have democracy,
capitalism, individualism, and apolitical, abstract, and elitist
modernism, while on the other side we have totalitarianism,
communism, an emphasis on the masses, and ideological,
realistic, and populist socialist realism. Regardless of the
value we give to the individual concepts (a Russian dissident,
for example, will be inspired by the western values in art and
society, while a member of the French Communist Party will
argue for a politically engaged realistic art as opposed to
decadent abstract formalism), these concepts remain the
basic, and self-evident, topography for the development of
art since 1945.

But there is yet another aspect to this symmetrical
opposition: we might say that the art discourse of the West
ensured its dominant position by means of a double ideological operation, in which the first step is to declare
modernism to be the cultural expression of humanity in
general, the universal artistic language, and the sole form of
high culture for its time. Thus Meyer Schapiro wrote of
modernist abstract art:

> "No other art today exhibits to that degree in the
> final result the presence of the individual, his sponta-
> neity and the concreteness of his procedure.
> This art is deeply rooted, I believe, in the self and its

relation to the surrounding world. The pathos of the reduction or the fragility of the self within a culture that becomes increasingly organized through industry, economy and the state intensifies the desire of the artist to create forms that will manifest his liberty in this striking way—a liberty that, in the best works, is associated with a sentiment of harmony and achieves stability, and even impersonality through the power of painting to universalize itself in the perfection of its form and to reach out into common life. It becomes then a possession of everyone and is related to everyday experience."[9]

It follows, then, that even in the East all true artists would create modernist art if they were not prevented from doing so by the ideological pressures of totalitarian society—the proof of this is, for instance, Kantor and other eastern modernists, and especially the dissidents, who risk persecution by their persistent use of genuine art forms. The second step in this double operation was to locate this universal language in the West and define it as something that is, in its essence, western. This was not merely a rhetorical figure: all the main institutions involved in the establishment of modernism and the modernist tradition were in the West—galleries, museums, art critics, art historians, collectors, and, of course, the artists. In this sense, modernism really was a western phenomenon, inasmuch as western institutions were the ones defining modernism and its lines of development. Here the role of New York's Museum of Modern Art was particularly significant: MoMA was perhaps the most visible example of how a museum collection, as a selection of works and their arrangement by chronology and development, could, so to speak, create a history. As Francis Frascina writes: "MoMA is regarded as the paradigmatic Modernist museum in that it most spectacularly represents a particular 'selective tradition.'"[10] MoMA and other institutions, then, selected those phenomena in the second half of the century that were deemed to be essential works and which, in their mutual connections, created a picture of historical development. Other phenomena either played the role of marginal confirmations of this development or were entirely pushed aside. A selection was made and a history was determined.

This, then, was the field Groys entered when he wrote his book: an already-defined art history in which the modernist tradition and socialist realism occupied solidly demarcated places. I suggested earlier that Groys's work defines the tradition retroactively, taking the Sots Art line as its starting point. I think one could also say that Sots Art is what created the need for such a work. In the mid-1980s, when there was a general interest in all things Soviet, special attention was also given to Sots Art, which, in fact, had been developing since the early 1970s and was also connected with other avant-garde phenomena in the Soviet Union.[11] Artists such as Ilya Kabakov, Erik Bulatov, Komar and Melamid, and others achieved international fame almost overnight. Their use of socialist-realist imagery in connection with images of everyday Soviet life (from communal kitchens to the particular green paint used in the hallways) and references to the historical avant-garde seemed exotic; it matched the phantasmatic images and expectations associated with the Soviet world that was just then opening up. But in order for this art to become something more than exotic decoration and a short-lived fashion outside its original setting, it would need a theoretical frame of reference; a tradition would have to be sketched out that culminated logically in Sots Art. And the only way to do this was for Groys to plot out a concept of art's development in the 20th century that was significantly different from the established models. More precisely, he defined the line that ran from the Russian avant-garde through Stalinism to Soviet Sots Art, not as the opposite pole of western modernism, but as a different, yet comparable, tradition. Thus Groys could no longer agree with the generalized notions about the inherent opposition between the avant-garde and socialist realism, socialist realism as kitsch, and so on. He underscored instead the implicit totalizing (totalitarian) dimension of the avant-garde—its inclination to move into the real social and historical world, which artistic vision would then shape into something new, out of nothing. But he also underscored the inner contradictions that prevented the avant-garde from truly implementing its vision in society. His central assertion is that Stalinism succeeded in realizing what the avant-garde had been trying to realize but could not because of inner limitations. Groys views the Stalinist system as a socially realized, complex work of art with an extraordinarily complex conceptual structure. In this context, socialist realism, which is itself established on a thorough theoretical foundation, assumes an entirely logical functional role. Only such a perspective makes it possible for us to perceive the inner complexity of the "post-utopian" Sots Art. And only thus does the spectacular —and for the western eye, exotic—use of socialist-realist elements acquire its conceptual and ironic, but also poetic, meaning.

The term "Sots Art," coined by Komar and Melamid as an analogy to western "Pop Art," speaks to both the parallelism and radical difference between the positions in the East and in the West. At the same time as the western consumerist world was visually inundated by mass culture, the visual appearance of the everyday world in the East, and especially in the Soviet Union, was saturated with images, placards, and other visual-art elements deriving from the socialist-realist tradition. In both worlds, too, there existed a peculiar tension between the image and the experience of everyday reality. Greenberg, to be sure, had included both these systems under the shared label "kitsch," but Groys showed that socialist realism is a complex artistic/conceptual system that is much different from the language of the popular mass culture of the West. (This is perhaps one of the reasons why Soviet conceptual art of the 1970s and 1980s had no difficulty using the medium of painting.) The immediate context to which works by representatives of Sots Art and other art trends were referring was the Soviet everyday reality and its inundation by post-socialist-realist imagery. If we take a work of this sort out of the context it refers to—if we strip it of this context—it becomes nothing but a pure visual sign of the unknown and the exotic. Kabakov, who like a number of other leading representatives of this art emigrated to the West, has written that the works he made in the Soviet Union lost all comprehensibility in their new setting. In order to compensate for the absence of the immediate context, and to keep on returning to the world of everyday Soviet reality, Kabakov developed a genre he called "total installation": he created—or rather, staged— a visual and emotional setting for the work that would again allow him to operate. But this kind of setting was no longer comprehensible in the original context: Russians in the Soviet Union would not have understood the total installations Kabakov developed for the western viewer. Apparently, the gulf between western and eastern experience is impossible to overcome.

For Groys, therefore, Sots Art has a conceptual and referential frame that is essential if we are to begin to comprehend its nature and quality. He also outlined a tradition for it: the line of development from which Sots Art emerged and to which it again returns. (It is interesting that neither Groys nor certain other writers conceal their revulsion toward Stalinism and its project; similarly, with regard to Sots Art, there is in his writing a very clear irony, even a self-irony, and, at the same time, an acknowledgment that Stalinism was truly a complex and complete "total work of art.") This formulation of the tradition demanded the reassessment of generally accepted notions. Groys's book is one of the first important works to show that, alongside the generally accepted tradition of modernism and the trends derived from it, we can also find different but no less relevant traditions in 20th-century art. The line that runs from the avant-garde through Stalinism to Sots Art is one of these.

[1] Boris Groys, *Gesamtkunstwerk Stalin: Die gespaltene Kultur in der Sowjetunion*, Hanser, Munich, 1988. The present essay was first published as an afterword to the Slovene translation of Groys's book: "Strategija zgodovinopisja," in Boris Groys, *Celostna umetnina Stalin: razcepljena kultura v Sovjetski zvezi*, trans. by Samo Krušič, Založba /*cf.*, Ljubljana, 1999, pp. 147–160. Groys's book was published in English as *The Total Art of Stalinism: Avant-Garde, Aesthetic Dictatorship, and Beyond*, trans. by Charles Rougle, Princeton University Press, Princeton, N.J., 1992. —Editor's note.

[2] *Partisan Review*, vol. 6, no. 5, 1939, pp. 34–49. The essay was reprinted in Clement Greenberg, *Art and Culture*, Beacon Press, Boston, 1961, pp. 3–21.

[3] Clement Greenberg, "The Late Thirties in New York," *Art and Culture*, p. 230. This is the revised version of a text that was originally published in *Art News* in 1957.

[4] Greenberg, "Avant-Garde and Kitsch," *Art and Culture*, pp. 7–8.

[5] *Ibid.*, p. 15.

[6] Max Kozloff, "American Painting during the Cold War," Francis Frascina (ed.), *Pollock and After: The Critical Debate*, Harper and Row, London, 1985, p. 108. The article was originally published in *Artforum*, vol. 11, no. 9, 1973, pp. 43–54.

[7] Eva Cockcroft, "Abstract Expressionism, Weapon of the Cold War," Frascina (ed.), *Pollock and After*, pp. 125-133; originally published in *Artforum*, vol. 12, no. 10, 1974, pp. 39–41.

[8] *Ibid.*, p. 132.

[9] Meyer Schapiro, "Recent Abstract Painting," *Selected Papers*, vol. 2, *Modern Art: 19th and 20th Centuries*, George Braziller, New York, 1978, p. 222.

[10] Francis Frascina, "The Politics of Representation," Paul Wood, Francis Frascina, Jonathan Harris, and Charles Harrison (ed.), *Modernism in Dispute: Art since the Forties*, Yale University Press, New Haven and London, 1993, p. 81.

[11] Not long ago, an anthology of literary and critical Sots Art writings was published in Croatian: Irena Lukšić (ed.), *Soc-art: Tekstovi i kritika*, Hrvatsko filološko društvo, Biblioteka Književna smotra, Zagreb, 1998.

Art and State: From Modernism to the Retroavantgarde

Contribution at the conference *Art and Ideology. The Nineteen-Fifties in a Divided Europe*, Filozofski fakultet Sveučillišta Zagreb; Društvo povjesničara umjetnosti, Zagreb, 1999, pp. 59–60.

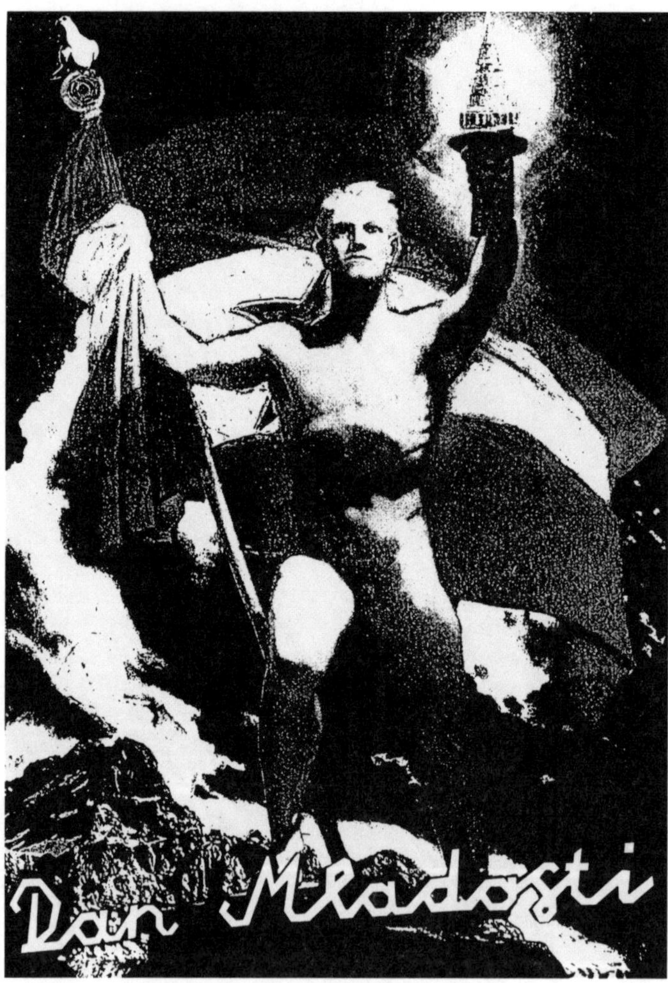

New Collectivism (Novi kolektivizem), *Youth Day*, 1987

What I want to suggest in this paper is that in Yugoslavia, since the 1950s, there was a particular symbiosis between modernist art and the party-and-state apparatus, as I will call it here. Not only did this apparatus tolerate, and even support, modernist artists but often even used modernism for its own public image. (Although I mainly refer to the situation in Slovenia, the situation in other former Yugoslav republics was, in general, comparable.)

I will, however, start much later, in 1987, with the so-called "Poster Scandal." A group of designers, called the New Collectivism (Novi kolektivizem, NK), won the competition for the visual concept of the Youth Day, which was, as we may remember, one of the major socialist festivals in Yugoslavia. Part of the concept was a proposal for a poster that was supposed to be distributed and displayed all over the country. The proposal, which showed a naked young man with the baton in one hand and Yugoslav flag in the other, was accepted by the federal Youth Day committee, but when it was published in the newspapers afterwards, somebody discovered that it was an accurate copy of a Nazi-Kunst work by one Richard Klein, entitled *The Third Reich*—with one significant difference: all Nazi symbols were replaced by the Yugoslav ones.

This event opens at least two interesting questions. The first question refers to the method of the New Collectivism (NK) group, described by the artists as the "retro principle." The second question is how it was at all possible that such a controversial group (it was obvious in advance that the New Collectivism group itself as well as the whole movement of Neue Slowenische Kunst,[1] to which it belongs, were highly controversial) won the competition for such an important and ideologically delicate commission. (As a matter of fact, the Youth Day poster was not the first provocation by New Collectivism. A few years earier, they designed a poster advertising the youth work brigades for the Socialist Youth of Slovenia. The poster included a detail from an Arno Breker sculpture. However, nobody discovered —or wanted to discover—this provocation.)

Both questions are tightly connected. Let me start with the "retro principle" as the working method and the "retrogardism" (or "retroavantgardism," both terms are used) as the ideological position of the group. "Retro principle" implies not only the use of already given forms and models for new needs, but also a conscious political position on which this appropriation is based. This position is made clear by one of the key statements by the rock group Laibach from the early 1980s: "Art and totalitarianism are not mutually exclusive. Totalitarian regimes abolish the illusion of revolutionary individual artistic freedom. Laibach Kunst is the principle of conscious rejection of personal tastes, judgement, convictions (...), free depersonalization, voluntary acceptance of the role of ideology, unmasking and recapitulation of the regime 'ultramodernism.'" Laibach add: "He who has material power has spiritual power, and all art is subject to political manipulation, except for that which speaks the language of this same manipulation."[2] So "retro principle" is essentially a strategy used in the conditions of political manipulation of art; in this case, against the attempt of the "regime" to appropriate a contemporary phenomenon such as the NSK for its own needs, just as it had before appropriated the "apolitical," "ultamodernist" art. It is therefore necessary to answer the second question, i.e., how was it possible that the NK won the competition for the Youth Day concept.

I believe that at least part of the answer lies in the fact that Yugoslavia had a long tradition of giving important commissions to modernists and other innovative artists (the Socialist Youth had a particular role in this respect). The commission to the NK group was clearly a continuation of this tradition.

An incredibly quick change in the cultural politics in Yugoslavia from the late 1940s to the early 1950s can be illustrated with some examples from the institution where I work, Moderna galerija Ljubljana. The new exhibition space of the museum was opened in 1947 with an exhibition presenting four masters of Soviet socialist realism (including Gerasimov and Deineka). Of course, the exhibition was generally praised as a perfect example of Socialist art which should be followed also by Slovene artists. Not much later, Moderna galerija started to prepare a historical show of Slovene Impressionist painters, and there was a strong negative reaction in the more conservative party circles. This art was accused of being reactionary, bourgeois, "l'art-pour-l'art-istic" and thus generally unacceptable for the new society. Nevertheless, the exhibition had its supporters that included intellectuals and artists who had outstanding positions inside the society and also the party itself, and the exhibition was opened in spring 1949. Only a few years after this event, in spring 1953, the same institution opened the first post-war exhibition of abstract art in Slovenia (Stane Kregar - Riko Debenjak). It is understandable that there were vivid discussions and also furious criticisms, but, as far as I know, no real political pressure comparable to the pressure in the case of Impressionist exhibition. In just about five years, the cultural politics has changed completely. Let us keep in mind that this first show of abstract art in Slovenia did not take place in any alternative or marginal place, but in the central state institution which had an important function for the cultural politics; therefore we can conclude that abstract art was not only tolerated but directly promoted by politics. Since then, modernist art, both abstract and figurative, was flourishing, and this development continued into the 1960s and 1970s. An important aspect of this development was a serious attempt to enter the western art world and also the international art market. (In the 1950s, western art was getting known through exhibitions and the newly established Graphic Biennial. Later, artists slowly began to exhibit in international context in museums or in commercial galleries in France, Italy and Germany. In the late 1960s, an association called Group 69, consisting of prominent modernist artists, was formed, proclaiming as its essential goal to enter the competition in the international art market.)

What made such a development possible? The history of Yugoslavia is not sufficiently researched yet and many details of its political history will have to be further clarified; I am sure further research could considerably expand our knowledge about the position of modernism since the 1950s, too. Nevertheless, I would like to suggest the idea that the development of modernism in the 1950s was connected to the growing power of the more liberal and enlightened wings of the Communist party, especially after the break with the Soviet Union in 1948. This break certainly did not have merely ideological and cultural consequences. Above all, it was a matter of economic survival and military security. Therefore, Yugoslavia was forced to open itself toward the West, and to develop an economic and cultural system compatible with the new situation (which would, however, not endanger the basic elements of socialism, the position of Tito himself, etc.); parallel to this development, the power of the liberal elites inside the system was growing, and I would like to suggest the idea that the importance of modernism was somehow connected to this development. The growing power of the party liberals culminated in the 1960s, when they even started to think about a "socialist market system," workers' shareholding etc. In the early 1970s, however, Tito replaced them with more conservative party members.

Of course, it is important to keep in mind that Yugoslav cultural politics was not liberal and permissive in every case. Obviously, there were important differences between liberals and more conservative politicians (many of them remained influential, also in the cultural field). The relation to modernism was changing over time. There was an attack against modernist art in one of Tito's speeches in 1963 that did not remain without consequences, although it did not really endanger this art. In the 1960s, there was also a campaign against elitism in the arts, proclaiming slogans like "art for working people" and "we are all artists." (Still, it is interesting that possible references for such a position are not only highly ideological positions of conservative party ideologists, but also contemporary radical and left-oriented movements in the arts in the West.) Still, one can generally say that apolitical and formalist modernist art was clearly supported. The relation with more critical representative art (not so much in the visual arts, but in literature, film etc.) was much more tense and uncertain. And any liberalism ended where a possibility for a political opposition was detected.

Modernism was not only supported by the party-and-state apparatus, but accepted as its own visual style. This is especially clear if we look at the number of monuments to the revolution and the partisans that were direct commissions of the apparatus and, of course, also directly controlled by it. Already in the 1950s, not only socialist realism, but any academic realistic tradition became outdated in monumental sculpture. In this field, the 1950s, can be seen as the transitional period from the realist models around 1950 to modernist figurative and abstract models around 1960. This development continued in the 1960s with several modernist monuments, some of them of very large dimensions.

It is interesting, however, that in the 1970s, when the liberal leaders were replaced by conservatives and when Yugoslavia turned much more towards the East again, modernism and other innovative artistic forms retained their central position; the movement of the "re-ideologization" of the Yugoslav society, moreover, used these forms, as well as the language of contemporary popular culture, directly for its needs. In this context, some really huge monuments by leading modernist sculptors were constructed.

In 1980, Yugoslavia appeared at the Venice Biennale exactly with these works. The theme of the pavilion was large monuments that were actually modernist landscape sculptures. It was one of the occasions when the link between modernism and party-and-state apparatus became especially clear. The pavilion system of the Venice Biennale, similar to the structure of a fair, indicates that the selecetd artists actually represent their states. With the selection of 1980, Yugoslavia was presented as a country that combines the Socialist system with a high level of modernist art; such a combination indicated that the structure of Yugoslav society was open, dynamic and contemporary (which was, at that time, certainly not true).

This was the context of the Youth Day poster scandal. The project of the New Collectivism was a result of their reflection on the symbiosis between modernism and the regime since the 1950s. In their view, the mistake of modernism was that it declared itself apolitical, pure and autonomous. This is exactly why it could be used for political aims. Today we often hear the opinion that modernist sculptors simply used the state commissions to build large-size sculptures that are supposedly just pure, autonomous works of art, untouched by their actual function and context. This is simply not true, and here I agree with the retrogardists. A pure form that is called *Monument of Revolution* is not a pure form anymore. (What is more, the reading of the very form is determined by the tradition of monumental sculpture; sometimes, we even find very traditional monumental clichés in these sculptures—however, in abstract form.)

The retroavantgardists knew well the writings of Max Kozloff, Eva Cockroft and other researchers of modernism who have pointed to the fact that modernist art was directly used in the cold war politics. And as they looked back at the long tradition of symbiosis between modernism and politics in Yugoslavia, retrogardists discovered that modernism, exactly because it was so "pure" and apolitical, could be used by different political and ideological systems. It is the particular political and ideological context which determines its actual role and significance. In this respect, therefore, it is not essentially different from traditional monumental art. Once we "purify" Richard Klein's work of the Nazi symbols, we get a work with no particular content, an "abstract" work. By giving it other symbols, we can re-contextualize it and give it a completely different meaning. And this is how the retroavantgarde was "using the language of political manipulation to avoid this manipulation."

[1] New Slovenian Art. The use of German was considered
     provocative within the post-war socialist context.
[2] *Neue Slowenische Kunst*, Milan Zinaić and NK (eds.), Grafički
     zavod Hrvatske, Zagreb, 1991, p. 21.

Commitment

First published as "Angažma" in *Prostori umetnosti*, *Društvo inovatorjev*, Ljubljana, 2002, pp. 161–169. Translated from Slovenian by Rawley Grau.

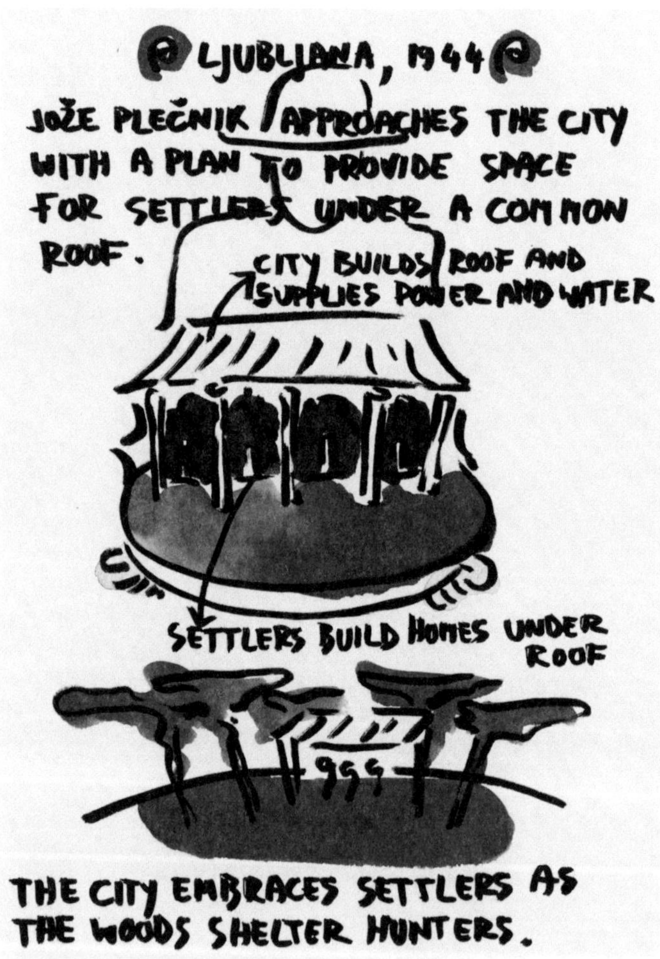

Marjetica Potrč, *Under a Common Roof*, 2005, 5/7

For more than a century, the production, nature, and function of art have been understood, in particular, in terms of art's relation to reality, which, in its essence, is social. This relationship has always been extremely complex and internally contradictory. The two concepts that, in their opposition, define this complex relationship are "autonomous art" and "committed art." More than eighty years ago, in 1920, George Grosz offered a very direct formulation of the dilemma that contemporary artists, curators, and critics must encounter, and respond to, even today. In comparison with social events, which are essentially a battle between oppressors and the oppressed, art seems inadequate and unimportant. Realizing this, an artist can no longer remain indifferent in his work but must recognize his social role; he must decide what position to take in this primary social conflict and then adapt his artistic language to this decision.[1] A few years later, Grosz and Wieland Herzfelde, in a famous essay entitled *Art Is in Danger* (1925), developed this basic view into a more general definition of the social role of art:

> "To summarize: the meaning, essence and history of art stand in direct relationship to the meaning, essence and history of society. The prerequisite for awareness and criticism of art in our time is awareness of the realities and relationships of real life in all its upheavals and tensions. Humankind has been in control of the earth's means of production, on a large scale, for a century now. At the same time, the struggle for possession of these means has grown ever more inclusive, drawing all men, without exception, into its storm. […] This struggle for existence, which divides humankind into exploiting and exploited halves, is called in its clearest and final form: class struggle."[2]

The consequences of such an understanding are obvious: if art is necessarily involved in a fundamental social antagonism—in class struggle—then artists must consciously and actively take part in it. This means they must "paint usefully," that is, they must use the medium of painting as a weapon in the class struggle. The only possible criterion, then, for judging their works is the social impact of these works, not their "autonomous" formal qualities. For this reason, the socially conscious artist will "measure the worth of his work in terms of its social usefulness and effectiveness—not according to some arbitrary, individualistic principle of art, nor by the work's 'success.'"[3]

If, however, we take the consequences of this thesis to their logical conclusion, we will have to admit that art, as art, is unimportant. It is meaningful only if it is socially useful. Grosz, like certain other artists and writers after him, explicitly acknowledged this: "The artist of today, if he doesn't want to evade the issues, or become an empty shell, must choose between technology and class-war propaganda."[4] Grosz's position, however, is internally contradictory, for his own paintings display artistic qualities that we can esteem regardless of whether the paintings are considered to be "class-war propaganda." Today his works are the highly esteemed property of museums and collectors. They have been incorporated into the canon of the art system, which, as Grosz himself stressed, is part of the economic and political system of power directly involved in the fundamental class war. Because of these works' artistic quality, the contemporary system of power is able to exploit them as symbolic value—and also use them for actual capital investments. By saying this, I do not want to imply that Grosz's works are not "revolutionary enough" or that they "failed" because they were unable to rid themselves of aesthetic qualities. I do not think that such artistic qualities are in themselves somehow "reactionary," but I do think that art, to the degree that it *is* art, also possesses qualities that are not directly socially useful as technology or propaganda (even if such works are trying to be one or the other of these). Because of these qualities, it is possible for systems of power to appropriate and exploit even art that is directly critical. Thus, in a sense, Grosz's works serve to confirm ideas that are antithetical to his own, such as those that were expressed by, among others, Man Ray in his *Statement* from 1916:

> "Throughout time painting has alternately been put to the service of the Church, the State, arms, individual patronage, scientific phenomena, anecdote, and decoration. But all the marvelous works that have been painted, whatever the sources of inspiration, still live for us because of absolute qualities they possess in common. [...] Accordingly the artist's work is to be measured by the vitality, the invention and the definiteness and conviction of purpose within its own medium."[5]

I mention this because I want to stress the fact that the idea of a consciously political or critical art practice contains contradictions that simply make it impossible for us to accept the concept of "committed" art as the assumed response to questions about the relationship between art and society. Both opposing concepts—"political art" and "autonomous art"—negate each other in their very opposition and expose each other's contradictions.

These are not merely academic questions. They are very practical, real issues that must be addressed by any artist, curator, or critic who wishes to reflect on their position and work. Anyone who wants to be sure that what they do is meaningful must confront these dilemmas and work out an answer to them, at least provisionally. Of course, the dilemmas faced by contemporary artists and curators are not exactly the same as those Grosz describes, although their basic structure has not changed. It was much easier for Grosz to see the world as divided into two opposite camps; thus, despite his pessimism and critical outlook, he could still possess a clear and all-encompassing vision of a political development that would transform the intolerable present and provide for a better and more equitable society. Consequently, he also had a clear sense of how he himself, through his art, could help to achieve this goal. Today, however, the power relations in society and the relations between art and society appear to be much more complex and contradictory. What was once seen as a single fundamental opposition, able to explain all other social antagonisms, today seems more like a web of antagonisms that cannot be fully reduced to one basic relationship. This web includes not only class conflicts but other antago-nisms as well, such as colonial and postcolonial relations and power strategies based on race, gender, culture, etc.[6] Grosz was able to formulate his notion of a relevant and effective art practice (or, perhaps, post-art practice) on the basis of a general theory of class relations. Today, however, politically oriented art critically analyzes discourses and power strategies on the micro-level, in their immediate and particular social functions. Instead of a general theory based on a clear and fundamental dualism, political art points to a heterogeneous and discontinuous conglomeration of discourses; only rarely does it also include more general concepts of social relations.

In addition, the historical prospect for any real alternative to the ruling system has also become much more uncertain and, indeed, almost vanished. The communist idea (which evolved into totalitarian systems—not "by mistake," as we are sometimes told, but from its own inner logic) has been discredited and no longer presents a mean-ingful social alternative. In recent decades, the economic system of global multinational capitalism and the democratic political system seem to have become the only alternatives to barbarism and totalitarianism.[7] The expansion of global capitalism appears inevitable and unstoppable; here, however, it reveals both its contradictions and its destructive nature. Global multinational capitalism, gradually freeing itself from ties to any particular nation, is increasingly displaying its true character: its alienated power and its irrational and unstoppable drive for perpetual self-accumulation.[8]

And finally, the experience of the past century has shown us how easy it is for the art system (as a constitutive part of the system of power and authority) to neutralize and subsume all practices that are consciously directed against it, that seek to be critical, self-critical, or subversive, or that even want to do away with art as a special "alienated" field of human practice.

It was during the war in Bosnia-Herzegovina that I myself became most immediately conscious of the dilemmas relating to the art world's position and function within social antagonisms. Reports about the aggression against the Bosnian state, about the mass killings and other violence, and about the wavering, slow, and ineffectual response of the international community provoked feelings of frustration, powerlessness, and shame. Like Grosz in the 1920s, my colleagues and I painfully realized that the world of art was a "secondary matter" in comparison with what was happening beyond the walls of studios and art museums, but we also realized that, nevertheless, we could not remain indifferent to these issues. When we talked with some artists who were then exhibiting at the museum, we saw that they too felt trapped in a very similar dilemma and were looking for a way out of the position of passive and powerless observers. When you are in such a position, of course, the first question you ask is: What can be done? Can we find an appropriate form of action within the world of art? When we were faced so immediately with such very real problems, our criteria for what was an appropriate response were very much in line with Grosz's ideas. We believed that a response would be appropriate and right if it could have an impact, if it could actually help Bosnia, directly or indirectly.

What we ultimately did was more on the level of the art system than on the level of artistic or curatorial strategizing. Our idea was to create a collection of important works that would be donated to Sarajevo.[9] We hoped that such a collection would be able to connect some "compensation" for our guilty consciences with the chance to give something of genuine value to Sarajevo. In our view, the symbolic value of such an act was based on the real market value of the collection. We believed that, although "humanitarian" aid might save lives, it could also prolong the status quo and turn the citizens of Bosnia into passive victims; for this reason, we also hoped that the cultural values embodied in the collection would be able to contribute to a material foundation for active strategies developed by Bosnian citizens themselves.[10]

As we wrestled with these dilemmas and sought answers to them, we could not avoid asking ourselves more general questions as well—about art and the art system and their relationship to the social reality. The response of the contemporary art world to the genocide in Bosnia-Herzegovina we felt was insufficient and unsuitable, and we wondered why that was so. Was it just the wrong thing, or was it related to certain internal contradictions within the contemporary art world itself? Can art have an effect on the world, and if so, how? Can it avoid becoming part of the power systems that create and perpetuate social antagonisms? Can it distance itself from these systems, and can it develop effective strategies of resistance?

The discussions we had among ourselves, as well as the international symposium we organized in order to widen the debate about these questions,[11] suggested certain positions:

– The notion that art can change the world in a momentous way became questionable, utopian, or even impossible. Art is powerless in the face of concrete and severe social problems; at the same time, however (or indeed, for this reason), it remains an effective part of the system of power and authority.[12]

– Political and critical art is trapped in the contradictions of its position within the art system, which allows such works only a limited audience and field of effect and which, moreover, can easily appropriate every attempt at criticism or self-criticism and exploit it.

– Artists do not necessarily have to respond to the social reality "beyond the studio walls" in the works themselves. They can, of course, always respond and take action as citizens. They are free to bring indirect references to actual social events into their work—or not. A number of the speakers at the symposium stressed that the only thing the artist "must" do in a crisis situation is make art.[13] Such a belief, I think, is also related to the idea that art is able to create specific values despite being trapped in political, economic, and other power systems that exploit it. This also suggests the possibility that even an autonomous art has a political function and can, in a sense, act as a point of resistance.

It is very interesting, I think, to reread Adorno's essay *Commitment* from this perspective.[14] Among other things, we find here two very interesting ideas. The first is Adorno's understanding of the relationship between committed and autonomous art. The essay underscores the tension and contradictions between the two approaches. Adorno does not think it at all necessary to combine the two poles into a synthetic and total view. Quite the opposite: his fundamental notion is that the two approaches negate each other. This contradiction remains just as strong today. On the one hand, in the light of critical art, we realize that a pure, autonomous art cannot remain outside political reality and that it is precisely the autonomy of this art that allows it to be appropriated by dominant—and sometimes repressive— political regimes.[15] On the other hand, it also appears that a critical and political art (which is based on a clear awareness of its social and political position and role) cannot escape being exploited by the system. Precisely because it is art, it can be appropriated by the very powers it tries to fight against. Adorno's understanding of art and also his manner of writing (and we mustn't forget that with Adorno it is impossible to separate the form of the writing from the content, and especially not in his *Notes to Literature*) are based precisely on the tension of negation between the two poles. Such tension and contradiction, however, are what still allow art to create values that cannot be completely absorbed either by the marketplace or by ideological functions, with the result that art continues to act as a point of resistance in society. Just as important, I think, is Adorno's recognition that the relationship between committed art and autonomous art is not fixed once and for all, but rather changes in accord with the circumstances. The tension between the two viewpoints remains essential; the structure of the tension, however, changes along with changes in the social relations.

The second essential idea in Adorno's essay is the demand for the politicization of autonomous art. Today, when the critical deconstruction of the practices and discourses of authority has become an extremely powerful current in contemporary art (which is in itself an indication that the art system has already managed to absorb quite a lot), the paradoxes of Adorno's theses acquire new importance:

> "The emphasis on the autonomous work, however, is itself sociopolitical in nature. […] At present everything cultural, even autonomous works, is in danger of suffocating in cultural twaddle; at the same time the work of art is charged with wordlessly maintaining what politics has no access to. […] This is not the time for political works of art; rather, politics has migrated into the autonomous work of art, and it has penetrated most deeply into works that present themselves as politically dead."[16]

I do not think we should somehow replace committed and critical political art with autonomous art, nor do I think that Adorno's idea is that autonomous art can, in general and in all circumstances, present the main opportunity for political struggle on the battlefield of art. Clearly, his statements refer to a particular historical moment and a particular type of art. But nevertheless, it seems to me that his demand for the political use of autonomous art continues to be (or is again) important today. The political use of autonomous art is perhaps possible precisely because of its relationship to committed art. At the same time I think that the politicization of autonomous art not only sheds light on the artistic ("autonomous") values of committed art; it also, in fact, allows for the political and critical dimension of autonomous art.

What are the possible curatorial strategies toward autonomous art and its political effects? Which aspects and properties bring about such effects? One of these properties, I think, is the "opacity" of art, which makes it impossible for us to consume it. It was this aspect that Greenberg, in the essay *Avant-Garde and Kitsch*, saw as containing the political potential of autonomous abstract artworks.[17] "Kitsch" is transparent; it does not resist the spectator's gaze and so arouses and directs his desire as determined by the demands of power. For Greenberg, these relationships were primarily spatial—surface vs. depth. Today, I think, this opposition has largely shifted into the temporal dimension of the work: it is the particular experience of "not-yet-colonized" time that acts as "the real"—the point of resistance that the system is unable to absorb and appropriate.

[1] "Today art is absolutely a secondary affair. Anyone able to see beyond their studio walls will admit this. Just the same, art is something that demands a clear-cut decision from artists. You can't be indifferent about your position in this trade, about your attitude toward the problem of the masses, a problem which is no problem if you can see straight. Are you on the side of the exploiters or on the side of the masses who are giving these exploiters a good tanning?" (George Grosz, "My New Pictures," Charles Harrison and Paul Wood (eds.), *Art in Theory 1900-1990: An Anthology of Changing Ideas*, Blackwell, Oxford, UK, and Cambridge, Mass., 1992, p. 270.)

[2] George Grosz and Wieland Herzfelde, "Art Is in Danger!" [*Die Kunst ist in Gefahr*, 1925], George Grosz, John Heartfield, and Wieland Herzfelde, *Art Is in Danger!*, trans. by Paul Gorrell, Curbstone Press, Willimantic, Conn., 1987, p. 59.

[3] *Ibid.*, pp. 58–59.

[4] *Ibid.*, p. 59. [The translation has been slightly revised to make it closer to both the original German and Igor Zabel's Slovene.—*Translator's note.*]

[5] Man Ray, "Statement," Harrison and Wood, *op. cit.*, p. 274.

[6] Let me mention one example of this complexity: the working class in the dominant country is, to be sure, exploited, but at the same time it also participates in the exploitation of dependent or vassal states. The rights and improvements in the position of workers, which the workers' movements fight for in the dominant countries, are, in part, possible because of the direct or indirect exploitation of other countries.

[7] The predominating position of the democratic political system is not as self-evident as it seems. We are witnessing a process that is replacing political activity, in the true sense of the term, with the idea of "management." In his book *Europe: Between Evolution and Euthanasia*, Tomaž Mastnak criticizes the process of European unification because it will gradually dismantle the state and subordinate Europe to the authority of the global market. The state guarantees its citizens the opportunity to participate in political decision-making and influence public concerns. The domination of the free market, however, destroys the state in this sense and transforms institutions of political decision-making into business corporations that compete among themselves and promote themselves on the free market. (See Tomaž Mastnak, *Evropa: med evolucijo in evtanazijo*, SH, Ljubljana, 1998.)

[8] Slavoj Žižek illustrates the Lacanian concept of *drive* using as an example the title character of the film *The Terminator*, "who, even when all that remains of him is a metallic, legless skeleton, persists in his demand and pursues his victim with no trace of compromise or hesitation. The Terminator is the embodiment of the drive, devoid of desire." (Slavoj Žižek, *Looking Awry: An Introduction to Jacques Lacan through Popular Culture*, MIT Press, Cambridge, Mass., and London, 1991, p. 22).

[9] At the suggestion of the Sarajevo artist Jadran Adamović, then living in Ljubljana, and the Irwin group, and after conversations between them and Zdenka Badovinac and myself, both curators at the Moderna galerija (Museum of Modern Art), the museum invited a number of artists to donate works for the new contemporary art museum in Sarajevo, which was then in development. The resulting collection consisted of works by thirteen artists or artist groups: Marina Abramović, Evgeny Asse, Vadim Fiškin, Dmitry Gutov and Viktor Misiano, Mirosław Bałka, Günter Brus, Sophie Calle, Richard Deacon, the Irwin group, Anish Kapoor, Marjetica Potrč, Thomas Schütte, Andres Serrano, Bill Viola, and the group V.S.S.D. The collection is part of the Ars Aevi Museum of Contemporary Art in Sarajevo.

[10] See Zdenka Badovinac, Igor Zabel, Irwin, and Jadran Adamović, "Museum for Sarajevo: Statement," *Living With Genocide: Art and War in Bosnia*, special issue, *M'ars* (Ljubljana), vol. 11, no. 1-2, 1999, p. 15.

[11] The symposium *Living with Genocide*, which took place 23-24 May, 1996 at the Moderna galerija in Ljubljana, had two parts: *Political Theory and the War in Bosnia* and *Art and the War in Bosnia*. Participating in the second part were Marina Abramović, Zdenka Badovinac, Dunja Blažević, David Elliott, Jürgen Harten, the Irwin group, Alexandre Melo, Viktor Misiano, Edin Numankadić, Peter Weibel, Denys Zacharopoulos, and myself. The papers from the symposium were later published in a special issue of *M'ars* magazine, *Living with Genocide: Art and War in Bosnia* (vol. 11, no. 1–2 1999).

[12] Jürgen Harten's contribution to the symposium *Living with Genocide* is of particular interest in this regard. In his paper "Commitment," Harten described the position of himself and his colleagues at the Kunsthalle Düsseldorf when they considered possible responses to the brutal attacks on foreigners, which had started happening in Germany. Their answer was to organize the exhibition *Deutschsein?*: "The problem started with the question of whether we should do anything at all or, rather, whether it would make any sense to react by means of an art exhibition to what had happened in the streets. The answer was: yes, we should create an exhibition, even if only in order to avoid our silence being misunderstood as ignorance. Of course, we did not believe in any direct effect—those who burn others are far away from the museum-world; nor did we intend to compete with the mass media, wondering at the same time about the silent by-standers whose attitude would not be changed by even the worst daily TV-news. But we strongly felt that there is a certain affiliation between politics and, let's say, an average mentality, which, ultimately, fosters a climate of oppression, hatred and xenophobia. It was at that level of opinion-shaping that we thought we should become involved, but we soon found ourselves inevitably confronted with the problem of how to understand our own nationality, particularly in terms of culture, and, eventually, which artists to invite." (Jürgen Harten, "Commitment," *Living with Genocide, op. cit.*, p. 30.) Harten thus expressed a shaky belief that art events could have an influence on public consciousness. The basic concern of the exhibition *Deutschsein?*, however, he described as follows: "The crucial issue of the *Deutschsein?* exhibition [...] was the relationship between the artistic identity of an artist and their identity as a *zoon politikon*." (p. 35).

[13] This was stated very clearly and directly by Denys Zacharopoulos, among others: "An artist can paint flowers during a war because it is not necessarily by painting cannons or weapons that you say something about the war" (*Living with Genocide*, op. cit., p. 47).

[14] Theodor W. Adorno, "Commitment," *Notes to Literature*, vol. 2, trans. by Shierry Weber Nicholsen, Columbia University Press, New York, 1992.

[15] Perhaps the most famous example of this is the case of abstract expressionism being used as a weapon in the Cold War.

[16] Adorno, "Commitment," *op. cit.*, pp. 93–94.

[17] Clement Greenberg, "Avant-Garde and Kitsch," *Art and Culture*, Beacon Press, Boston, 1961, pp. 3–21; the essay was originally published in 1939.

Intimacy and Society: Post-communist or Eastern Art?

Contribution at the conference *Post-communist Conditions*, 10.–12. June 2004, Berlin, Kulturstiftung des Bundes and Zentrum für Kunst und Medientechnologie, Karlsruhe.

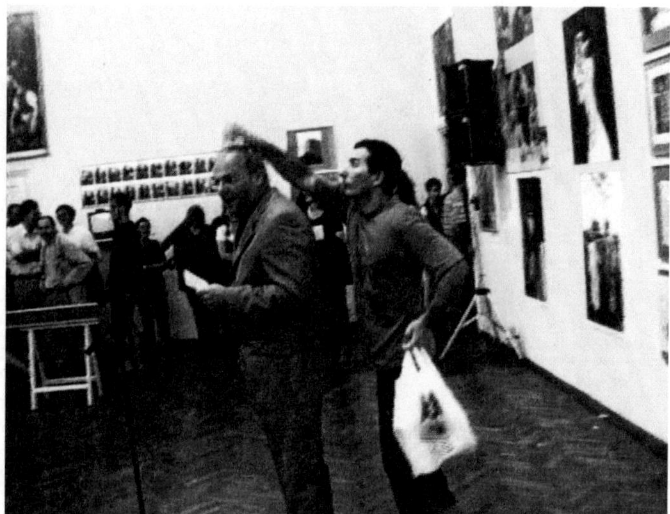

Alexander Brener, performance at the opening of the exhibition *Body and the East*, Moderna galerija, Ljubljana, 1998

When we speak about post-communist art and culture, we usually take for granted that the two concepts, post-communist art and eastern art, are tightly connected if not indeed identical. The very "Easterness" of eastern art seems to be determined by political relations and divisions rather than by the geographical position or indeed any assumed "cultural essence." This becomes quite obvious when Eastern Europe is politically correctly described as "former East." Why "former"? The geographical position, and also cultural traditions of the "former Eastern" countries remain the same. What can be called "former" is the socialist system that has been abolished. This system, in spite of being abolished and absent, obviously still determines the identity of these countries and their cultural production. Eastern Europe now belongs to the same political, economic and cultural frameworks as the western countries, yet inside that framework it remains essentially different from them. The parallelism with the idea of the post-communist condition is, I think, obvious. The end of the communist system, introduction of market economy, a democratic political system etc. do not put the post-communist countries on the same level with the democratic western society. Communism has obviously not been replaced by a fully functional system of democracy and free market, but by a post-communist system that is and is not equal to the system on the West. Yet one cannot fully explain the idea of the eastern (or "former eastern") art and culture only through the changed social, political and economic context. It is essential that it also implies (more or less openly) a particular "eastern" cultural identity.

The case of Slovene art and its relation to eastern art and culture, although particular in several aspects, might contribute some aspects that could help us to better understand the idea of the eastern cultural identity. Nowadays the idea that Slovene art belongs to the Eastern European art seems to be more or less naturally accepted. Especially younger artists, curators, critics etc. seem to have no particular problem with that; rather, they almost take it for granted. There are, of course, other artists and intellectuals who still feel the necessity to stress that Slovenia has to return to Europe (meaning, of course, Western Europe) where it belongs, or even that it, in fact, does not need to return, as it has always been part of it. Somehow paradoxically, such understanding sometimes seems to be outdated and conservative. On one hand, acceptance of Slovene art's close connection with the East appears to be realistic (i.e. a recognition of the state of things as they actually are). On the other hand, however, there is a conviction that the particular position and tradition of eastern art and culture doesn't necessarily mean an inferior value and that it rather offers certain qualities, advantages and possibilities.

Still, it would perhaps make sense to question this natural connection. Why should it be taken for granted that Slovene art belongs to the eastern art and culture? Has it always been eastern, and when and how did it become so? And, even more important, what does its "Easterness" actually mean and what are its characteristics? We can assume that this is not only an issue of Slovene art and that the question about its Easterness actually refers to the much broader context of Eastern European art and culture.

If we ask about when Slovene art has become eastern, the most obvious answer would perhaps be in 1945, following the end of the Second World War and the victory of the socialist revolution. Still, this answer is not so obvious as it seems. If we look at the development of art in Slovenia since the early 50s, at its tendencies, trends and influences, we clearly see that these influences are predominantly, if not exclusively, western.

The same is true for art in other federal republics of former Yugoslavia. Although there were certain differences in its traditions and developments, art in Yugoslavia was essentially determined by the same general political framework (including a general cultural policy). Due to the particular political position of Yugoslavia after 1948, this framework was different from the political circumstances of artistic production in other Eastern European countries. After the quarrel with Stalin, Tito found support in Western Europe and the United States. Later, he was looking for an in-between position between the two blocks, especially with the so-called movement of the non-aligned countries. Although Yugoslavia slowly re-approached the Soviet Union, it generally remained more open for western influences in culture and even economy. The impact of Soviet influence oscillated, but it was never unimportant. Still, the Soviet Union did not directly control Yugoslav culture, and the cultural policy was gradually becoming more liberal and less directly controlled by the state and party ideologists.

An important comparative study of Slovene modernist art of the second half of the 20th century, written by Jure Mikuž, is characteristically entitled *Slovene Modern Painting and Western Art*. The book deals with the essential period of Slovene modernism, from the first post-war abstract works in 1953 to the late 1960s. Its introduction, with the title *The Problematic of Relation—a Problematic Relation*, is particularly interesting in our context. Here Mikuž precisely formulates the understanding of the East-West relation in Slovene art; this understanding was still prevailing in the 1980s. The "problematic relation" is, of course, the relation of Slovene art to western art. If we simplify and sum up Mikuž's arguments, we can say the following: Slovene art of the first half of the 20th century used to be a natural part of western art, although a peripheral, or rather, a provincial one. The revolution and the introduction of the ideologically dictated and controlled socialist realism disrupted this connection. The political changes after the conflict between Tito and Stalin in 1948 opened the possibilities for more subjective approaches in art, first for fantastic and surrealist art and then for modernism with abstract art. Modernism was directly connected to western sources. Since the early 1950s, artists started to travel abroad, especially to Paris; there was more information available in books, magazines and catalogues, as well as travelling exhibitions. Mikuž's book clearly shows how wide the range of influences and sources of Slovene art in the 1950s and 60s was. Nevertheless, as Mikuž stresses, these artists were under a constant pressure, as they were limited by those political powers that still demanded ideological art and opposed modernism and (political and cultural) modernization. As an important evidence of such attitude he mentions Tito's attack on abstract art in 1963; we will return to this event a little later.

Mikuž characteristically understands Slovene art since the 1950s as art that belongs essentially to the West, but is limited by a conservative political system and cultural policy as well as the provincial position of Slovene culture. Or, if we put this very shortly: art is essentially western, limitations and threats to this genuine art are eastern. In such interpretations, socialist realism and similar currents are never considered to be genuine art; at best, they can be taken into account as cultural artifacts. And it is precisely socialist realism that represents eastern spirit in art in its developed form.

The position of art in Yugoslavia was therefore significantly different from the position of art in other Eastern European countries. Still, in these countries, too, existed a connection with developments in western art, and it was sometimes quite significant. There were, in fact, relatively big differences in the situation of modernist tendencies in art in different Eastern European countries. In some of them, abstract art was tolerated or even supported to a certain extent. This was often connected to the apolitical nature of modernist art. Formal experiments were more or less tolerated; what was prohibited was direct political criticism.

In other countries, however, modernist language was not tolerated, and the mere use of, e.g., the language of abstract art had a direct political (i.e. oppositional) meaning. But even in such situations forms of (western) modernist art continued to exist in the work of the non-official, dissident artists.

It is, therefore, impossible to reduce relations in post-1945 Europe to a simple dualism of modernism (in the West) and socialist realism (in the East). Eastern European art was based on complex relations of socialist realist and modernist approaches. Socialist realism is therefore important for the idea of Easterness of Eastern European art, but it is not sufficient. We have to complement it with its relation with modernism, both on the international and on the internal level, i.e. both in the relations between eastern and western art and in the relations between official and dissident art (or, in some cases, like in Yugoslavia and Poland, more advanced and conservative art). In both cases, however, the relation between the two systems is one of opposition and total exclusion.

As Mikuž's book proves, this understanding was still very strong in the 1980s when his work was written. Still, in this time important changes in Slovene and Yugoslav art could be noticed, in its position as well as in its understanding and self-understanding. The relation of Slovene art to the West was not taken for granted anymore. Artists started to feel excluded from it, although the information was still available, they could still travel abroad, etc. The international art world seemed to become much less receptive, and art in Slovenia (and Yugoslavia in general) became more isolated. In the 1960s and still in the 1970s, the use of western forms indicated an organic connection with western art and culture. The 1980s, however, introduced a strange shift in understanding of such use. It actually became a sign of separation. Artists' attempts to be natural ("normal") representatives of international (i.e. western) art were by themselves understood as a proof of their Easterness. In other words, the eastern nature of art demonstrates itself exactly in these (unavoidably inadequate) attempts to adopt a foreign artistic idiom, i.e. the visual language of western art. The more hysterical these attempts were, the more obvious their Easterness was. Slovene art had suddenly become eastern.

The transformation of Slovene (and Yugoslav) art into an
eastern art had complex, internal and external reasons. Tito's
death in 1980 was a symbolical point in the development of
Yugoslavia. It indicated a break that started earlier, but
became completely obvious in the 1980s. Yugoslavia entered
a crisis that was both economic and social. For the social
crisis was, generally speaking, an important confrontation of
two opposite tendencies. On one side there were attempts
to liberalize the society, develop at least elements of market
economy and political democracy etc., on the other hand
tendencies towards a much more centralized, politically
controlled and ideologically strict system. Because of such
processes, the situation in Yugoslav society was becoming
more and more comparable, even structurally, to that in the
countries of the Soviet block. Conservatives
in the communist party aimed at a society that would
be much more centralized and ideological and in fact much
more similar to Eastern European countries. The democrats,
however, were not satisfied anymore with the limited
reforms and demanded a complete transformation of the
society into a western-type democracy and developed
market economy. In these efforts they were often criticizing
Yugoslav society as being totalitarian and actually eastern.
They thought that the attempts at social reforms that would
introduce more elements of market economy based on
private property while keeping the essential elements of
the socialist social structure untouched were illusory and
actually a maneuver of the ruling forces to keep their
positions while accepting some compromises regarding
the economic and political system.

The three general tendencies in Yugoslavia in the
1980s, communist party conservatives, liberal opposition
and those who attempted liberalization in the framework
of the existing socialist system, roughly corresponded to the
tendencies and processes in Eastern Europe. The 1980s were
a time when both the Soviet Union and Eastern European
countries were in a strong and decisive process of
transformation. One aspect was the attempt at (economic,
cultural and political) liberalization and democratization
that was conducted within the system and "from above."
Gorbatchov's reforms, running under the code words of
"perestroika" (reform) and "glasnost" (freedom of speech),

were essential for such processes in other socialist countries as they practically legalized them. The leaders trying to carry out such reforms, however, were under pressure from two sides, from the conservatives in the communist parties who were still strong, and from the democratic movements (often combined with national movements) that demanded complete transformation of their societies into western-type democracies. Encouraged by the atmosphere of liberalization, these movements were quickly becoming stronger and generally supported.

On the global scale, the decade represented a fundamental change of the existing geo-political relations, i.e. of the bipolar world order. During the time of strong tension between the two blocks, the West thought it primarily important that Yugoslavia prevented a direct Soviet presence on the strategically important area of the Adriatic, and therefore easily tolerated the fact that it remained a socialist country. As the bipolar opposition of the two superpowers disappeared, however, Yugoslavia lost its crucial strategic in-between position. What prevailed was the fact that its system was clearly a socialist one, in spite of all the differences with the countries of the Soviet block. Therefore, in international relations (and especially from the perspective of the West, which was, as it has often been said, "winning the cold war"), Yugoslavia was now understood primarily as a socialist, and later post-socialist country, i.e., an eastern country. The new relations between the two superpowers, and thus between two antagonistic social systems, also affected the position of the movement of the non-aligned countries that was so important for Yugoslav foreign policy. The idea of a strong third group of countries, besides the two blocks, lost its importance in the new situation. The movement was in decline in the 1980s, and Yugoslavia lost a strong basis for its differentiation from the Soviet block countries.

The progressive "easternization" of Yugoslavia in the 1980s was thus a result of both its international situation and of the processes in its society. Partly because of the economic crisis and partly because of aspirations of the conservative segments of the party and the state, Yugoslavia was becoming progressively isolated. Even the possibility of free travel, one of the most important achievements that differentiated this country from those under the direct Soviet influence, was substantially reduced. Cultural relations with the West were seriously diminished, too. In the first part of the decade the movement of the so-called New Image still kept a relation with the international art developments, but later the country slid into a relatively strong cultural isolation. In such a situation, the international art scene was replaced by pseudo-international activities inside Yugoslavia, i.e., between its federal republics. This was of course important for the circulation of art at least inside the Yugoslav space, but it was also a clear sign of the fact that Yugoslav art was all but excluded from the international art scene. It therefore functioned as a surrogate for an international dynamics and thus even contributed to its isolation. It was only in the late 1980s that Slovene (and Yugoslav) artists began to enter the space of international art again; but now already as a part of Eastern European art.

The process of "easternization" of Slovene (and Yugoslav) art in the 1980s is of course particular and local, but it also indicates a more general process in the European cultural space, a transformation that also strongly influenced the position of Slovene art. The reforms introduced by Gorbatchov started a process that radically transformed the position of Eastern Europe and the structure of its societies. The idea of a bipolar world came to an end in a new, declarative political partnership of the two superpowers ("new world order"); but this was, in fact, victory of one side (the West and its system of political democracy, capitalism and consumer society) over the other. By the end of the decade, the communist system has collapsed, and Francis Fukuyama felt he could declare the "end of history": in his opinion, western liberal democracy has become universal and, at the same time, the final form of human government. There was a strong demand for re-unification of Europe, meaning the political, economic and also cultural (re-) integration of Eastern Europe into the western system as the "final form" of society.

It was, however, essential that the end of the bipolar system did not mean that the essential differences between the West and the East have disappeared. In this situation, the basis for the difference has shifted from political to cultural differences. Samuel P. Huntington, among others, has formulated this shift very clearly: "In the post-Cold War world, the most important distinctions among peoples are not ideological, political, or economic. They are cultural."[1] In other words, the difference between the East and West was not based on the "outer" condition of the political and economic system, but on the "inner" condition of cultural identity. If we simplify: In the first case, people are essentially equal, the differences between them are based on the conditions in which they live and act; in the second case, people are essentially different, and the essential differences between them remain, even if they live in comparable political and economic systems.

The 1980s brought a strong interest in Eastern European, and especially Russian, art. This interest was clearly connected to the changes in the Soviet system and the new role of the Soviet Union in the global political order. It could be argued that this interest also corresponded to the needs of the art market. But it was also an expression of the necessity to restructure cultural relations in Europe.

In the context of the bipolar world of the Cold War, both modernism and socialist realism claimed a universal value and validity. The defenders of modernism claimed that it was a universal artistic language, that it corresponded to the very essence of human creativity, and that it would certainly be prevailing in Eastern Europe, too, would it not be balked by political and ideological pressures. This corresponds to the insight we have found in Jure Mikuž's book: genuine art is western, the obstacles for it are eastern. In such context, the western art system was interested primarily in those works that demonstrated a clear link with its own, modernist art. This can be well illustrated by the often quoted passage from Eva Cockroft's essay *Abstract Expressionism, Weapon of the Cold War*, where she speaks about the active role of New York's Museum of Modern Art in the Cold War context: "Especially important was the attempt to influence intellectuals and artists behind the 'iron curtain.' During the post-Stalin era in 1956, when the Polish government under Gomulka became more liberal, Tadeusz Kantor, an artist from Cracow, impressed by the work of Pollock and other abstractionists that he had seen during an earlier trip to Paris, began to lead the movement away from socialist realism in Poland. Irrespective of the role

of this art movement within the internal artistic evolution of
Polish art, this kind of development was seen as a triumph
for 'our side.' In 1961, Kantor and 14 other non-objective
Polish painters were given an exhibition at MoMA. Examples
like this one reflect the success of the political aims of
the international programs of MoMA."[2] This example
indicates at least two essential issues that have to be taken
into account here. First, modernist artists in the East
were considered to be representatives of a general artistic
approach; particular contexts, meanings and traditions of
their work were ignored. Second, such an attitude was
certainly not neutral. It was closely connected to the power
relations between the two systems, as the cases where
politics was directly involved in art events prove.

By the late 1980s, however, the western art world became
attentive to those artists and works that could be seen as
representatives of a particular eastern experience, tradition,
culture and identity. The magazine *Flash Art*, for example,
published several articles and reviews dedicated to (primarily
Russian) art in the second half of the 1980s. Among them
was a relatively comprehensive supplement on Russian art,
entitled *An Eye on the East* (no. 137, November–December
1987). In the following issue, Giacinto di Pietrantonio
published an article dedicated to the new interest in Eastern
European art and its importance. Di Pietrantonio argued for
the re-integration of the eastern art into the European one—
a process made possible by the political changes in the
Soviet Union and elsewhere. But for him, this reintegration
did not mean a liberation of a politically repressed universal
artistic language, but a possibility for a particular cultural
tradition and identity to develop and express itself fully and
thus enrich the cultural situation in Europe: "It is only
natural that this perestrojka should be conductive to new
cultural developments and the consequent return of the
East to its place in the international debate. It is clear that
culturally it belongs to Europe and that the caesura created
at Yalta and symbolized by the obscenity of the Berlin Wall
is nothing but the tragic outcome of a farce determined
by conventions of global politics. [...] Art too is at stake
here, for even when it is not in itself 'political,' it is at the
mercy of political affairs. If, in fact, current political
developments should go so far as to guarantee freedom of

artistic expression, the artists of the East will once again be able to vie with the rest of the world in full awareness of their own cultural heritage and with no needs to conform to the demands of a regime or to imitate the West (which would in any case be the same thing)."[3]

This article not only indicates the critic's positive attitude towards eastern contemporary art and its tradition (an attitude that was actually not very frequent). It is also an example of the position shortly before the actual political changes in Europe. The writer is already attentive to the particular eastern tradition and cultural identity; he also hopes for a re-integration of this tradition with the western one and has big expectations about the level of eastern artistic and cultural production and its tradition. What will be liberated from political pressure, however, will not be universal (and in fact western-like and western-based) modernism, says Di Pietrantonio in a very explicit way; rather, it will be the particular cultural tradition and artistic language of the East.

The development of the relations between western and eastern cultures in the 1980s and 1990s, however, was actually more complex and contradictory. One aspect could be, very roughly, described as a double dynamics of integration and, at the same time, increasing of cultural differences. Another aspect, connected to this, concerns the eastern cultural (but also social and political) identity that has been constructed not only out of its particular traditions, but also through a system of divisions and exclusions that has been understood as the experience of the (cultural) Other. This is confirmed by actual and direct experiences of artists who have been faced with the fact that their works become incomprehensible in the new cultural circumstances, since they refer to experiences and contexts that the new audience does not share. The works of Sots art, in their aspiration for the deconstruction of the modernist universalism, in a sense still remain universal. This tendency towards universality, however, gets lost in the tensions of cultural differences. In the new context, works like the painting by Eric Bulatov, *Glory to the CPSU* of 1975 (I mention this work as it was published on the cover of *Flash Art* no. 138, January–February 1988) became spectacular, but essentially illegible signs of the cultural Other. There is, I believe, a continuous line leading from the Cyrillic letters on the *Flash Art* cover to understanding Kulik's performances as representing the "Russian dog," i.e. the wild, irrational, primordial, illegible, threatening and fascinating essence of Russia (or the East, for that matter).

This already indicates that the processes of constructing the identity of the cultural Other reformulated the eastern cultural identity and tradition in a very particular way. It is not only illegible and exotic; it is also deeply archaic and irrational. Communism understood itself (and in many aspects indeed was) a heroic process of modernization. But the post-communists societies have now been understood as deeply pre-modern. Boris Groys, in his essay *Back from the Future,* describes this process of "re-exoticizing, re-orientalizing, and re-antiquitizing former communist countries." In this text, he says: "Where communism once used to reign we must now have the Orient. The redefinition of Eastern Europe by the media is currently being performed as a purported 'rediscovery' of its varied archaic, pre-modern and ethnically shaped cultural identities, which are alleged to have remained the same as they always were. Yet what is quickly forgotten about communism is that under its rule the campaign to combat and eradicate regional and ethnic cultural identities in Eastern Europe was waged with far greater vehemence and thoroughness than in the West." Groys also demonstrates that the purpose of such re-orientalization is "to inscribe the process of simultaneous westernization of Eastern European countries into the currently dominant discursive framework. Had post-communist countries—then and now—always been oriental, then this process of westernization could reasonably be described in the usual categories of modernization, namely as the opening up of pre-modern, closed communities and as a transition from isolation to globalization. But what is mostly ignored is that all these countries—and not just Russia—possess their own avant-garde traditions that are marked by uninterrupted continuity both in the official culture of the communist era as well as in dissident circles. The other fact that is overlooked is that these countries were all once fully integrated within a shared internationalist and globalist venture—the project of communism. Thus the real transition now being undergone by post-communist

Eastern Europe, namely a passage from a militant form of modernity towards modernity in a moderate guise, is being symbolically displaced by an alleged transition from an oriental, pre-modern condition into western modernity."[4]

The transformations that by the late 1980s re-defined Slovene art as an Eastern European art demanded new strategies and new approaches from the artists. This included a rethinking of one's own position as a representative of the eastern art and culture, as well as a search for possible ways of developing one's own activities in response to such a position. In this, the Irwin group and the NSK movement had the crucial role in Slovene art. Roughly speaking, their strategy could be described in three steps. Their starting point has been to accept the position of eastern artists that has been assigned to them essentially from the outside. Second, they have reflected this position in their art and social activities (inasmuch as we can differentiate between the two at all): its difficulties and advantages, but also the political and ideological foundations on which the strategies of the East-West division are based. In the third step, they have tried to affect the situation and eventually deconstruct the very idea of the West-East opposition.

An essential step in this direction was Irwin's project *NSK Embassy Moscow* in 1992. The group has continued the work in this vein till today in the still ongoing project *East Art Map. NSK Embassy Moscow* was a series of events organized in Moscow in 1992, a process of discussions between artists, writers and critics from two quite different cultural contexts who, nevertheless, discovered a lot of common issues and experiences. Russian and Slovene participants eventually drafted a document called *The Moscow Declaration*.[5] In it, they acknowledged a common experience and a specific subjectivity as a result of "history, experience and time" in Eastern Europe. This was accepted as a basis for a specific eastern identity, albeit with a universal importance and meaning. The participants also suggested some common practical goals, especially the "formation of new infrastructures." *The Moscow Declaration* marks the moment when Slovene art not only accepted its eastern identity (which had been developed during the 1980s), but accepted it in an active and also strategic way.

The strategic issues of the group's activities are precisely analyzed in Viktor Misiano's essay on Irwin's project *Transnacionala*. In 1996 the group organized a one-month trip from Atlanta to Seattle during which they discussed issues of contemporary art, theory, politics etc. The participants of the trip were, among others, Russian artists Alexander Brener, Vadim Fiškin and Yuri Leiderman. One of the main topics of the discussions was the issue of art in relation to the East-West opposition in the contemporary world. Misiano analyzed the positions of Brener, Leiderman and the Irwin group regarding this issue and the relations between them. He demonstrates that Irwin's aim is primarily "to understand the nature of the difference between East and West, not to define it. They do not perceive the existing margin between East and West as something stable, but as a convention, a construct. For them, the most interesting task is to understand the internal dynamics which produced this margin, and compare it with other margins dividing the East and the West internally."[6] Misiano also points at the strategic value of the concept of the East in the group's work: "The need to reveal its eastern identity is a natural way for Slovenia to enter the European and global markets of identity. Slovenia perfectly understands that its chance to become West lies not in demonstrating itself as an absolute West, but in revealing the conventional character of the borders created by the West, therefore relativizing the western idea by proving its multi-dimensional character. This is why Russia is so important for Slovenia. It is the light reflected by Russia's mirror of Otherness that provides an identity to the countries which don't seem very western to the West otherwise. Relativizing Western ideas implies destabilizing the eastern idea. That is why Irwin is not trying to preserve the myths of the communist epoch. Their intellectual platform does not function through reversal, but through the deconstruction of their own misleading concepts."[7]

Although *NSK Embassy Moscow* brought an important new level to the group's work we could also say that it is, on the other hand, a consequent continuation of their previous issues. From the very beginning of their work in the early 1980s, the Irwin group and the NSK movement questioned the idea of the universal validity of modernism and the organic connection of Slovene (and Yugoslav) art with western art. This critique could, among other things, be understood as a response to the changed role of modernist language in the East-West relations in the 1980s. Here, the group could refer to the analyses of the role and function of American modernist art during the Cold War (in the texts by Max Kozloff, Eva Cockroft and others), but they could also critically rethink the political role of modernist art in Yugoslavia since the 1950s.

Their understanding of the position of modernism in Yugoslavia has been essentially different from the one represented by Jure Mikuž. They stressed that modernism, while presenting itself as apolitical (and, to a certain level, even dissident) art, practically functioned as official art. Modernism was not only supported by the party-and-state apparatus in Yugoslavia, but actually accepted as its own visual style. This is especially clear if we look at the number of monuments to the Revolution and the partisans that were directly commissioned by the apparatus and, of course, also directly controlled by it. As early as the 1950s not only socialist realism but also any academic realistic tradition became outdated in the field of monumental sculpture. The 1950s can be seen as the transitional period from the realist models around 1950 to modernist figurative and abstract models around 1960. This development continued in the 1960s and 1970s with several modernist monuments, some of very large dimensions. Even Tito's aforementioned speech against abstract art from 1963 could be used as evidence for a growing importance of abstract art. Tito actually complained that abstract art had prevailed in Yugoslavia, that realist artists had been marginalized, that all official prizes were given to abstract artists, etc. And, as he said, responsible for this situation were the communists who allowed it.

We could, perhaps, search here for one of the possible meanings of the concept of post-communist art. The work of the Irwin group (and the whole NSK movement) in the 1980s deconstructed the established understanding of relations between East and West, between modernism and socialist realism (as well as Nazi-Kunst), between modernity and totalitarianism etc. They performed this deconstruction through several operations. First, they pointed at the mutuality of modernism and socialist realism; not only at the parallelism of their functions inside the political, economic and cultural confrontations and struggles, but also at the mirroring of the two universal and total artistic (and ideological) perspectives. An important implication of this is that both modernism and socialist realism can be understood as two forms of modernity, or even as manifestations of two different, albeit corresponding modernities. In their work they have shown that the putatively apolitical modernism not only had (sometimes very direct) political functions, but also that it could perform such functions for different political systems. Similar abstract forms can have different meanings, depending on the political contexts in which they are used. In this, however, they are similar to the totalitarian propaganda art. If we replace the symbols in such a work with other symbols, we can completely change its message. Works of totalitarian art are thus abstract, too, and only receive their actual meaning from their context. The Irwin group, however, were not satisfied merely with the presentation of the basic parallelism of these two artistic systems. What they wanted to achieve is a tension between the political and artistic meaning. In a kind of circular motion they both demonstrate the political function of art and purify this art of such function, returning it to art.

It is important to notice that this deconstruction took place inside a still existing and functioning socialist system. We could mention other, earlier cases of such deconstructivist approach to the "communist condition" (Sots Art etc.). In this context, the communist condition may be understood not merely as the engaged, ideological, eastern art, but also as the tension between this and the pure, formal, western art. "Communist condition," therefore, implies not one, but two cultural and artistic systems, mutually exclusive, both claiming to be total and universally valid. Let us take the well-known case of Kosolapov's combination of Coca-Cola and Lenin. This act might seem banal at first glance, but this is because of the banality of the systems that the artist is dealing with and disclosing in his seemingly naive work. Actually, the work is a complex deconstruction that uncovers at least two essential issues: first, that the total and universal modernist project of communist society and culture exists only in opposition with another, equally universal modernist system of capitalist market economy; and second, that there is, at the same time, a certain parallelism between the two of them. Post-communist works use this conflicting parallelism as a double mirror. The nature of one system reflects itself in the mirror of the other, opposite one. Soviet socialism and American capitalism are, of course, two opposing social concepts. This opposition finds its visual expression in two visual systems—in the world of commercial advertising on one side and the world of ideological propaganda on the other. But when Kosolapov places the main icons of both systems, Lenin and Coca-Cola, on the same level, when the red color represents both the color of revolution and an element of a protected trade mark, the functional parallelism between both becomes obvious. Coca-Cola is Lenin's truth, and vice versa, Lenin is the truth of Coca-Cola. Revolutionary rhetoric is an instrument of advertising and advertising is ideological manipulation. The approach of these artists demonstrates that the two opposing modern systems are, in spite of their aim for totality and universal validity, heteronomous. They are based on each other, and they are each other's suppressed truth. In this sense we could also describe post-communist art as post-modern—not in the sense of art that would be liberated of restraints and asceticism of the total modernist project, but in a sense similar to one of Lyotard's definitions of the notion of the post-modern, as described in his book *The Postmodern Explained to Children*. Post-socialist art in this sense would thus correspond to Lyotard's idea that the post-modern represents modernity's "working through" (Durcharbeiten) itself. He described the meaning of the prefix "post-" not as "going back," but as "working through" in the psychoanalytical sense, i.e. as a process of "ana-lysing, ana-mnesing, of reflection."[8]

The fact that Slovene art by the late 1980s already belonged to Eastern European art and that Eastern European artists supposedly represented a particular eastern cultural identity included an interesting paradox: Eastern European cultural space did in fact not exist. "Another point of interest is that where I come from art does not circulate. There is no publicity concerning art and no information concerning art is widely disseminated. Information about any exhibit is generally restricted to the town where it is held, and when we came here to prepare the show together, we discovered that we didn't know what was going on elsewhere in Eastern Europe. I did not know what has been happening in Poland or in Czecho-Slovakia, for example. Not only is there no distribution in the West of news from the Eastern European art world, there is no distribution of news in the East either." This quotation, taken from a discussion with Marjetica Potrč at the *Points East* conference in Glasgow in 1990, indicates the actual situation by the end of the 1980s. While the idea of the cultural difference between western and eastern art and culture (and the lack of eastern representation in the West) formed the main framework of thinking about eastern art, the actual contacts between artists, critics and institutions from the eastern countries were very few and the knowledge about the contemporary artistic production as well as the tradition of modern and contemporary art from those countries was poor. It was not only the time of the first exhibitions of eastern art in the West, but also the time of the first attempts at contacts and collaborations between eastern institutions. The process of establishing the eastern cultural space had therefore two interconnected aspects. One of them was the approach from the West, i.e. the search for a common Eastern European cultural space and identity, different from the western one. The other were the attempts of the eastern artists, curators and institutions to create contacts, find common (eastern) ground and perhaps develop common (eastern) strategies.

Perhaps we should indicate here another possible context of the process of constructing the cultural difference between the East and the West and of a particular Eastern European cultural identity. We might compare it to the concepts of difference and identity in political and cultural studies, as well as in practical political activities. These concepts, too, involve a deep contradiction. They have been interpreted as a way of liberating minorities and repressed groups, indeed of formulating their particular traditions and interests, needs and demands that have been repressed by the (ideological) concept of a universal human experience. But they have also been understood as results of strategies of ethnicization and thus of a reformulation of the power strategies in post-colonial conditions. Just as it has been with eastern identity, this is not an "either-or" situation. It probably demands careful strategies that both promote and question these concepts, and eventually deconstruct them.

These contradictions can be illustrated by two examples. The first is the well-known essay by Cornell West about *The New Cultural Politics of Difference* (1990). Here, West argues for a politics that replaces the "false universalism"—actually a form of domination—with a new importance of difference. "Distinctive features of the new cultural politics of difference are to trash the monolithic and homogeneous in the name of diversity, multiplicity, and heterogeneity; to reject the abstract, general, and universal in light of the concrete, specific, and particular; and to historicize, contextualize, and pluralize by highlighting the contingent, provisional, variable, tentative, shifting, and changing. [...] To put it bluntly, the new cultural politics of difference consists of creative responses to the precise circumstances of our present moment [...]."[9] It should be noted, however, that West does not connect the new importance of difference to any rigid notion of identity. Speaking about the difference between blacks and whites, he emphasizes the necessity to avoid both the "assimilationist" tendencies and the "homogenizing impulse" (that assumes that all black people are alike and thus erases the differences between them). The West aims at a deconstruction and explanation of oppositions such as whiteness-blackness, i.e. at disclosing the manner of the political construction of such notions and their actual function.

The second text we could mention here is Rasheed Araeen's critical analysis of multiculturalism and the concept of cultural difference. While Cornel West understands the cultural difference as a liberalizing force, Araeen, on the other hand, understands the discourse of the cultural difference basically as "a cultural tool" of the West "to ethnicize its non-white population in order to administer and control its aspiration for equality. [...] As for the dominant discourse, it is so obsessed with cultural difference and identity to the extent of suffering from an intellectual blockage, that it is unable to maintain its focus on the works of art themselves. [...] The obsession with cultural difference is now being institutionally legitimized through the construction of the 'postcolonial other,' who is allowed to express itself only so long as it speaks of its own otherness."[10]

It would be wrong to understand the idea of the East-West relations as something static and simple. It has been internally complex and contradictory as well as in a constant transformation. We should, for example, not neglect the fact that the end of the Cold War era fundamentally changed the situation in Europe. Cultural differences did not simply re-establish the former bipolarity. The representatives of today's middle and young generations of artists have shaped their approaches in a world where the opposition of the communist East and capitalist West is history; in a world which is often called—and in many essential aspect indeed is—global. The experience of such a world is obviously present in their works.

In his text *Art after Communism?*, written for the catalogue of the *Manifesta 2* in Luxembourg in 1998, Robert Fleck pointed at disappearing differences between eastern and western young contemporary art in the post-communist context. "The disappearance of communism from the cultural and political map," says Fleck, "has deeply influenced recent art throughout the world. Since the 1990s, the environment is no longer divided between conflicting alternative social systems. Today's artists need no more take positions in the ideological battle, which marched through European landscape from 1917. It is, however, no longer possible to choose between different perspectives."[11] It is important that for him the term "post-communism" refers not only to Eastern Europe, but is used as a more general description of European society and culture of the 1990s. The disappearance of the political division, the processes of integration and the loss of any reasonable alternative to the capitalist system affect western societies perhaps not less strongly than the eastern ones. The artistic parallel to these new conditions in Europe is what Fleck calls "the new international style." This style is critically oriented and can be connected with the fact that for the "children of the implosion of communism" there is "no longer any alternative to capitalism." And what had once been experienced, from the part of the West, as a "typical eastern aesthetic" has become obsolete or has even disappeared. Today, says he, one cannot perceive any differences between the works of art produced in the East or in the West. "Whoever, today, travels all parts of the continent, determines no fundamental difference in the aesthetic paradigms of younger artists from the various regions." Young Eastern European artists never really experienced the communist system; the "same advertisements, the same television channels, and the same social values and dreams as in the West, were for them the only concrete experience."[12]

Since one still, even today, meets the idea that Eastern European identity finds its expression in a particular, genuine eastern aesthetic and visual language, Fleck's descriptions of the post-communist 1990s and his pointing at the "disappearance of the fundamental aesthetic differences between the various parts of Europe" are particularly important. Yet, his statements did not pass undisputed. (There were many discussions about them— much more discussions, in fact, than there were written responses.) Some of the critical responses—especially those that implied the idea of static and fundamental cultural essences of the West and the East—are not particularly relevant. More interesting were those that questioned Fleck's optimistic attitude, e.g. when he speaks about a "return to normality" and a "genuine liberation."

On the other hand, several texts and discussions that appeared in Eastern Europe about the same time, but also later, show rather different feelings. It would, for example, be interesting to compare Fleck's essay to the texts published in the issue of the *Moscow Art Magazine* entitled *East is Looking at the East, East is Looking at the West*.[13] These texts display a painful feeling of being trapped in a radically divided world where the West-East opposition still fatally determined their writers. The notion of the Other as the most basic principle of the East-West relations is a recurrent issue in them. Reading the texts, one can't help noticing that these writers feel the division of Europe not to have disappeared after the fall of the Berlin Wall, but to have changed its character and forms of appearance. The writers do not know the feeling of liberation, although several of them might be counted among the representatives of the "international style." Moreover, the basic feeling seems to be one of being pre-determined within the West-East relations, of the impossibility to step out of them. It seems, then, that the

divisions in Europe have not yet been overcome and that they have been, after the radical changes of the geopolitical situation in Europe, only transformed and re-arranged.
It should be further noticed that the writers of the *Moscow Art Magazine* describe these differences as a part of strategies of power and dominance in contemporary Europe—a game in which they themselves obviously play the role of the weaker party.

Faced with the contradictions between the demand for a universal (actually western-based) artistic language (such as the new "international style" is supposed to be) and the experience of the impossibility of communication between eastern and western artistic approaches (actually, the impossibility of eastern works to be properly understood in the West), Piotr Piotrowski suggested the concept of "framing." The concept of the "frame," based on ideas of Jonathan Culler and Norman Bryson, replaces the notion of the "context." It is "structurally an element of the text, although […] it is not given, but derives from the adopted interpretative strategy." [14] Although one would find in different cities seemingly similar works of art, articulated in the western-based artistic language, one's interpretation can disclose differences in their meanings. "Even though sometimes the perceived forms resemble one another, they acquire their meaning because of our 'framing' so that we ought to pay more attention to the 'frame' than to the 'ideolect.' It may be that art all over the world, or at least in the East and West, speaks similar languages, but in fact it communicates diverse meanings dictated by the 'frame' that we activate." [15] An aspect that might be related to this concept of framing is the fact that the same work of art can be understood in very different ways, depending on the circumstances of reception.

In discussing different aspects of the eastern, post-communist contemporary art, we have met several possible meanings of its concept. Here, we will propose another possibility. Very simply we could say that the post-communist art is art of the post-communist societies. It is art produced in a world that has relatively recently underwent a deep transformation of its social, economic and political fundaments and is determined both by processes of integration and of differentiation, of identity and otherness.

The most basic transformation is the introduction of the
capitalist and market-based system and the world of the
developed consumer society.

Perhaps one should determine post-communist art
as art that refers to such conditions (is "framed" with them)
and, what is even more important, reflects them and
responds to them. In this sense, we could also speak about
a particular tradition of the post-communist art that
sometimes goes back to the 1960s and 1970s. Here we should
take into consideration primarily those artists and movements that critically (although often ironically or playfully)
responded to the bi-polarity of two universal ideological,
social and cultural discourses during the Cold War situation.
As we have indicated before, transformations have not only
been happening in Eastern Europe. The end of the bi-polar
structure, the lack of opposition or alternatives to the
existing capitalist system and the processes of globalization
have transformed western societies as well, although this
change hasn't been so obvious. Yet we will not go into this
problem further, except mentioning that those aspects that
seem to be characteristic for eastern post-communist
culture should actually be understood as a part of, or at least
in connection with, the "new international style" in art,
mentioned by Fleck.

I would like to propose some issues that are, in my
opinion, characteristic for recent art in the post-communist
condition.

Exoticism

The issue of exoticism in post-communist art is connected
to the construction of Eastern European identity and its
characteristics. It is, thus, based on a set of preconceptions
that determine this identity. Through the "orientalizing"
attitude in the post-communist situation, an exotic eastern
identity is shaped out of the elements of the communist
past, picturesque poverty and archaisms, the excesses of
the new rich, Mafia, nationalisms, folklore and a particular
spiritual and mystic tradition. Not that such and similar
issues weren't actually present; the function of such
"orientalizing" view is to select them, combine them into
a firm essence that determines the understanding of eastern

identity and its cultural manifestations. It excludes and suppresses a number of issues that are not compatible with it and neglects the differences, not only between different countries, but also inside individual societies. One could, for example, notice how often, despite the recent interest in the Balkans, its rational, constructive dimension, both in contemporary culture and tradition, is completely ignored.

Dealing with these and similar issues does not necessarily imply an exoticist position. But we can speak about such a position in those cases when artists produce works that respond to the supposed desire of the Other (that is, in this case, the West) by deliberately accepting the role of a representative of the eastern essence.

Besides, it often happens that something gets a particular exotic value when seen outside its context or "frame." The meaning of the Campbell soups, for example, has been essentially different in those contexts where such soups have not been banal every-day items from the grocery store. Similarly, monumental slogans in Cyrillic alphabet necessarily function very exotic in the societies where banners and posters with such slogans have never been a normal every-day experience. Such works, too, have often been appropriated by the "orientalizing" approach and turned into manifestations of an exotic culture and its essence.

But we might also speak about an inverse exoticism, when the artists are dealing exactly with such preconceptions, disclosing the mechanisms of their construction. Often, such works are structured in such a way that they speak to the viewer: "This is what you expect and want to see, so we are showing it to you." Because of such shift, exotic imagery ceases to be the expression of the artistic cultural identity, it becomes a reflection of the viewer's own desire. Yet, we cannot really divide the approaches of exoticism and inverse exoticism, they belong together and are linked with a wide range of in-between forms.

Consumerism, advertising strategies, and mass culture

The experience of the developed consumer society and of its marketing strategies, and the impact of mass culture have been essential for the younger generation of artists in the "former" Eastern Europe. Robert Fleck pointed at the fact that young eastern artists now grow up surrounded by the very same mass imagery as their colleagues in the West. Therefore, their art doesn't differ essentially from the art produced in the West.

Nevertheless, the relations of (even young) eastern artists to such issues often show certain particularities. For them, the spectacular world of consumerism is less natural and their distance towards it is bigger. They experience it more intensely; what sometimes seems to be a naive identification with this world might just be the attempt to cross the gap and to reach a "normal" relationship with it. The result of such an attitude can be a certain heroization and fetishization of mass-cultural products. On the other hand, the relations towards the mass society often enable a closer look at the mechanisms and strategies of advertising and consumption.

The (young) artists are not faced only with the seductive powers of imagery and objects of the contemporary mass market. They are also involved with the developing (but often still undeveloped) art market; and because they cannot take it for granted and natural, they are able to reflect its mechanisms and contradictions very precisely, and sometimes quite radically.

Speaking about the relation to the market system, we often mention two types of artists: those who (sometimes quite naively) aim for market success and those who try to avoid the market, since they believe that art should not be a commodity. The alternative to these two types is not so much a "normal" artist's relation to the market, but the approach of those who admit their fascination with its spectacle and power without being naive about it. Deliberately assuming the roles of producers of commodities or of advertising agents, they are prepared to follow the consequences of their decision until they reach its fundamental contradictions and the limits of their own (also moral) position. In such a way, they respond to the alluring power of the consumer society and display their way of functioning and their contradictory consequences.

Technology and the new media

The opening of Eastern European space for consumerism coincided with the expansion of new technological means that have become widely available. (Such availability is, of course, a necessary part of the expansion of the market and its search for new commodities.) There has been an enthusiasm for the new, spectacular visual, acoustic, and virtual worlds, as well as for the technical means that make them possible. New technological media have been particularly appropriate for art that refers to the mass media and consumer society. Technology has entered Eastern Europe in a developed form, and the artists responded by a keen interest in it. Therefore they have not only achieved a high level of technical skills (although their resources have been fairly limited, compared with the artists and institutions in the West), but also a critical understanding of the nature of the new media and their social function. The critical and political use of the media can range from an over-simulation of seducing, spectacular and manipulative effects, characteristic for contemporary mass society, and from exposing its mechanisms, to attempts at developing possibilities for political, rebellious and subversive use of such means and finally to utopian projects where technology offers possibilities to transcend the present.

Body

We might understand the role of the body in the post-communist context through at least two aspects. First, it is very obvious that the transition from the socialist societies to the post-communist condition also involves a deep-reaching transformation of the role of the body and of the ideals and norms that define it. The ideology of "physical culture," the more-than-human efforts of the heroic workers or the strictly disciplined body of the spectacular mass events have been replaced by obsessive ideas of beauty, care for the body, relaxation etc., all in the context of the new, highly competitive society. Since the new models and norms have entered these societies so abruptly and forcefully, it is possible to study their functioning and their underlying ideologies. A comparison of two different bodily regimes enables the artists to question them both and to present their constructed nature as well as their role in the mechanisms of the reproduction of power.

Another aspect is connected to the issue of representation. In her essay *Body and the East* Zdenka Badovinac returns to the question of the representational role of eastern artists. In her opinion, art that is based on an artist's body offers a particularly clear insight into this issue. This is "because the artist's body is necessarily defined only in terms of the relation with the other, and because—due to its inherent intersubjectivity and performativeness—it can be a model of another representational economy."[16]

Intimacy and society

The communist system was never only a matter of general historical events and of global geopolitics. It functioned essentially on the micro level of every-day life and its details, from the choice of objects that surrounded people at home, at work and in the city to the way the passengers were communicating on a city bus. Politics, the structure of society and the most banal as well as the most intimate details of daily life were inseparably connected. Therefore, analysis and reflection of one's personal circumstances, every-day life and experience necessarily involve also an (implicit or explicit) research of the social, political and ideological structures that shaped such experiences. Works that deal with experiences and memories of the communist past should not be understood simply as nostalgic. They often demonstrate quite precisely how the system used to function through the intimate micro-level. (Memories indicate the issue of time that is a recurrent theme in such works. Again, we can very often differentiate among different time structures, e.g. abstract time, personal time and social time.) In such a way, these works function as paradigms and means for reading also the newly developed, post-communist social structure and their effects and aims through the details of the everyday reality.

Institutional and political criticism

When Robert Fleck, in the above-mentioned essay, discussed the "new international style," to which also young Eastern European artists belong, he connected it to a critical intention of the artists. In Fleck's opinion, this "international style" has been characteristic both for eastern and western artists. Young artists, however, did not express their criticism universally, but made it "explicit to specific points, pictures and processes." Methods and means of such critical approach are therefore numerous and heterogeneous: "Criticism as artistic content can in this context be built up by uncovering of social processes, by own or fictitious biographies, by forms of self-examination and self-portrayal, by scientific methods, and by a criticism of the media picture."[17] We could add that political and critical art can't be isolated into a particular art field. Rather, it is an attitude that is present in very different forms of contemporary art.

In spite of the heterogeneity and diversity of the critical artistic practices in the East and in the West, and a certain similarity of their results, it could be misleading to assume that this general style has the same role and meaning in both contexts. From the outset, an eastern artist is in a position that is different from that of a western artist. Regardless of the fact that they both refer to similar sources, an eastern artist is still caught in the system of preconceptions and representations. His/her position could perhaps be described as "conditional inclusion"—inclusion through a system of representations that connect him/her to the idea of the eastern cultural identity. This conditional inclusion is not simply a matter of symbolic relations, but also of possibilities, technical and institutional infrastructure, income etc.

We should not neglect the fact that the East-West relations are in transition and that the process of political, economic and cultural integration essentially modifies the position of the Other and its representation. Still, such differences, although often hidden, are still present and effective. Moreover, the strategies of the East-West division can be regarded as a paradigm. Critical approach and deconstruction of this division opens insights in the strategies of power in other, similar contexts, too.

If we can speak about politically critical post-communist artists, then we have to suppose that such artists do not necessarily deal with "typical" post-communist themes, such as the long-reaching effects of the communist past, the culture of the new rich, the new radical nationalist right etc. Rather, their main subject is the strategy of division, representation and control that defines the "former East."

[1] Samuel Huntington, *The Clash of Civilizations and the Remaking of World Order*, Simon & Schuster, New York, 1996, p. 21.

[2] Eva Cockcroft, "Abstract Expressionism, Weapon of the Cold War," *Pollock and After: The Critical Debate*, Francis Frascina (ed.), Harper and Row, London, 1985, p. 132.

[3] Giacinto di Pietrantonio, "Wind from the East," *Flash Art*, no. 138, Jan.-Feb. 1988, p.67.

[4] Boris Groys, "Back from the Future," *Third Text*, Routledge, London, vol. 17, no. 4, December 2003, pp. 323–331.

[5] *NSK Embassy Moscow: How the East Sees the East*, Eda Čufer (ed.), Obalne galerije, Piran, 1993, p. 46.

[6] *Transnacionala. Highway Collisions Between East ad West at the Crossroads of Art*, Študentska založba, Ljubljana, 1999, p. 188.

[7] *Ibid.*

[8] Jean-Francois Lyotard, *The postmodern explained to children: correspondence, 1982-1985*, Power Publications, Sydney, 1992.

[9] Cornel West, "The New Cultural Politics of Difference," *Out There: Marginalization in Contemporary Cultures*, Russel Ferguson, Martha Gever, Trinh T. Minh-ha, Cornel West (eds.), The New Museum of Contemporary Art, New York; MIT Press, Cambrige, Mass., 1990, p. 19.

[10] Rasheed Araeen, "New Internationalism, or the Multiculturalism of Global Bantustans," *Global Visions: Toward a New Internationalism in the Visual Arts*, Jean Fisher (ed.), Kala Press, London, 1994.

[11] Robert Fleck, "Art after Communism," *Manifesta 2—European Biennial of Contemporary Art*, Luxembourg, 1998, p. 193.

[12] *Cf.* "Art after Communism," *op. cit.*, pp. 193–197.

[13] *Moscow Art Magazine. East is Looking at the East, East is Looking at the West*, no. 22, Moscow, 1998.

[14] Piotr Piotrowski, "'Framing' of the Central Europe," *2000+ ArtEast Collection. The Art of Eastern Europe*, Orangerie Congress, Innsbruck; Folio Verlag, Vienna-Bozen, 2001, pp. 15–22.

[15] *Ibid.* p. 20.

[16] Zdenka Badovinac, *Body and the East: From the 1960s to the Present*, Moderna galerija, Ljubljana; The MIT Press, Cambridge, Mass.; London, 1998, p. 10.

[17] Robert Fleck, *op. cit.*, p. 196.

Haven't We Had Enough?

First published in *BAK, Basis voor actuelle kunst newsletter*, no. 3, Utrecht, 2004, p. 17; 19.

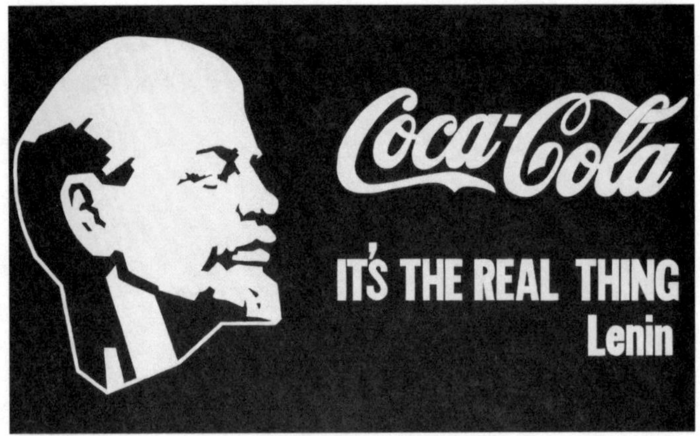

Alexander Kosolapov, *Lenin—Coca-Cola*, 1980-2000

After Moderna galerija in Ljubljana presented, during the opening days of *Manifesta 3*, the *2000+ Arteast* Collection, in which the majority of works are by Eastern European artists, I spoke to an art critic and curator who didn't seem to be too enthusiastic about the event. "Why this East again?," he said. He almost seemed insulted somehow. "Haven't we had enough of that in the last years?" Indeed, have we or haven't we? One could hardly say that Eastern European art—even now, a few years after this conversation—has been over-represented in the world of international contemporary art. Why then this feeling of being fed up with Eastern European art? When the curator said, "we have had enough of that," what exactly did he mean? I believe he actually had two different things in mind. First, by that time Eastern Europe was not fashionable anymore. Well informed as he is (or considers himself to be), he probably had the feeling that the whole event was somehow obsolete, not in accordance with the latest trends in art. He has always tried to follow such trends and respond to them immediately. His need to be always up-to-date with the new events is connected to the second reason why he disliked the exhibition of predominantly eastern artists. Actually, he did not like the idea of Eastern European art as something separate at all. Coming from Eastern Europe himself, throughout his professional career (that started sometime in the 1960s) he has been trying to oppose the idea that there is any essential difference between eastern and western art. His position has always been: There is only art. If the situation in Eastern European art had been different in any way, it was because genuine art had been repressed, limited, or even replaced by political propaganda disguised as art. He had always felt that it was his mission to confirm himself and the art scene he belongs to as "natural" parts of the international art scene. The idea that this art scene (or even himself) belongs to Eastern Europe is exactly what he wanted to resist.

Normal

So, once again, what did he actually mean by claiming that there had been "enough" Eastern European art? I guess he had in mind that art recognizable as Eastern European and appearing in a context that would point at its Easterness somehow represented a minor, "ethnic" type of art. He could tolerate it as long as it remained fashionable (I have known him long enough to be able to say that), but once the concept of the East seemingly went out of fashion, he felt only embarrassed or almost humiliated by it. What he wanted then (and still wants today) is to belong to the art world in a "normal" way. Simply, he wants to be a part of the normal art scene, not the Eastern European one. Art and criticism produced in the West are his ideals, but he is not interested in them because of any particular Westerness, but because they are "normal." His words, "We have had enough of eastern art," therefore meant, "We simply want to produce normal art and criticism. We are interested only in art, not in any ethnic Eastern European art. In such a way, we want to be one with the West." It seemed then, and to a certain extent still seems today, that the West has the unique ability to produce "just art," while all other parts of the world produce culturally specific types of art. Representatives of marginalized communities are often confronted with this dilemma and frustrated by it. Such frustrations, in Turkish culture for example, as described by Orhan Pamuk, correspond well to the situation in Eastern Europe:

"The Kurdish youth whose uncle lived in Germany was the most outspoken on this point: 'When they write poems or sing songs in the West, they speak for all humanity. They're human beings—but we're just Muslims. When we write something, it's just ethnic poetry.'"[1]

But there is, I think, a hidden contradiction in said curator's wish to be "normal." This wish only indicates that we are, in fact, not "normal"—otherwise we would probably not be aware of this issue at all. What is, then, the reason that Eastern European art cannot be normal art, art as such, just art, etc.?

The Trauma

I think that the basic answer is rather obvious. There is no "art as such," since art is always produced, distributed, and consumed in particular circumstances. These circumstances are not only an outer framework that does not touch the essence (as the person I talked to would probably like to believe). They determine not only the choice of the materials, subject, ideas, and issues, but also the meaning of the work; not only its means and sources, but also its availability, distribution, and conditions of reception. It is clear therefore, that—even if we speak about art that is "just" art—we have to speak about its particular context and conditions, as well as those conditions that determine it as "just" art.

One of the most basic facts of post-war Europe was the political division and balance of the two superpowers and their political, economic, and cultural systems. Even in today's Europe, the division is felt as a trauma that demands endless repetitions and re-enactment. If contemporary research points to the fact that the divisions of the Cold War period were more complex than it seemed (e.g. that the parceling out of Europe and the rest of the world between the USA and USSR was based on an agreement that both sides, in spite of occasional crises, basically respected and which kept the situation balanced), it nevertheless confirms that the division was very radical and that there has been very little communication or exchange, economic or cultural, between the two sides.

The Power of Exclusion

The political and cultural division of Europe was based on a balance and tension between powers. The strategies of division were therefore also strategies of power. Even if the two superpowers remained in agreement about dominance over their respective zones, thus avoiding a direct (armed) conflict, they nevertheless developed these strategies of division in such a way as to ensure their own side a certain primacy or advantage. They used these strategies to increase their political, military, and ultimately, economic power. In this context, art and culture, too, were used as strategic means. Not only artistic production as such was important here, but also its conditions and contexts. It was, for example, possible to use the strategies of division, i.e. of inclusion and exclusion, to secure a globally dominant position for ones own artistic and cultural production. Strategies of inclusion and exclusion are effective if they produce the idea of the primacy of the space they regulate. We could therefore say that the cultural power of the West was (and is) based on the fact that it promoted its own dominant artistic language(s) as "normal" art (i.e. established it as the norm of art), as "just" art.[2] For those excluded from it, it became not only a norm, but also the space of desire.

The Two Art Systems

Europe's political division found its expression in the dualism of the two systems of artistic language and production that could be roughly described as modernism and socialist realism. I do not want to imply that the two systems are somehow equal, in the sense that they have produced equally strong and important art. In fact, it is hard to speak about terms of equality between the two art systems. They imply essentially different value systems and mutually exclusive aims. From the point of view of cultural theory, of course, there are, in principle, no basic differences between them, as they are clearly two cultural forms in two types of societies. But for someone dealing with art and not primarily with society, works of art cannot be merely cultural and social documents. They have their particular value which transcends their role as a document. We may know that the value system on which our own appreciation of art is grounded is socially based; yet we are nevertheless determined by it. Socialist realism should not be mistaken for a simple and naive system; it was, at least at its best, a complex theoretical apparatus based on a developed social theory and critical aesthetic thought. For us, however, the values developed by modernism and subsequent currents seem more natural than those advocated by socialist realism.

The trouble with socialist realism, however, is not only that it represents a different conceptual and aesthetic system that does not generally correspond to those artistic values we take for granted. An even bigger problem is that it has been, by its very essence, an actual and rather effective tool in organizing and disciplining a society we felt was extremely repressive, even directly totalitarian.

For a long time, socialist realism has only been understood as a cultural document, if not merely as pseudo-art used to repress not only any genuine artistic production, but also any aspiration toward a meaningful and free life. Only after the breakdown of the communist regimes in Eastern Europe, when the structures and approaches derived from socialist realism lost their actual political function, did it become possible to perceive it differently and to allow even the possibility to think about it as art.

The Strange Case of Socialist Realism, Part One: Is it Art?

I remember very well a discussion with Joseph Backstein, who came to Ljubljana to give a lecture connected to his project *Monumental Propaganda,* which was presented at the Moderna galerija. The project dealt with the then highly urgent issue of what to do with the numerous monuments from the time of the Socialist regimes—the topic was important for the relation to aesthetic and cultural concepts from the immediate past. The discussion naturally moved towards the issue of socialist realism (Joseph had just recently prepared an exhibition of Soviet socialist realist art which had been on tour through the United States and had enjoyed enormous success with the public there), and I was very surprised to realize that his statements seemed to indicate that we should treat such works as "art" in the full sense of the word. I remember asking him about that, and he answered that he personally was not yet ready to look at the works in such a way because the experience of their function in the communist system was still too close. But he believed that in time (and since these works had no political role anymore), they would indeed be perceived as art.

For the art critic with whom I spoke at the opening of the *2000+ Collection*, such an idea is still absolutely unacceptable. He firmly believes that socialist realism cannot be considered art but quite the opposite: as something that needs to be eliminated, a threat and limitation for real art in the socialist countries, an obstacle for it to become "normal." This is of course not his personal misunderstanding; rather, it can be understood as characteristic of the position of pro-western intellectuals in Eastern Europe in the last decades. As such, it directly reflects the dominant cultural concepts of the time of political division in Europe. And his wish to be recognized as a "normal" curator and critic is of course an expression of his reluctance to accept the marginal and excluded position of somebody either politically compromised or ethnically exotic. On the other hand, the new interest in Socialist realism indicates a slow, but actually very radical transformation of European cultural space and its governing concepts. The Socialist realist works lost their original meaning and function, and they have been filled with new aesthetic and cultural content. They can indeed be enjoyed as art, not only because of their execution (which is sometimes quite excellent), but also because of their theoretical and conceptual foundations. These works have become conceptual art of a sort. Thus, the long dominant structure of cultural division, according to which art produced in the West became "normal" art, while artistic production characteristic of the East remained an ideological threat to genuine artistic expression, kitsch, or, at best, a cultural phenomenon, has been challenged.[3]

The Strange Case of Socialist Realism, Part Two:
A Re-Interpretation

It was perhaps the "discovery" of the Russian avant-garde
in the West that indicated that the relation between avant-
garde art and politics in the Soviet Union was actually more
complex than it seemed before. The exhibition *Paris—
Moscow* at the Centre Georges Pompidou in Paris in 1977,
one of the first large-scale exhibitions of Russian and Soviet
avant-garde art, demonstrated that the relationship between
the adventurous and experimental avant-gardists and the
representatives of the official Soviet art of the Stalin era
was not just one of mutual exclusion. It presented
transformations from one type of language into the other,
and surprising parallels between them.

  The intriguing relation between the avant-garde and
socialist realism is a central issue in Boris Groys's book
The Total Art of Stalinism.[4] He developed an interpretation
of an important artistic tradition that meaningfully included
socialist realism, shedding new light on its conceptual
complexities and acknowledging its central position
in Russian art as one of the three main points in a triangle
formed by the avant-garde and Sots Art. The book, however,
is not only a far-reaching reinterpretation of socialist
realism and Soviet art from the avant-garde to Sots Art, but
also of the dominant representations of European cultural
space and the cultural division between East and West.
Implicitly, it was also a strategic move that challenged the
primacy and universality of western modernism and its
traditions. Through his interpretation, Groys established, so
to speak, a particular artistic tradition, very different, but
no less important from the one in the West. In such a way he
also questioned the "natural" and "universal" values
promoted by modernism, and introduced an artistic tradition
that has been highly complex and radical in its approaches
and its ideas about art, politics, and society. It is not
unimportant that this interpretation is based on the
experiences of Sots Art and Moscow Conceptualism. These
approaches, being a direct and deliberate response to
their own political and cultural contexts, also demanded
a reinterpretation of this context and tradition.

The Strange Case of Socialist realism, Part Three: Deconstruction

The deconstruction of the East-West opposition, as implied in Groys's book, includes two main aspects. On one side, the very dualism of East and West is questioned. This does not mean that the differences are ignored or denied; rather, the complex nature of this opposition is rendered visible. Representatives of Sots Art themselves have indicated not only the differences but also the parallels between eastern and western (and particularly, American) society. The very term "Sots Art," a play on "Pop Art," indicates certain parallels between these two visual systems. (A well-known example is Kosolapov's mixture of Soviet and US "pop" icons, i.e. Lenin and Mickey Mouse or Coca Cola.) We could connect this to critical analysis of the political role of western modernism, which began with the writings of Max Kozloff and Eva Cockroft. As is well known, these analyses pointed to the fact that Modernist art, while declaring itself to be apolitical, was directly used as a "weapon of the Cold War."[5] Another excellent example of work that refers to the hidden political parallels between these two very different systems is the series of Lenin portraits painted by Art & Language in the style of Jackson Pollock, or the work of the Irwin group and the NSK movement in Slovenia which also deals with the parallel visual systems and power structures in East and West.

A possible (and rather far-reaching) consequence of these explorations could be a changed understanding of the concept of modernity. Politically, socially, and culturally, Eastern Europe was one of the most radical realizations of the modern zeitgeist. Therefore, we should perhaps start to think about modernity as something internally split and heterogeneous, not to mention essentially contradictory.

On the other hand, the idea that art in each of the two halves of divided Europe could be completely identified with its respective system has also been critically challenged. The need for a new interpretation of the art of the Stalin era already indicates its major role as a general reference for the whole field of eastern art. Yet, it has also become clear that this field was rich and varied, and certainly not without strong differences or conflicts.

Divisions and Identities

Groys' book, furthermore, is a critical response to the idea that political divisions and even radical changes in the structure of society remain somehow external to art and culture, and do not affect its essence. In fact, we are confronted with a number of examples that clearly demonstrate the opposite. The Mediterranean region (to mention only one example, important for the idea of Europe) has for centuries been perceived as a unique economic and cultural space, in spite of conflicts between states, religions, etc. Today, however, we take it for granted that this region is actually radically divided. The northern Mediterranean belongs, so it seems, not only to a very different political context (as the countries of the Middle East and North Africa), but also indeed to a very different culture. If we think about Spain, for example, it seems natural to us that it is more closely connected to Sweden than to Morocco, the neighboring country with which Spain has had very close connections for centuries. Eastern Europe, too, has had such an identity, created by the strategies of political division and internal cultural homogenization (based, of course, on social structure). This also means that the changes of the dividing lines and strategies, and transformations in the social and political structure in the Eastern European (or post-communist) countries open the possibility of reconstructing this particular identity. Again, I should mention here the idea of a particular Eastern European cultural essence that has supposedly been the basis and source of art that comes from the region. This is, in fact, a reformulation of the strategies of inclusion and exclusion (and therefore domination) developed after the political dualism of the Cold War lost its importance. Based on this idea, Eastern European (and other non-western) cultures have been "ethnicized" and "exoticized." Artists from such cultures have been admitted into the western (dominant) cultural space as representatives of a particular (strange, peculiar) culture. The hierarchical difference implicit in this division is not unlike the separation between artworks and cultural artifacts. Such works, of course, often arouse interest and admiration for their particular wisdom, emotional intensity, or picturesque nature. But they are not universal; for example, they demand a special knowledge about their original cultural context to be enjoyed at all. Western art, on the other hand, declares itself as one of a number of different cultural productions that exist today, but through its dominant position in the global world, it still remains universal, "normal."

Resolving the Trauma?

In thinking about cultural difference, and also about European cultural identity, we have to avoid two main traps in particular. The first is considering western (or European) cultural identity as homogeneous and universal, and the second is to think about cultural essence as something unchangeable, firm, basic, and essentially separated from other cultural essences with a dividing line that can never really be overcome. I believe that the changes in the way socialist realist art is understood which I outlined above indicate a different model of how cultural identities, and the way in which they are represented, can be transformed. It indicates a possible common context through which western and eastern artistic traditions can be connected, although they remain separate and sometimes contradict each other. And this is a possible basis for the idea that European cultural space (of course, not without political and social changes) could be transformed in such a way as to actually include such different and seemingly mutually exclusive traditions into a common context. Such changes could perhaps slowly resolve the trauma of European division that still marks our experience of so-called European identity.

I believe that this trauma cannot be solved in a way that seems to be indicated by two essential texts of the post-Cold War and "new world order" era: Samuel Huntington's *The Clash of Civilizations* and Francis Fukuyama's *The End of History*.[6] These two essays could be understood as programs of a political and social re-arrangement of Europe, and indeed the world, in a time when the dualism between the two superpowers is no longer the basis of the world order. Leaving aside the complexities of Huntington's and Fukuyama's arguments, we might say that they indicate a new position of the West inside a world divided according to cultural and religious identities. As far as Europe is concerned,

Huntington does not predict its unification, but rather a redefinition of the East-West division. He believes that the new division will be (or already is) based on the cultural and religious fault-lines between the two civilizations that meet there: western and orthodox. This restructuring of Europe demands, as Huntington indicates, a certain cultural and political unification and homogenization of the West. We could connect this to Fukuyama's arguments and presume that, in the context of this re-defined West, the system of democratic and liberal capitalism remains the only reasonable basis of social organization. The re-unification of Europe, based on Huntington's and Fukuyama's ideas, would be a process of total assimilation of Eastern Europe (or, more precisely, of those post-communist countries that historically belong to western culture) into the western cultural block and the putatively final social form of historical development: democratic and liberal capitalist society.

What seems more productive to me (and perhaps not totally utopian) is an attempt to reformulate European identity in a way that would connect elements of both western and eastern social and cultural systems into a new unity. Unavoidably, such new unity will be highly complex and heterogeneous, and not without contradictions, struggles, and conflicts. Also, such an identity would necessarily be understood as something variable and changeable, and without definite outer limits.

Yes and No

"Haven't we had enough of Eastern Europe?" Yes and no. "Yes," if we mean the political and cultural divisions and strategies of marginalization, ethnicization, exclusion, and (controlled) inclusion. But one cannot resolve such divisions by pretending that they do not exist and that they are simply an external circumstance that does not touch the "essence." It is only through repetition, through returning to and reworking the trauma, that it can perhaps be slowly resolved, and not by repressing, ignoring, and forgetting it. "No," if we mean a re-evaluation of the social and cultural potentials of Eastern Europe and their ability to transform themselves and thereby transform European identity.

[1] Orhan Pamuk, *Snow*, trans. Maureen Freely, Faber & Faber, London, 2004, p. 286.

[2] The effectiveness of the ideological appropriation of modern art in the West was based on a double operation. Modern art has been presented as both universal and essentially western. It comes as no surprise that Eastern European achievements in modern art have long been (and partly still are) marginalized or tendentiously forgotten. Malevich, for example, was practically unknown for a large part of the last century, and is at present only slowly receiving his deserved central position in 20th century art.

[3] This does not mean, however, that the strategies of division, inclusion, and exclusion have been eliminated. To a great extent, they have been replaced by an idea of an essential cultural difference. In such a system, the non-western artistic production becomes an expression of alien cultural identity, and thus, as the quotation from Pamuk's novel indicates, "ethnic" and exotic.

[4] Boris Groys, *Gesamtkunstwerk Stalin. Die gespaltene Kultur in der Sowjetunion*, Carl Hanser Verlag, Munich, 1988. English edition: *The Total Art of Stalinism: Avant-garde, Aesthetic Dictatorship, and Beyond*, trans. Charles Rougle, Princeton University Press, Princeton, N.J., 1993.

[5] Eva Cockcroft, "Abstract Expressionism, Weapon of the Cold War," *Pollock and After: The Critical Debate*, Francis Frascina (ed.), Harper and Row, London, 1985, p. 132.

[6] These essays can be found in the following publications: Francis Fukuyama, "The End of History," *The National Interest*, Summer 1989; Samuel P. Huntington, "The Clash of Civilizations," *Foreign Affairs*, Summer 1993: see also Samuel P. Huntington, *The Clash of Civilizations and the Remaking of World Order*, Simon & Schuster, New York, 1996.

II. STRATEGIES AND SPACES OF ART

Exhibition Strategies in the 1990s:
A Few Examples From Slovenia

First published in *Theories of Display. The World of Art: Curatorial Course for Contemporary Arts*,
Soros Center for Contemporary Art, Ljubljana, 1998, pp. 58–71.
Translated from Slovenian by Ljubica Klančar.

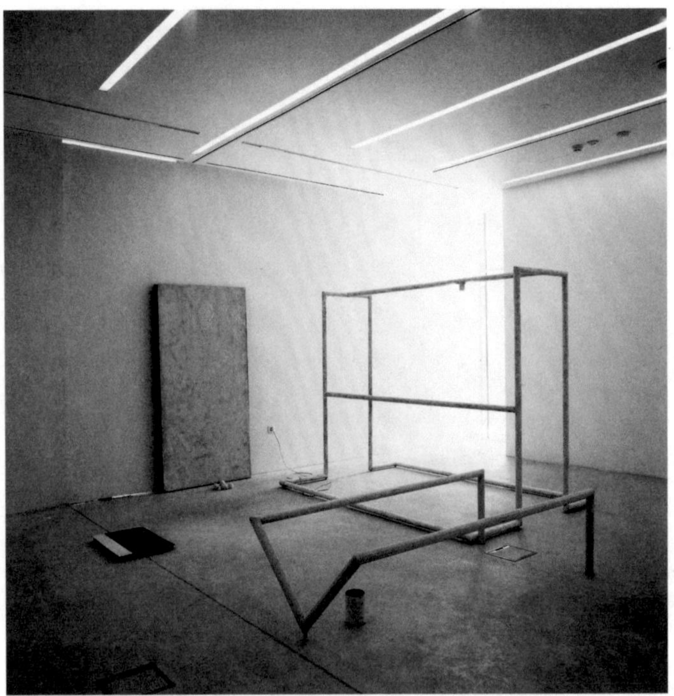

Mirosław Bałka, *Winterhilfsverein*, 1994
The Present and Presence, Museum of Contemporary Art Metelkova, Ljubljana, 2011

Introductory Note

"Strategy" is a word we tend to use with some frequency and authority when talking about contemporary art, e.g. "art strategies," "the strategy of audience relations," "exhibition strategies" and in similar contexts. These and comparable terms have become such an obvious component of artistic jargon that we consider their meanings obvious as well. Still, perhaps it would not be entirely out of place here to begin by looking up the actual meaning of "strategy."

If we investigate the origin of the word, we see that it stems from the military. Such is also its etymology, as it originates from the Greek words stratos—army and agein—to lead; strategos therefore means military commander. Besides its narrower meaning of actually leading an army, the term "strategy" also encompasses the broader meaning of skillful and prudent handling of affairs in an unarmed battle, e.g. political, and finally in the figurative sense: of the serious handling of matters particularly those directed towards a purpose. It seems that it is this figurative meaning or term that fits the idea or concept of "the strategy of exhibiting." Nevertheless, the general usage of a term such as "strategy" certainly indicates that the art field is not neutral, that it is saturated with a kind of "agon," therefore competition, conflict or even struggle and that its main meaning (although not always entirely explicit) is also a battlefield.

Exhibiting or displaying work for the public always implies a kind of strategic relationship, even if the work is wholly anonymous and self-contained and if the exhibition space seems completely neutral (the so-called "white cube," for example, only seems neutral as it is related to a specific public, institutional network, group of experts and collectors). Art as such can only realize itself in relation to an audience and it is precisely in the act of defining this relationship that we inevitably encounter a kind of global strategic idea, an idea that determines the individual aspects of the work appearing in public, from the exhibition design details (lighting, dominant or marginal positions, etc.) to the question of which institutional (or non-institutional) space to mount the work in, for which public it is primarily targeted, and the like. In short, in the most general sense of the term, "exhibition strategy" is a global concept, a sensible collection of procedures and approaches aimed at ensuring that the work will be seen in the right light by the right viewer.

In this essay, I do not intend to deal with this broader notion that is a component of every exhibition. I would rather confine myself to art that expounds and perhaps even incorporates this dimension in its effect. Such projects all consciously revoke the dualism between the artwork and the act of exhibiting. In short, the work is no longer a kind of autonomous given for which suitable surroundings must be found and organized. Rather, it occurs within the tight and dynamic relationships between artifacts, surroundings, viewer, curator, institutional framework and so on. Artists, work, surroundings, audience, institutions—these are not abstract entities, but are defined by ideological, political, class, gender, linguistic and other factors and their

discrepancies; and this expounds the "agon" that demands
a strategic approach in exhibiting art, among other things.

I suppose this is the approach towards "exhibition
strategies" that is particularly characteristic of what we call
the "art in the 1990s." By this, I do not mean to say that
exhibition strategies are also entirely a thing of the 1990s,
on the contrary. The numerous strategic approaches
appearing over these past few years were developed in the
1980s, 70s and 60s and even earlier. The 1990s have
reaffirmed, appropriated and adapted these approaches,
incorporated them into a different context and have given
them a somewhat different meaning.

Up to now I have spoken about the strategic aspects
of exhibitions as if they only concerned the artist in his
or her relation towards the exhibition space, institutions and
audience. But just as a field of "agon," the field of art is an
area in which different interests cross paths, thus resulting
in the development and cross-breeding of different strategies. When speaking about exhibition strategies, besides
mentioning the artists, we must, at the very least, also
mention the curator and exhibiting institution, which in line
with their strategic interests can also firmly define the
context of an exhibition and manner of putting the work on
display and, in doing so, significantly influence the meaning
of the work.

The Strategy of Exhibiting in a "White Cube": the Mala Galerija Example

Over the past decades the notion of the art exhibition space
has been essentially determined by the concept of the
so-called "white cube." This was developed during the
Modernist period as the ideal environment in which to view
individual pieces of art which themselves were seen as
self-contained, freestanding and autonomous entities. It is
primarily a neutral space as independent as possible of
external circumstances such as the time of day or the change
of seasons. This includes the historical, political and social
contexts. Harmonious architectural forms, white walls,
neutral floors, evenly distributed and constant light (indirect
or artificial lighting) were thought to ensure that the works
of art on view would achieve full expression on their own,

as autonomous and purely aesthetical entities. With several examples taken from a single exhibition site–Ljubljana's Mala galerija (Small Gallery)—I would like to show how certain artists tackled the neutral and thus impersonal space (in many ways Mala galerija is the typical white cube), how they made use of its possibilities and at the same time perverted its neutrality and thus accentuated some of the possibilities of a strategic approach towards a "white" gallery such as this example.

The first case is that of Miroslaw Balka, who appropriated the space by means of a symbolic act: at the entrance of the gallery itself, he placed a "doorstep" made of material from his own burned-down studio in Ottwock. This doorstep functioned as a symbolic threshold turning the interior of the gallery into the artist's own personal space into which he moved a house (a metal construction based on his body's measurements). This transformation of space was necessary, because, among other things, Balka had transferred into it his own personal story linked to the real time of his exhibition—namely the period close to Christmas.[1] (With this very act the artist rejected one of the fundamental requirements of the "white cube"—independence of external circumstances. The gallery's large windows–as the characteristic making the greatest departure from the ideal "white cube"—acquired a special role as a connection between the interior and exterior.) With the gallery space marked out in this way, the reality of the Christmas season was transformed through the artist's vision of winter as something hovering between good and evil, so to speak; here winter on the one hand was shown as a time of want, suffering, death and destruction, and on the other as a time of salvation, sublimity, new beginnings and mercy. (This dualism is present in the title of the exhibition itself: *Winterhilfsverein.* The title alludes to the suffering and dying during the Second World War, particularly in the winter, but also to the idea of solidarity and aid.) Through this transformation of the gallery space, the gallery's whiteness completely lost its impersonality and neutrality by acquiring a special, meaningful, emotionally and sensorial charged essence.

Petra Varl inhabited this space in a different manner. With a project dedicated to her mother, she completely annihilated the characteristics of the white cube: she covered the floor with linoleum and the walls with vividly colourful wallpaper, and placed elements belonging to the kitchen (a refrigerator, table, chairs) into this space. But this was not really a kitchen nor some truly intimate space. We could sooner say that the artist created a setting, a stage; in it, by means of a system of selected objects and other elements (drawings, notes) functioning as signs, she literally staged a domestic environment or, at the very least, the personal experience of it. (The fact that two actors performed at the opening of the exhibition only further emphasised this theatrical dimension.)

Vadim Fiškin was confronted with a situation similar to Balka's: he was to mount his exhibition in a space that was empty, neutral and impersonal and that in itself did not offer him any visual clues. And so his first step was to locate the space. Fiskin marked the space's precise geographic coordinates on the gallery's floor. By doing this he not only installed the site in strict geographical terms, but in an implicitly cultural sense as well. At the same time he located his project in another way—institutionally. Through his approach to this exhibition he opened the issue of the gallery space and exhibition (in a dialogue with Viktor Misiano, the curator) as an institution. In line with this fundamental approach to the exhibition, which was the act of locating, he decided to take the term "one-man show" seriously and literally. Thus, he exhibited the entire body of work he had created up to that point by means of slide projections. Viktor Misiano, too, set out his role analogously; he gave thought to the basic role of the curator and decided it was to pose questions. He asked the visitors of the exhibition several questions concerning the exhibition, its author and the viewers' response towards them. In the middle of the gallery, at the very point determined by Fiskin's geographical coordinates, stood a wooden construction orientated to the four corners of the sky. This construction held the slide projectors that projected the artist's work onto the darkened walls of the gallery. If the viewer chose to step inside, a light would switch on and a tape recorder relayed Misiano's questions, recorded the viewer's responses and in doing so, also radically located and activated the viewer. The gallery space continues to be an abstract, impersonal framework, yet always filled anew with content which subsequently disappears again.

Rene Rusjan reflected this invisible history of the gallery space in a project titled *Yesterday, for example...*in which she exhibited the documentation of exhibitions that had been mounted during the previous years in the Mala galerija. She borrowed from two exhibitions which had been presented immediately prior to hers: an exhibition of the *photo-ceramics* of Michelangelo Pistoletto and an exhibition by Uri Tzaig entitled *Two Balls* (she found the title for her exhibition in Tzaig's: the words appearing in the title were one of the subtitles of Tzaig's video film and accidentally appeared on a photo of the display). She kept the video projector and the chairs for the viewers from Tzaig's exhibition, only this time the screen showed a presentation of the exhibitions, vernissages and other events held in the gallery. At his exhibition, Pistoletto had presented a series of ceramic plates bearing photos of pieces from his series *Oggetti in meno* that he created in the 1960s; Rene Rusjan displayed similar plates with photographic representations of various past exhibitions held in the Mala galerija. And just as Pistoletto re-actualised his own works through transformation, "recycling" and, so to speak, re-appropriating them, Rene Rusjan brought certain past exhibitions back to life, thus appropriating them, or, in other words, identifying with them and in a sense proclaiming them her own.

Ulf Rollof approached the gallery space and the institution of the exhibition in a somewhat different manner. The exhibition itself did not essentially modify the "white cube"; Rollof filled it rather densely with fir trees that were covered in wax and placed in concrete stands that allowed the trees to sway to and fro. In doing so, the artist exploited the whiteness and neutrality of the Mala galerija, of its "art," to emphasise the contrast with nature which itself had been subdued, reworked and turned into a toy. What is important here is that Rollof's project reached beyond the borders of the gallery and the exhibition. The artist realised the exhibition in Ljubljana; the production process, which is normally concealed from the public, was opened to an audience. Bart De Baere, who curated the exhibition, used three words to describe this expansion: *production* (the process of creating the work); *reception* (the opening of the exhibition itself as a social event and also as the point at which the work is displayed before an audience); and *exhibition* (the exhibition and its life). He set up a temporary studio in one of the exhibition rooms of the Moderna galerija (Ljubljana Museum of Modern Art). By doing this he took an environment otherwise open to the public and rather than closing it changed it into a half public and half private space, similar to the 19th century studio which was also a semi-public space, a space open to friends, art connoisseurs, critics and buyers, a place for viewing, discussion and business transactions. Visitors to the gallery were able to walk into Rollof's studio, view his work, talk to him, sit down and leaf through catalogues and other material. Part of the exhibition was also realised outdoors in front of the gallery. Thus the exhibition grew into a process that offered new opportunities for cooperation with the audience. At the same time, Rollof creatively made use of the practical aspects of the preparations for the exhibition by deconstructing the established principles of exhibition institutions. Instead of the "white cube," he constituted a different example of exhibiting and communicating with the audience.

Art in Context

Art in the 1990s is often no longer considered as a prod-uction of autonomous or even purely aesthetic pieces. It consciously operates within various social and historical contexts and establishes a reflexive or even directly active relation towards them. This does not necessarily mean that such pieces must be realised outside the gallery; on the contrary, sometimes they make good use of the traditional exhibition site. For example, it is possible to create different or even incompatible surroundings within these "neutral" exhibition surroundings; the effect of such pieces is often based on this incompatibility and the incongruity of codes itself.

Earlier on I described how Miroslaw Balka had moved into the Mala galerija and set up his own symbolic "house." Rirkrit Tiravania also placed a "house" within the gallery, this house, however, was somewhat different. Tiravania created his work of art for an exhibition titled *The House in*

Time; the theme of the exhibition related to the issues of location and dislocation, home and exile and also to the experience of war refugees from the regions of former Yugoslavia for whom the issue of dislocation and exile had become a reality in a painfully concrete and radical way. When the artist received an invitation to participate in the exhibition he began to collect issues of *The New York Times*. He took out pages from the collected copies referring to the war in the former Yugoslavia and created a house out of them (and so he literally built a house of "time," namely a newspaper called *The Times*). He had built another space within the gallery space. The visitor could enter it, make a cup of tea, sit comfortably and leaf through the newspaper pages not used by the artist to build the house. Tiravania created a personal, intimate space for the viewer, literally building it out of time and history—conveyed through the newspaper as his eminent medium.

At the *2nd Triennial of Contemporary Slovene Art* titled *U3*, Rene Rusjan also built an intimate area, which was simultaneously a space of time and history. She closed off part of the exhibition hall and organized a reading room. The visitor had access to diverse answers to questions she posed to a number of her acquaintances concerning the period of the past five years, their personal and historical aspects and the role of art in it. These replies took the form of written responses and also objects, tape tracks, photos, works of art, etc. Here, too, the daily newspaper appeared as an important element available to the viewer. The reading room was also envisaged as an interactive space: the viewers had the opportunity of responding to the artist's questions themselves, of bringing an object of their own, etc.

Some artists brought even more heterogeneous spaces into the gallery. Janja Žvegelj organised a squash court in the Škuc Gallery (as a response to the unusual shapes and measurements of the gallery rooms) at which she actually played a tournament with the gallery's artistic director. These features should probably have not only been read as *ready-made* art; they were an about-turn in which the artist (who was not actually a professional squash player) exposed herself, at the same time bringing onto the scene the gallery's art director—an element of power who ordinarily does not perform in front of an audience in such a direct manner. By introducing *squash* to the gallery the established relations of power were also shifted—at least as long as the tournament went on. And so it is understandable that the artist so strongly emphasised the gallery's institutional framework for her project, even including a ceremonial opening speech.

Some of Darij Kreuh's projects have introduced different kinds of spatial order into the gallery space altogether. At the *2nd Triennial, U3*, he thus "exhibited" an object that was completely immaterial, as it was only a spatial segment defined by coordinates in a three-dimensional coordinate system. The coordinates of this object were transmitted by three different radio stations as part of the signals that appear on radio receivers; each station transmitted the coordinates of one axis. In a way, the object thus existed in the gallery space and at the same time was distributed across the immaterial realm of radio signals and information where it became senseless noise. (Not only was the serendipitous radio listener able to see the coordinates of only one axis on his or her display, he or she would be ignorant of the context of these numbers which would thus make no sense to the listener.) The "exhibited object" was presented as the Tower of Babylon, the point when the full swing, differentiation and specialisation of communication systems turns into the opposite—the incomprehensibility and incapacity of communication. Kreuh expanded the theme of entwining different spatial systems, or we could even say systems of reality, in a project prepared for the Kapelica Gallery. Here, through an "information helmet," the viewer stepped into a virtual world while at the same time moving around the real space of the gallery. The viewers thus moved physically in one space while they visually "moved" in another. With the aid of technology, other viewers in neighbouring premises found themselves in the position of the "impossible" viewer, as they were able, via monitors, to concurrently follow both sequences. On one monitor they observed the movement across objective space and on the other the perception of virtual space.

Up to this point I have primarily spoken about exhibition space and the modification and deconstruction of its established principles. In the projects I've mentioned it has already been made clear that space was defined by its institutional framework, by its system of values and requirements. An exhibition, in short, is not merely the artefact mounted in a physical space, but also the whole process that leads up to this—the system of selecting, directing and mounting, etc. Some projects are directly orientated towards this aspect. Here I will mention two examples, both taken from the most recent *U3* exhibition; both projects, each in their own way and independent of each other, dealt with the role of the exhibition selector and curator, who in this case was Peter Weibel.

Nika Špan prepared her *Presentation* by explaining projects she had carried out up to that point in time by drawing for the curator, who in turn observed her in the act of drawing on a television screen. Through a different monitor the artist was able to observe his reactions (he expressed by nodding whether or not he understood). At the exhibition, both recordings were confronted in such a way that the curator observed the artist's hand drawing from an elevated position. This work is obviously concerned with communication (mediated and transformed via media technology)—not merely with anyone, but just the selector, the curator of the exhibition—and also the element of power. The work is actually a staging of a situation typical for the contemporary art world, in which the artist is continuously obliged to show, describe and explain his or her work.

As her project, Maja Licul exhibited the process through which she was selected—a process which, though of such vital importance to the exhibition, is not otherwise visible within it. The artist exhibited the portfolio of her work with which she applied, the letter informing her of her inclusion in the exhibition and the recording of the conversation between her and the curator during which the curator discussed the works, anticipated projects for the exhibition and finally decided on the artists' participation in the exhibition.

Here, I must certainly mention the activities of Tadej Pogačar or rather his institution called The P.A.R.A.S.I.T.E. Museum of Contemporary Art. This institution does not have its own premises or art collection, but acts according to parasitic and parallel principles. It moves into a host institution, intervenes and exploits its structures. By doing this it explicates the hidden ideological suppositions the activity of the host institution is based on and which we consider natural and self-evident. One of the most characteristic of Pogačar's interventions took place at a museum that, among other things, held a collection of African "aboriginal" art. Pogačar placed these works of art face to face with objects characteristic of western rationalism and pragmatism, thus developing a critical discourse on the ideological suppositions (for example the idea of cultural differences) which the West takes advantage of to build, maintain and establish a dominant position in relation to the Third World. Pogačar's interventions revealed the concept and structure of the mentioned collection as the result of these ideological mechanisms.

All of the mentioned projects dealt with gallery space that, in spite of its critics and deconstructions, continues to be very important. However, the most diverse range of other surroundings can emerge as exhibition premises. Unlike the white cube, these do not even seem to be neutral, although on the other hand a public sculpture can also behave as if it does not properly relate to its surroundings (think of the numerous sculptures in pedestrian zones, parks and the courtyards of business buildings, etc.). To intervene in non-gallery surroundings means to step in to or become involved in complicated semantic groups, the principles of day-to-day life, the historical, ideological and institutional contexts and so on. Here I will mention only two examples of many.

The first is a project mounted by Marija Mojca Pungerčar in the French Cultural Center in Ljubljana. She took the Center's windows and turned them into shop windows in which she exhibited white Chanel outfits with highly minimalist black decorations. The mounting and lighting of these garments were so effective that the Center truly appeared to be a haute couture boutique. It was only after the observers came nearer and took a closer look at the garments that they could realise that these were in fact replicas—very large ones made of plastic. Each of the outfits bore a label with the name of an important woman in French history, and the project, appropriately enough, was titled *Cherchez la femme*. In addition to the displays with the outfits, one window showed quotes by Coco Chanel and ascetic saints (for example Ignatius Loyola) on the value of reserve and asceticism appearing side by side. Inside the Center, the artist exhibited lounge tables on which she presented the various roles of women through pictures taken from (fashion) magazines. All this shows sufficiently that the artist took advantage of the context in which she exhibited: in pursuit of her own interests, yet she also dealt with notions and stereotypes relating to the idea of French culture, the role of fashion in it, the function of women in the representations of French tradition and culture and so on.

A somewhat different project was prepared by Alenka Pirman in the large reading room of the National University Library (NUK) in Ljubljana. For a long time the artist had collected "Germanisms" appearing frequently in everyday Slovene conversation, but which are not allowed in the written or formal usage of the language. (The project was part of a larger process that the artist concluded with the publication of a dictionary of these words. The project was titled *Arcticae horulae* after the first grammar book on the Slovene language.) On the tables in the reading room she displayed little banners onto which examples of the collected words had been embroidered. (These little banners had a decidedly homemade appearance reminiscent of traditional primary school "handicrafts.") The location of this project was in no way accidental. The Slovene language is the foundation of the Slovene national identity, the "Slovene essence of being," so to speak, and this foundation is most expressively realised in the form of the book. When architect Jože Plečnik designed the library building he emphasised its symbolic function even at the cost of its functionalism. In the architectural designs this symbolic function is most strongly stressed in the line running from the portal via the monumental stairway to the grand reading rooms. The National and University Library is, in a way, the central temple of the Slovene book, Slovene literature and language and thus the Slovene national essence. So, the artist was introducing into this temple a kind of heterogeneity, a damaged language that has been spoiled, a deformation adopted directly from foreign languages, particularly German. And yet this act should not be seen simply as an anarchic assault on established values; her

subversion is actually much more refined. The unusual paradox to which she draws attention lies in the fact that these
inadmissible, borrowed words are sensed as something
genuine. Whenever we wish to speak directly, "genuinely,"
in "everyday language" or in the vernacular we can hardly
avoid them. Contrary to this we perceive the correct usage
of the language as something manufactured, artificial or
laboured; we do not have the sense of direct and genuine
expression from a speaker expressing him or herself in
this language, but rather sense a sort of distance between
the act of pronouncing and the pronouncement. If, therefore, language is the foundation of our national identity,
then registered in the very heart of this identity, where it is
most genuine, are foreign languages and foreign identities.

The Curator and His or Her Strategy

Recent developments in art have highlighted the role of the
curator as selector, as author of the exhibition, interpreter
and co-creator of an exhibition's context. The figure who
within the context of high modernism was analogous to the
contemporary curator was the art critic. He or she would
depart from what would seemingly be an objective position
yet which in truth concealed the actual partiality or even
arbitrariness of his or her judgments and decisions; in this
the art critic was truly analogous to the "white cube." The
emphatically personal or even arbitrary nature of the work
often characteristic of the contemporary curator is actually
the deconstruction of the position of power and selection.
(Speaking about "deconstruction," I am not trying to say
that curators can eliminate their role as the instance of
power in the institutional system of the world of art, but
rather that they reveal this role clearly and no longer present
it as something "objective" or "natural.")

Although curators are often said to turn into artists,
this statement is incorrect. What is actually true is that their
role is probably becoming more "dialogical." The term
"dialogic relationship" signifies that though the curator does
not create the works nor defines them (although he or she
can have a practical influence on them), he or she can
decisively determine the viewpoint from which we observe
them, emphasise a particular aspect and so on. By selecting

the work the curator is placing it into a certain environment, supplying it with additional information and interpretations, etc. The curator is actually defining the context of the work through which it might acquire an added value, but this context does not also determine how it is received.

The idea of the curator as artist probably arises because in this dialogic relationship the curator can have quite an active role while at the same time he or she starts from personal preferences, concepts or even obsessions more plainly than before. And this picture also emerges because curators today frequently attempt to avoid conventional forms of presenting art and instead look for new environments, forms and contexts which are to provide art with new possibilities and at the same time enable a more intense relationship with these works as a result of their being different and unconventional.

I will try to clarify some of these aspects in a project which I have titled *Inexplicable Presence* and subtitled *The Curator's Office.* As the subtitle indicates, through this project I have tried to give thought to some of the aspects of the curator's role in contemporary art. I approached the project by sending eleven artists a copy of a photo showing a place in Ljubljana and a brief text explaining why I chose this particular spot. The place on the photograph is tied to a very personal and yet expressly marginal experience of mine. But as often happens, this marginal experience has been unusually permanent. I asked the artists to create a piece that would somehow originate from the photo and text. With the exception of the request that the work be a response to the picture and story, I did not want to determine the motif nor the medium of the artists' work. The only limitation was that their work was to be sent to me by post. Of the eleven artists, ten responded positively, nine of whom actually sent me their work. These were Lewis Baltz, Jože Barši, Jochen Gerz, Angela Grauerholz, Per Kirkeby, Yuri Leiderman, Mladen Stilinović, Uri Tzaig and Heimo Zobernig. (Suchan Kinoshita chose not to send me her work because she was not happy with it, but I nevertheless counted it as part of the exhibition as an "absent piece.") The works I received were extremely diverse; most of them were no direct, impulsive responses, but in some cases very carefully conceived pieces that were, of course, small in format and in their outward appearance often closer to studies than exhibition material. I then prepared a sort of exhibition with these pieces. The chamber-like and partly study-like character of the works required an appropriate space. For this reason I used a room that was ordinarily not used as exhibition area, located right next to the underground exhibition rooms of the Ljubljana Museum of Modern Art. I moved my office there (for two weeks) and built a kind of personal space with these works. Every day I spent several hours in the space carrying out my daily assignments; of course I was prepared to speak to any visitor who desired to.

Through this activity, I slowly discovered how important not only my general discursive points of departure and world outlook were to my projects, but also my personal reactions (sometimes vague and uncertain) and memories, and what a major role coincidence plays. In the role of the curator itself, I am increasingly attracted to the peripheral, ephemeral, accidental and general. I am fascinated by the traces of fleeting thoughts and transient feelings, which sometimes (not always, even less frequently so) linger on as something curiously permanent and can have far-reaching consequences. This of course does not mean that I have anything against large-scale projects and major exhibitions and I am definitely not of the opinion that these should be "replaced."

It is just that I am particularly interested in the possibilities of marginal fields of art, attention, etc. A significant aspect here (which is also tied to all the other aspects) is the issue of the opportunities offered by low-budget projects. (The entire project was very low-cost and set out in such a way that I was able to manage it by myself.) I am convinced that a conscious exploitation of the possibilities of a project like this creates specific qualities that large-scale and costly projects cannot offer. This is why I was interested to discover whether it was possible for a project that would really be founded on a very private and marginal point of departure to develop a dialogue neverthe-less. I decided to begin with a little personal experience as described. I opted for this point of departure because I believe it contains issues that strongly interest me: the decisive influence of something I do not understand and the permanence of an ephemeral experience and its influence on comprehension, understanding and assessment. Of course, I do not consider my personal obsessions, preferences and the like important enough to justify such a project in itself. Moreover, I do not consider them to have been their center, but rather just a point of departure; above all I wanted to unveil a specific field, an active interactive space for works of art. I did not appropriate the role of the artist, but merely posed a question and a problem while at the same time striving not to conceal the circumstances of my own position.

To be sure, I was also faced with the question of which criteria to apply when it came to deciding which artists to ask for cooperation. I was convinced that these criteria were an essential aspect of the overall project and that they should, in a way, be tied to its initial ideas. That is why I invited artists who above all were important to me personally (that is to say I do not only objectively consider them to be good artists, but I am also personally drawn to their work), whereby my attraction to their work is linked to the fact that it contains something which I do not fully comprehend or understand. The invitations were therefore not a "selection" based on a "concept"; they were meant to be direct and personal. This is why I did not share the list of the other invited artists with the participants. Instead, in addition to the photo, story and description of the project, I included a personal, handwritten letter in which I explained which aspect(s) in their work I found particularly fascinating and why I chose them in particular.

One aspect that in view of the overall project seemed highly important to me was how to establish an environment for a more intimate and attentive relationship to art. As a possible model of such a surrounding I envisaged the position we find ourselves in as visitors to an office or study and observing the works hanging there. It is more likely that in this case the works would be drawings, sketches and smaller pieces instead of real "museum pieces," but the smaller distance and more personal relationship to them can encourage a more attentive investigation, contemplation and discussion than can be triggered by large, major pieces hanging in the museum halls. And yet, again, this kind of discussion is ultimately just an episode, an ephemeral event which nevertheless can have more permanent consequences sometimes. In the museum surroundings I was, of course, able to establish a space that was only partly private and partly public (after all this was a kind of exhibition and not a private visit); but as discussions with the visitors indicated, the environment was stimulating. It was highly stimulating for me as well; in the hours I spent there and in the conversations with the visitors I returned to the exhibited works, studied them and always discovered new dimensions.

The Changes to Institutional Settings and New Opportunities of Exhibition Sites

Institutions played a role in all these shifts. The changes within the institutional setting span from the more or less cautious relativity of the museum's role as selector and enforcer of hierarchies via ideas regarding the museum and exhibition space opening up to the social and natural environment, its contradictions and changes (in program and approach as well as in terms of architecture) to the new roles being assumed by the specifically non-institutional institutions and spaces which in the 1990s have acquired a special place or status within new constellations.

Over the past decades criticism of the "white cube" and equivalently of the museum and exhibition institutions has taken several routes, and in many ways current institutional practices stem from these findings. One critical route has been directly orientated toward the supposed objectivity and neutrality of the traditional premises/institution; these authors and writers have, for instance, drawn attention to the ideological or even concrete political backgrounds of the institutions supposed neutrality, to the social functions of selection and presentation mechanisms, and so on. On the other hand, the fact that art itself consciously began to place itself in specific spaces with specific social, historical and aesthetic dimensions could not help but have an influence on institutions.

These and similar tendencies have shaped the institutional structure of the "world of art"; the formerly rigid, hierarchic pyramid structure has become much more open. On the one hand, possible areas in which to exhibit have even increased in number, and on the other, museums and galleries are now seen as functional components of a kind of societal entity, its internal conflicts, domination systems, etc. Needless to say, this does not mean that institutions are no longer the center of power and point of codification. However, this codification is not the same as physically bringing art into an institution's exhibition space anymore. It actually occurs in a wider field in which "marginal" scenes can also be incorporated. Moreover, institutions themselves are spreading out to scenes such as these and appropriating them. At the same time, an opportunity has opened for specific exhibition sites or institutions that no longer appear to be something strictly alternative, marginal or pushed to the side, but are rather seen as key component of the art field.

I can illustrate these shifts with several examples taken from institutional and non-institutional spaces. It is possible to observe a tendency towards a "dialogic" relationship towards artistic tradition in the museum practice of the Ljubljana Museum of Modern Art. This is probably best seen in the arrangements for retrospective exhibitions of the key artists of 20th century Slovene art, which are far from neutral. On the contrary, these arrangements actually emphasize the historical distance, the aspect of interpretation and appropriation as well as the tendency to breathe new life into the works on view. The mounting of exhibitions such as these are, as a rule, entrusted to contemporary artists (exhibitions have thus been mounted by Jože Barši, New Collectivism and Tadej Pogačar) who are expected to establish a dialogue with the historic pieces, add their own commentary, place them in a new light and shed further light on them, etc.

In the Slovene art scene of the 1990s a number of specific spaces have created their own profiles with expressive programs and their own "styles"; these have ranged from the more or less established galleries to different media centers and alternative sites. I will mention two very specific exhibition sites or "institutions," sites that in their very concepts and practices are highly characteristic examples of exhibition and (conditionally) institutional activities in the open and diffused space of the 1990s.

One of these is Vila Katarin—a private residential house with a garden. For ten years now the owner, Mrs. Milena Kosec, has prepared exhibitions and other events. The dimension for which Vila Katarina is certainly relevant in the context of the 1990s is that it does not put itself forward as an "alternative" or "underground" space in its program. That is to say, it does not define itself by contradicting institutional and established practices. On the contrary, this is a project where personal interest has been teamed with the utilisation of the specific possibilities offered by the premises itself. The fact that these are private, residential premises creates a particularly intense relationship with the artists themselves who must adapt their production and mounting to the special character of the space as well as to the viewers.

Another highly specific space is Sestava, which operates in premises within the former military barracks on Metelkova Street in Ljubljana. Sestava can be seen as a unique exhibition space and at the same time as a continuously developing project, a discussion (Sestava's key component is an area allocated for discussion both within the group's members as well as other interested individuals) and an attempt to establish an open social space. The Sestava project derives from deliberations about the building it inhabits—a former military prison. The project's initiators had the idea to take this space with its traumatic connotations and transform it, but not by erasing its historical dimension. Their idea was to change the prison cells by giving the individual rooms to various artists who, departing from their own experiences and interests and from a contemplation of the space itself, would establish a habitable space which would eventually become a youth hostel ("The Cell").

[1] Mirosław Bałka, *Winterbilfsverein*, Mala galerija, Ljubljana,
      15. 12. 1994–10. 1. 1995.

The Para-Mirror of the New Parasitism

First published in *Absolute One. Vuk Ćosić, Tadej Pogačar, 01001011010101101.org., 49. International Art Exhibition. La Biennale di Venezia, The Slovenian Pavilion*, Mednarodni grafični likovni center, Ljubljana, 2001, pp. 142–153. Translated from Slovenian by Igor Zabel.

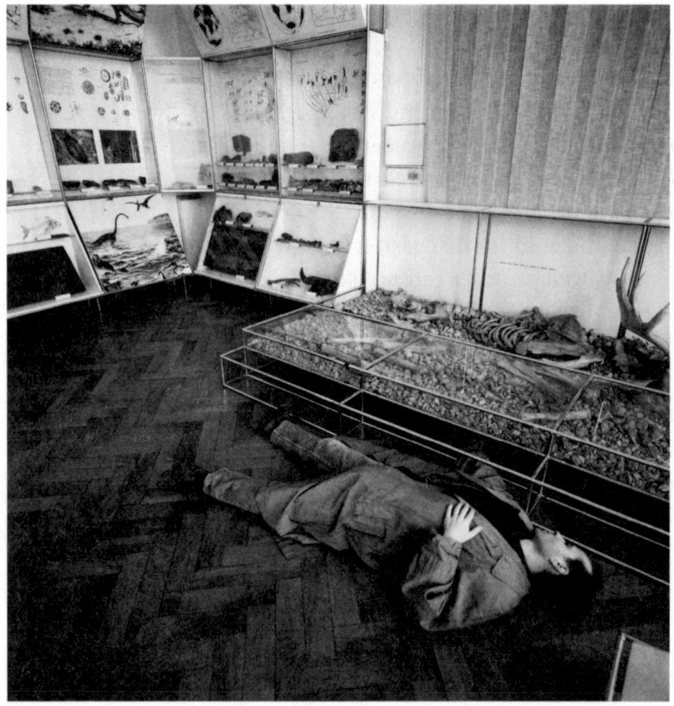

Tadej Pogačar, *Visit II c- No Event Action (Sleeping with a Deer)*, 1993

The two levels of the New Parasitism

The strategy that Tadej Pogačar describes as the "New Parasitism" (to differentiate it from the parasitism as a biological phenomenon) appears in several different forms. Pogačar establishes fictitious systems and institutions, enters actual institutions (museums, schools, etc.) and operates in them, and is also active in researching and presenting the hidden or overlooked phenomena, social groups, practices and relations. All these forms and activities, however, are included in one basic concept - the museum. The museum institution established by Pogačar, The P.A.R.A.S.I.T.E. Museum of Contemporary Art (below, I will refer to it as PMCA), is not just one of the forms of appearance of the New Parasitism; it is its institutional base. The Museum is an institutional form that has, as such, became independent even from Pogačar himself as a person and artist (e.g., PMCA can appropriate and use his own works of art). This institution gives the basis and meaning to other forms of the New Parasitism (which include scientific and pedagogical discourse, commercial activities, etc.). Being compatible to other institutions, it is able to enter them, to adapt to their structures and to operate within them. It is also the institutional form which structures the attempts to research and reveal the hidden, suppressed and parallel, and organises the space of visibility for it. Pogačar's "New Parasitism," therefore, operates on two levels. One level is his entering into systems, institutions and relations; but this level is only possible because of a more fundamental parasitic operation: the appropriation of the form of museum and therefore a mirroring, a duplication of the institutional space of art.

Art is what is on display in the museum

Of course we have to ask ourselves why he did choose exactly the museum for such an institutional basis. The answer is probably connected to the definition of art and its radical transformation in the past century. The traditional aesthetics was able to define art through its specific media (painting, sculpture, drawing etc.), the specific activities inside these media ("imitating," "depicting" etc.), and the specific values that were thus produced ("the beautiful," "the sublime" etc.). In the last century, however, art has expanded far beyond these limits, transforming its own character and definition radically. Even more, in the 20th century we repeatedly witness attempts to abolish the autonomous character of art and to amalgamate art and life completely.

Art can now appropriate any object, phenomenon or activity (and often attempts even to abolish itself as art and to become a part of the so-called "life practice"). Therefore, new criteria have to be established, according to which one can reliably judge whether something can be treated as art or not. It turned out that the criteria for art (although not of the artistic quality) can be external or formal rather than internal or structural. The field of art is, to put it simply, determined by its institutional framework. It can be defined as the world or system of art; whatever enters this system becomes artistically relevant. An artist can appropriate and use any part of the non-artistic reality, or even works by other artists, and turn them into (his/her) art. The art status, however, does not depend entirely on the artists' decisions anymore; to a certain extent, the art system became autonomous. If it used to hold true that artistic relevance depended on the decision of an artist (e.g., the well-known example of a "bus drive" which can be art if it is performed by an artist and used for his or her artistic statement), it is now enough that a certain fact—which originally and by its intention is not art—enters the art system (represented by an artist, but also a curator, critic, historian, museum director, etc.) to gain such a relevance. Therefore, we often see on exhibitions, on equal level with the works of art, most diverse exhibits, such as medical models, erotic devices, police photographs, reconnaissance photos from the military satellites, etc.; none of these objects was produced as a work of art, and often no artist used them for his/her statement. It is one particular institution that has gained a special, dominant position inside the world of art: the museum (especially the museum of modern and/ or contemporary art). We can say that the museum often, in a sort of metonymical way (as a pars pro toto of the whole system) represents the world of art. It has been granted this key role because of its position in the hierarchy of the system, because of the diversity of its activities, possibilities and structures, and because of its role in selection and regulation of the field of art. The museum stands on top of the pyramid of public spaces (with this I mean all the spaces, physical as well as institutional, where art is publicly displayed); the mere physical presence of a work in the museum space is by itself a confirmation that the work is not only a work of art, but a work of art with specific qualities, worth dealing with more thoroughly.

If the mere presence in the museum confirms that the object in question is a relevant work of art (or something which is not a work of art by its intention, but is somehow equivalent to such a work), we must perhaps pose the question about the structure of the museum space; and this will hopefully show us a clearer picture of the parasitic strategy towards the museum as a space and institution.

The ground plan and the discipline of knowledge

When the architect Edvard Ravnikar, in the second half of
the 1930s, worked on his first big project, the building
of Moderna galerija in Ljubljana, he carefully studied recent
museum buildings; not so much their formal properties, as
a matter of fact, but rather their structural aspects and
functional organization. He collected a number of examples
of architecture that enabled a rational, clear and meaningful
arrangement of the exhibits, a simple and logical way
through the exhibition and a quick and easy access to any
point of the exhibition space. If we look at the ground plans
Ravnikar published in 1939 as reference materials in his
article on the project of Moderna galerija, we can easily see
that the form of these plans has more than just strictly
functional value; their geometrical perfection expresses the
order of the knowledge represented by the museum. Spaces
are often connected in a system of fields and disciplines;
when an object enters a museum room, it also enters an
ordered and hierarchical system of knowledge, a system that
is just as clear, perfect and accessible as the museum spaces
themselves. It is remarkable that the ground plans that were
especially interesting for Ravnikar seem to be quite similar:
they represent the form of a wheel, i.e. a round building
with connections reaching from the center to the rim in an
ordered beam form, as spokes (it makes no essential
difference if the plan presents a full circle or just a half of it).
This is an archetypal form, rational, clear, perfect, functional
and aesthetic, and with a strong metaphorical potential.
But it is also a form with a very specific history and specific
connotations in the western world. It is directly connected
to the ordered and hierarchical architecture of prisons,
hospitals and similar institutions, reaching back to the 17th
and 18th century, to the architecture of ordering and disciplining as described by Foucault, especially in his *Surveiller
et punir*. In this sense, we can understand the notion of
"disciplines," which the museum connects, orders and
represents, in a more literal way, and connect the museum
with the systems of managing and disciplining—in this
case, of managing and disciplining the knowledge.

The materials Ravnikar published in his article make
us aware of how in the ground plan of Moderna galerija

(with a central room from which one can directly enter
almost any exhibition space), the system of the hierarchically-
disciplinary institution—jail, hospital, etc—is still present,
although hidden.

It seems, however, that the museum of modern art is
not based on an ordered system of knowledge, i.e. on a
scientific system, in the same sense as the so-called general
museum or the museums based on specific fields of science
(natural history, ethnography, history); this is why Ravnikar
was able to conceal and modify the hierarchical structure of
the ground plan and allow for a more flexible, less hierarchical and systematical, even more heterogeneous character.
Perhaps, the function of the museum of modern and
contemporary art is mainly to accept certain practices
and knowledge into a special field where they gain a specific
"artistic" value, become objects of observation and
contemplation, while at the same time they lose the primary
function they used to have in the non-artistic world.
They become, with the expression used by Peter Bürger,
"folgenlos," i.e. they have no real effect on the world anymore—apart from the actual social role of representations
and images, of course.

Museum as mirror

In a sense, the museum, especially the museum of modern
and contemporary art, functions as a mirror—it can capture
in itself the "whole world," but what we see in it, regardless
how real, how identical to the "external" reality it seems
to be, is only a reflection, an image, a representation of this
reality. Just as the mirror selects a certain detail or fragment,
cuts it out from the continuity of the reality and thus makes
it really visible for the first time, the museum accepts
certain objects and practices of the outer world, and these,
as they enter the institutional field of art (e.g., as they are
on view in the rooms of a museum of modern art), lose their
reality and turn into the reflections and representations of
the reality, but gain visibility, form and structure, meaning
and new contexts. They enter visibility, and at the same
time a system of knowledge. As the example of Ravnikar's
plan for Moderna galerija proves: the "mirror" of the
museum is not neutral or innocent; its structure is, openly

or secretly, the structure of a disciplinary and hierarchical institution. As the museum of modern art "mirrors" the world, its numerous practices and realities, it at the same time brings order and discipline to it, turns it into a system of knowledge, establishes structures of power through it.

Now we can return to the parasitic strategy of the PMCA. As any museum, PMCA produces visibility and brings it into systems of knowledge, but it does so on a certain meta-level. As it is a parallel and delocalised entity (literally "para-site"), it has no substance of its own, no material basis for such a production, merely the institutional form through which it sticks itself onto the host's body and starts to explore its potentials. It is only through its hosts that it incarnates and localizes itself, using the hosts' resources for its own basic museum function: the production of visibility/ knowledge. Only a host can provide the space, the "mirroring surface" for this task. But, since the PMCA as a parainstitution doubles these hosts while itself remains essentially non-localized and non-materialized, it introduces a certain dualism into the hosts' view. It uses the host's "mirroring structure" to catch reflections of the world, but at the same time it displays the surface itself and its structure, i.e. the strategies and methods by which the host produces visibility. This relation of duplication, the self-mirroring of the host in its own mirror appropriated by the parasite (i.e., in the parasite's "para-mirror") is uncertain, fragile and permanently in danger of turning into its opposite. (There is always the danger that the host will appropriate and use the parasite, just as it happened to a number of critical attempts to attack and undermine the institution of the museum—although it is also true that the museum, which had to adapt to these attacks and response to them, has transformed itself essentially in the process). The "hidden ground plan" of the power relations that define the museum thus appears only in fragments, and on the edges of this duplication.

Making Art Visible

First published in *Words of Wisdom. A Curator's Vade Mecum on Contemporary Art*, Independent Curators International (ICI), New York, 2001, pp. 175–176.

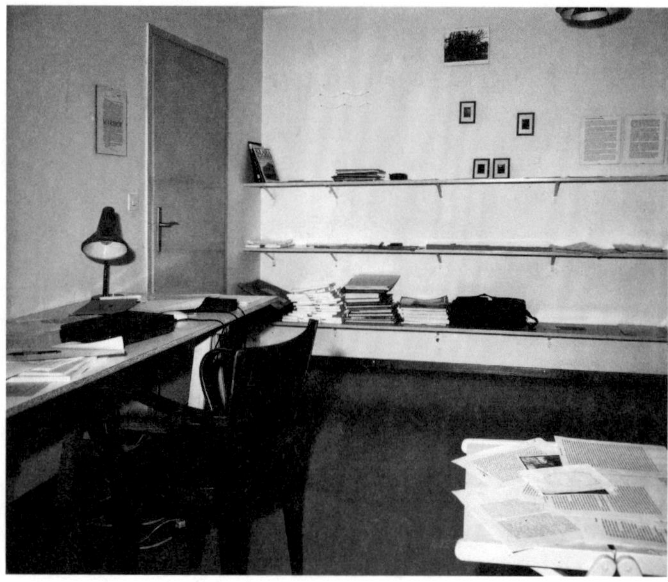

Inexplicable Presence. Curator's Working Place
Installation view of the project, Moderna galerija, Ljubljana, 1997

It has often been said that one essential task of the curator is to construct a space for the work of art—physical space as well as mental, social, etc. A work can only be seen and experienced in an actual context; its existence per se (i.e., outside any such particular context) is only an abstract idea. The curator can therefore essentially affect the reception of the work without actually becoming an artist.

Of course, today, when the idea of art is no longer connected only to a specific type of object but often to constellations, relationships, and interventions into different contexts, the division between artist and curator is less clear, especially since both activities tend to meet in an intermediate area. Still, I would say that curatorial activity cannot replace artistic production, and it cannot exist if there is no artistic production; the task of a curator is not the production of works of art but the production of the conditions for their display and visibility (in the broadest sense). This is a polyvalent and multilayered activity. Simultaneously, it includes a wide range of attitudes and approaches, from the very rational and pragmatic to more emotional and even irrational ones.

A curator never works in a clear and neutral space; his or her activity is therefore a response to particular determining conditions. For example, as somebody coming from the area of so-called Eastern Europe, I experience how the work of artists, critics, and curators from this area is a priori caught in a specific system of assumptions (of cultural difference, etc.), and how often we are expected to "represent" a particular "identity," etc. It therefore seems almost unavoidable to reflect these ideas and to build an effective strategy to deal with them.

In my own practice, I experience repeatedly how decisive small, accidental, and marginal events can be. One is often haunted by images or expressions seen or read somewhere, by uncertain memories, and small personal obsessions. Coincidence, too, can be a decisive factor. I often ask myself whether it is possible to deliberately and actively incorporate this aspect of the marginal and coincidental into the process of constructing a show, thus exposing the decisive but hidden pre-conditions of this process and consciously dealing with them.

Certainly, the question is, why should one's marginal personal obsessions and preferences be so important that they can form the basis for the curatorial construction of the space for art? I believe that, in order to turn them into something of more general interest, one should basically use them as a starting point for a dialogical process with art and artists. Only through such a dialogue and the relations within it can they be developed into a more generally interesting field, eventually (and this is essential) throwing a particular and, hopefully, fresh light on the works of art themselves.

The Return of the White Cube

First published in *The revenge of the white cube. MJ–Manifesta Journal: journal of contemporary curatorship*, no. 1, Moderna galerija, Ljubljana; International Foundation Manifesta, Amsterdam, pp. 12–21, Spring/Summer 2003.

We often hear about a "return" of the "white cube," and indeed, it seems that there is a new interest in this type of exhibition space. A number of recent exhibitions, including the last *Documenta*, have employed the neutral, white exhibition space. How can we understand this interest? Is it a sign of some new conservatism in art after the adventurous experimental work of the 1990s—art that precisely strove to break out of the white gallery space and enter, as directly as possible, a wide diversity of situations and contexts? Or have artists and curators discovered new and challenging possibilities in this sort of exhibition environment?

But can we indeed speak about the white cube's return? Has it ever actually gone away? I would rather say, instead, that the white cube has represented the norm, the most common type of exhibition space in the past decades. Even the site-specific projects and other works "beyond the white cube" have implicitly or explicitly used it as a sort of a generally valid reference point.

We think that we know this sort of space and its characteristics completely:

> "A gallery is constructed along laws as rigorous as those for building a medieval church. The outside world must not come in, so windows are usually sealed off. Walls are painted white. The ceiling becomes the source of light. The wooden floor is polished so that you can click along clinically, or carpeted so that you pad soundlessly, resting the feet while the eyes have at the wall. The art is free, as the saying used to go, 'to take on its own life.' The discreet desk may be the only piece of furniture. In this context a standing ashtray becomes almost a sacred object, just as the firehose in a modern museum looks not like a firehose but an esthetic conundrum. Modernism's transposition of perception from life to formal values is complete. This, of course, is one of modernism's fatal diseases."[1]

This precise and vivid description is taken from the text that actually established the notion of the white cube, Brian O'Doherty's essay *Notes on the Gallery Space*, later reprinted in his book *Inside the White Cube*. As described by O'Doherty, this space and its atmosphere seem so well-known and omnipresent that it is almost strange to consider that the white exhibition space is a relatively recent innovation and that when it was introduced, it was experienced as something radically new and immensely challenging:

> "When Sandberg had the walls painted white, it was a deed of activism, in collaboration with artists wanting renewal. Before he painted them white, they were colored, as they had been since the museum existed. Walls were simply not left white; thus neither were the walls upon which paintings were hung. The color of walls in a museum formed an interesting tangential problem. It was a possibility to create a new, art-historical context for the work. When Sandberg

painted the museum walls white, he brought the museum from the past into his present."[2]

The white walls of the Stedelijk Museum in the late 1930s were thus experienced not as the general norm, but as a particular aesthetic statement that brought a new perspective to the artwork. The white walls could be understood as an active curatorial strategy. A few years later, white walls in exhibition spaces were a generally valid norm.

One result of this development was that there appeared to be a general agreement about what the white cube was. This idea, in turn, was subjected to criticism and dissent, in artists' strategies, in curatorial practice, as well as in museological theory and architectural concepts. The main target of the criticism has been the artificial, neutral, aseptic, and isolated nature of the white cube. Such a space is so neutral it almost seems to disappear. Anything that might interfere with the works is excluded. In a space defined by white walls, neutral floor and lit ceiling, we are unaware of the season of the year or the time of the day, of the space's location and its natural, cultural, social, and historical context. Such spaces are transformed into separate, perennial entities, and we, the visitors, are given a sort of "pure eyes"—as if we left our social, cultural, gender and other particularities outside the gallery door. As O'Doherty observed:

> "The ideal gallery subtracts from the artwork all cues that interfere with the fact that it is 'art'. The work is isolated from everything that would detract from its own evaluation of itself."[3]

It seems to have been primarily the frustrating feeling of isolation from the world that made critical strategies against the white cube so urgent. It was felt that, in order to enter the peaceful enclave of the white cube and to experience and appreciate the exhibited works, one had to pay an exorbitant price. This price, of course, was essentially to forget the world outside the gallery walls; taken metaphorically, this meant to forget the world outside the art system. It also meant that art was banished from the world into the isolated realm of the art system. Robert Smithson, in

Cultural Confinement, his critical textual contribution to *Documenta 5* (1972), sharply attacked the white cube space and the art system for being an isolating force that separated art from the "world outside of cultural confinement." (Smithson understood this world primarily as the "dialectic of nature," but this dialectic includes, of course, also the huge transforming impact of human society.)

> "Artists themselves are not confined, but their output is. Museums like asylums and jails have wards and cells—in other words, neutral rooms called 'galleries.' A work of art when placed in a gallery loses its charge, and becomes a portable object or surface disengaged from the outside world. A vacant white room with lights is still submission to the neutral. Works of art seen in such spaces seem to be going through a kind of esthetic convalescence. They are looked upon as so many inanimate invalids, waiting for critics to pronounce them curable or incurable. The function of the warden-curator is to separate art from the rest of society. Next comes integration. Once the work of art is totally neutralized, ineffective, abstracted, safe, and politically lobotomized it is ready to be consumed by society. All is reduced to visual fodder and transportable merchandise. Innovations are allowed only if they support this kind of confinement."[4]

Smithson's statement demonstrates how deeply the understanding of the white cube space has changed. (Such changes in understanding represent, of course, changes in art and the fundamental ideas that determine works of art.) What was once considered the ideal space for observing, experiencing, and evaluating art—the only possible space in which works of art could disclose all their essential qualities—had now become an asylum and a prison.

The most direct critical reaction to the isolated white exhibition space has been to abandon it altogether and to search for a different kind of space to present art, very often with the idea that art should somehow become a much more immediate part of life. Art has moved into a great variety of contexts and appropriated them for its own purposes.

There have also been modifications within the traditional exhibition space. (One such modification was Rudi Fuchs's decision to paint the walls in the Stedelijk Museum light gray, thus reviving in a way Sandberg's active relationship to works of art and giving the exhibited pieces a more active, and also more appropriate, context.) But there has also been a strong tension within artistic and curatorial practices to develop new critical strategies *with* the white cube space. One essential strategy could be described as (re)localization of such a space and thus its (re)contextualization. There have been ongoing efforts over the past few decades to reconnect the exhibition space with its context—environmentally, historically, culturally and politically. Furthermore, there has been a recurring effort to deconstruct the apparently neutral and generic nature of such a space and to disclose the ideological background on which it is constituted, as well as the function and role of such a space (and related curatorial approaches) within the actual power relations in society.

This approach may also be seen in the work of architects who have considered changing the traditional white exhibition space by permitting more subtle connections to its natural and social context. In some cases, they even tried to make visitors critically aware of the nature and function of the exhibition space. In some cases, the modification of such elements as lighting have essentially changed the nature of the space, as Kenneth Frampton proposed in his vision of a "critical regionalism" in architecture.

"Until recently, the received precepts of modern curatorial practice favored the exclusive use of artificial light in all art galleries. It has perhaps been insufficiently recognized how this encapsulation tends to reduce the artwork to commodity, since such an environment must conspire to render the work placeless. This is because the local spectrum is never permitted to play across the surface: here, then, we see how the loss of aura, attributed by Walter Benjamin to the processes of mechanical reproduction, also arises from a relatively static application of universal technology. The converse of this 'placeless' practice would be to provide that art galleries would be top-lit through carefully contrived monitors so that, while the injurious effects of direct sunlight are avoided, the ambient light of the exhibition volume changes under the impact of time, season, humidity, etc. Such conditions guarantee the appearance of a place-conscious poetic—a form of filtration compounded out of an interaction between culture and nature, between art and light."[5]

To paint the walls gray or change the character of the light might seem relatively small modifications, but they indicate a transformation in our understanding of the white cube space that is quite far-reaching and deep. These are not so much changes in the physical environment of the space, but rather in its conceptual framework. The issue was never merely the form and character of the exhibition space but, rather, the concept of art, its constitution, and its position in society, which become self-evident in the character of the gallery. O'Doherty and others have clearly pointed to this relationship:

> "The history of modernism is intimately framed by that space; or rather the history of modern art can be correlated with changes in that space and in the way we see it. [...] An image comes to mind of a white, ideal space that, more than any single picture, may be the archetypal image of twentieth century art; it clarifies itself through a process of historical inevitability usually attached to the art it contains."[6]

The isolation of a work of art in a white cube space is something more than the work's physical placement in a closed and supposedly neutral room. It corresponds to the autonomous nature of the modernist work of art. A discussion about the characteristics of the white exhibition space is, implicitly or explicitly, a discussion about modernist art, and perhaps about modernity itself. Criticism directed toward the isolation and confinement of art in a neutral white space is actually aimed at the autonomous status of art and the fact that, as such, art has been considered only in terms of its formal values and, thus, socially neutralized, pacified, and turned into commodity. Attempts to break out of the white cube are, by the same token, attempts to make art more relevant for society and an essential part of life.

Is it fair to assume that the new importance of the white cube space indicates a new importance for the notion of art's autonomy? In my view, the response to this question cannot be a simple one. First, the white cube has gone through a process of transformation, critique, and deconstruction that is implicitly present in the way we understand it today. Second, the idea of the autonomy of art seems much more complex than the simple opposition, "autonomous" vs. "engaged" art. This, indeed, was obvious at the last *Documenta*, which used the white cube space to present art that often dealt with direct social and political research and criticism. This in itself indicates a change in the structure of the white cube. But does the white cube still have the power to change anything that enters it into art, and moreover, into autonomous art?

In the same article in which he discusses Sandberg's white walls, Bart De Baere also writes: "*The* white space does not exist. There are countless white spaces with different behaviours."[7] He is speaking from a position that, after the experiences of the 1980s and early 1990s, no longer understands the white space as a general condition for the presentation of art (in either a positive or a negative sense). There is a multitude of different exhibition spaces, and the white space is one of them. Moreover, the white space has ceased to be uniform and timeless. The mutual relationship, valid for modernism, between the white cube and the nature of art has disappeared. One perceives not the general idea of the white cube, but rather the particular qualities and differences that determine the behavior of each space. The white cube is also seen as something constantly developing, parallel to the development of art. And now that the heterogeneity and plurality of art have been expressed in the plurality of the contexts and spaces in which art can be presented, it seems that art has been liberated from the "cultural confinement" Smithson spoke about:

> "Every context is a good context for art, an artistic context as well. The museum can continue to claim that it is the place par excellence for art to be exhibited, but artists have tended for some time

already to believe that it is possibly one of the places par excellence to allow art to exist. The same goes for the gallery. Both infrastructure models have a character of their own, with its own advantages. Like other places."[8]

The plurality and heterogeneity of the white cube indicates the disappearance of the rationale behind its uniformity—the modernist concepts that established and shaped this type of space. Yet, despite such relativization, the white cube has kept a particular status. To exhibit in it means, directly or indirectly, to allude to modernist concepts. Furthermore, despite the pluralism of art, we continue to refer to *the* white cube, *the* white space. The white cube simply cannot be understood as just one of many spaces for art. Even if there obviously are a great variety of spaces, the white cube still has a determining role. Sometimes it almost seems one could reduce the entire rich diversity of art spaces to two types: "white cube" and "not white cube." (It might be possible to apply the Klein group to this opposition and extend it into the "extended field," as Rosalind Krauss did with sculpture; still the first opposition would remain essential.[9])

To what extent, then, does the new interest in the white cube indicate a new, or renewed, importance for modernist concepts? And what role do these concepts play in contemporary art? The ambiguous role of the white space, which is both one space among many and yet something more than that, could suggest an answer. Modernist concepts, especially the concept of the autonomy of art, cannot be the final horizon of this art, but they remain essential within the heterogeneous complex of conflicting aspects and contradictions that determine the position of contemporary art. *Documenta 11* has demonstrated this clearly. One could not describe it as a show of autonomous art, but neither was it unequivocally political. The works were dislocated into the world of art and academic discourse, as represented by the white cube, but, by the same token, there was obviously a very clear desire to establish a relationship with the contexts to which the works referred. Like Smithson's *Nonsites*, the works were both inside and outside the gallery, both autonomous and concrete, both maintaining a distance and establishing a strong link, in a tension that was, at least for me, one of the most important achievements of the exhibition.

The acknowledgement that there exists no white cube space as such (except as an idea), and that white spaces are different from each other and also historically structured in different ways, would suggest something else, as well. Modernism, too, is internally heterogeneous, plural and non-coherent, despite the idea of modernism as such and *the* modern. There are, perhaps, even different modernisms (which are, however, all still modernisms), and even different modernities (which are still modernities).

There is no simple answer to the question about the new interest in the white cube. It is true that it can be used from a conservative position and as part of the process of the commodification of art. But it can also have other uses. Today, the white cube can no longer be taken for granted. It has been transformed and loaded with numerous references and traditions, and thus cannot be used in a "natural" way. It demands an active strategy from artists and curators, a reflection of the possibilities, limitations, and meanings it embodies, and of the importance of its fundamental concepts for today's art. So it could, perhaps, regain the active role it had in the days when the walls were first painted white.

[1] Brian O'Doherty, *Inside the White Cube. The Ideology of the Gallery Space*, expanded edition. University of California Press, Berkeley, Los Angeles and London, 1999, p. 15.

[2] Bart De Baere, "Joining the Present to Now," *Kunst & Museumjournaal*, vol. 6, double new year issue, 1994-1995, (pp. 59–20), p. 62.

[3] O'Doherty, *op. cit.*, p. 14.

[4] Robert Smithson, "Cultural Confinement," Charles Harrison and Paul Wood (eds.), *Art in Theory, 1900–1990*, Blackwell, Oxford (UK) and Cambridge (USA), 1992, pp. 946–948, quotation p. 947. The text was first published in the catalogue of the *Documenta 5*, Kassel, 1972.

[5] Kenneth Frampton, "Towards a Critical Regionalism: Six Points for an Architecture of Resistance," Hal Foster (ed.), *Postmodern Culture*, Bay Press, Port Townsend, Wash., 1983, pp. 16–30, quotation p. 27.

[6] O'Doherty, *op. cit.*, p. 14.

[7] De Baere, *op. cit.*, p. 63.

[8] *Ibid.*, p. 67.

[9] Rosalind Krauss, "Sculpture in the Expanded Field," *The Originality of the Avant-Garde and Other Modernist Myths*, MIT Press, 1985, pp. 276–91.

Contemporary Art and the Institutional System

Contribution at the conference *What Contemporary Art Demands from Its Institutions?*, Moderna galerija, Ljubljana, 1–2 March 2003. Translated from Slovenian by Rawley Grau.

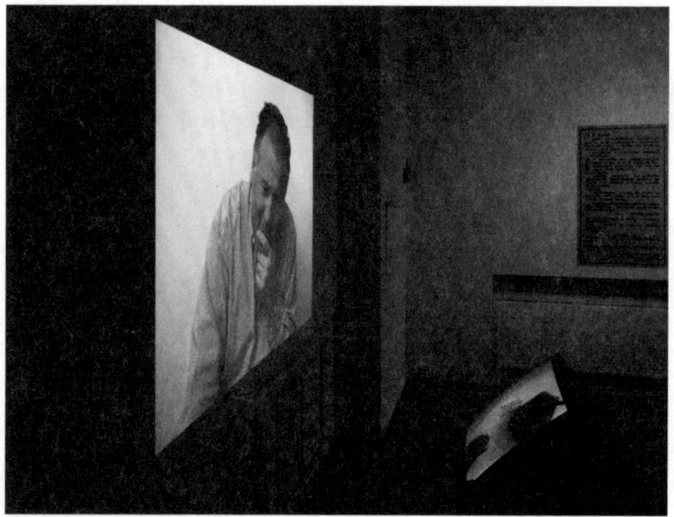

Nika Špan, *Video ne video*, 1997
The Present and Presence, Museum of Contemporary Art Metelkova, Ljubljana, 2011

The theme of this symposium is concerned with the relationship between contemporary art and the institutional system. To illustrate how important this system is, let us go back a century to the time when Slovene modern art was first becoming established and grounded. This process is usually associated primarily with Rihard Jakopič, not only because he brought new forms into Slovene art—forms that were very modern and progressive for the provincial Slovene culture of the time—but especially because he realized that he needed to organize an appropriate context for his art production if it was to be at all meaningful. He strived to establish his painting as a national art, but a national art is possible only if there exists an institutional system that can set it within the society and at the same time enable it to be reproduced. It is astonishing to realize just how active Jakopič was in this regard and how many different segments of the system he (more or less successfully) sought to develop—a system which, in the modern sense of the word, had not existed at all in the Slovene lands before that time but which Jakopič saw as necessary in order for his actual painting practice to have any chance of a context in which it would be meaningful, in which it could be understood (and if possible, of course, also highly valued). He tried to organize like-minded artists, prepared exhibitions, created an exhibition venue along the lines of the German *Kunsthalle* (the famous Jakopič Pavilion), managed the sale of artworks, made suggestions for historical exhibitions and the national collection, wrote art criticism, established an art school, and so on. Thus he designed, at least in its basic outlines, the structure of the modern (national) art system that is still active today and that consists, in particular, of the following elements: above all, of course, artists and their works and activities; then, a system of presentation and interpretation (exhibition spaces from alternative and nonprofit spaces through *Kunsthalle*-type venues to art centers and museums; curators, theoreticians, and critics; publications intended for the general public and those intended for a more specialized readership; museum collections and other collections, museological processes and the establishment of artistic and cultural traditions, etc.); the system of the art market (galleries, art fairs, auction houses, collectors, etc.); and the educational system, both specialist programs (for artists, art historians, theoreticians, and critics) and those for the general public (such as art education in non-specialized secondary schools), whether presented by the school system or by museums, exhibition venues, and other similar institutions. Finally, an essential component of any such system is the public—and also private—funding that makes its functioning possible.

It would probably not be wrong to say that this system is the true subject of cultural policy for the field of contemporary art. In other words, we can define cultural policy as a series of state measures (regulations, direct and indirect financial support, etc.) that foster and develop the system, especially in areas where certain deficiencies are seen to exist; at the same time, these measures allow the system as much open space as possible in which its generative, but also self-modifying potential can develop. It goes without saying, however, that in its broader concept cultural policy is concerned with how this field is placed within the total system of the national culture and to what degree it will exploit the exceptional potential of contemporary art.

As an indication of just how crucially art today is intertwined with the system in which it originates, reproduces itself, and enters into relationships with the public, let me mention one of the fundamental art-theoretical notions of recent times, which was put forward by Arthur Danto.[1] Put simply, his thesis is that today the criteria for whether something is or is not a work of art can no longer be based on content, form, or genre, but rather, it can be determined only in the context of the art system, or, as he calls it, "the artworld." I mention this thesis in order to underscore the fact that today it is simply no longer possible to limit art to the production of art as a closed, autonomous activity; instead, art must be understood as the interweaving of production with strategies of presentation and interpretation, which is something that happens, of course, within social, political, and economic frameworks. We might perhaps connect Danto's thesis about "the world of art" with Luhmann's ideas about the system of art as an autonomous and autopoietic system. This system is materialized precisely through a network of institutions, influences, and initiatives, i.e. through the institutional system of contemporary art in its broadest sense. This is the system that makes possible the practice of art, its production, and its reproduction.

If we speak about the system of "contemporary" art, we of course need to define what "contemporary" means. The concept of "contemporary art" has a very specific meaning, which took shape especially in the 1980s and 1990s. The art of the modern era developed by means of the continual defining and redefining of "modernity"; this developmental logic was for the first time put into question explicitly by the appearance of the concepts "postmodern" and "postmodernism." With them, the concept of "modernity" was suddenly shown as a specific historical, and therefore already exceeded line of development. The "modern art" from which "contemporary art" distinguishes itself is understood primarily as modernism—that is to say, the tradition that extends from the late nineteenth century

into the second half of the twentieth century. This, of
course, does not mean that we cannot also speak about
"contemporary" art as a specific historical tradition,
one that also reaches back several decades.

Summarizing the definitions of the "main current"
of high modernism as presented by Charles Harrison,[2] we
can say that the following aspects, among others, are crucial:
for modernism the concept of quality is essential as an
absolute value given in the viewer's experience; in the
modern period, modernism is a necessary condition for
quality in high art; and the standard for this quality is found
in the paradigmatic works of high modernism. By thus
defining the "central current" of modernism, critics simplified the modernist tradition, excluding or marginalizing
those phenomena that involved precisely such things as
critical thinking about their own social position and function
and reactualizing the political, critical, and subversive
dimensions in art; attacks on auratic art; shifts in value that
placed in the foreground what was marginal, ephemeral,
or partial; a new interest in narrative, decoration, irony, and
play; and so on.

The concept of "contemporary art" does not merely
relativize such ideas as the autonomy of art, its originality,
its confessional and contemplative aspects; it is also based
on a very different understanding of time and the historical
position of artistic activity. One might say that, in the view
of modernist criticism, the history of art since the second
half of the nineteenth century is conceived in teleological
terms, with art gradually approaching its final and absolute
truth and fundamental irreducible form. The concept of
contemporaneity, conversely, is not constituted as a logical
succession of achievements that get closer and closer to the
absolute, but rather as a contingent position and a constellation in an endless state of transformation. Contemporary
art today is no longer what it was five years ago (which,
however, does not mean there are no connections between
then and now). At the same time, the concept of "contemporary art" offers—in a seeming contradiction of terms—a
reevaluation and recoding of the tradition which high
modernism suppressed or marginalized because it did not
fit into the teleological construction of the logical and
necessary development of modernism; contemporary art

reactualizes these artists and movements, for it uncovers in them tendencies and perspectives close to its own. (Thus we should hardly be surprised at the renewed and very animated interest in such phenomena as Situationism, Fluxus, conceptualism, and the avant-garde art movements of the 1960s and 1970s, and efforts to return to them.) In short, we might say that when we speak of "contemporaneity" in art, we mean both the kind of production we can have no distance from but must be constantly defining our position toward as well as a specific tradition that is connected with our own interests and positions. (Here the paradox is that modernism is not yet so integrated into the prevailing norms of taste that it does not still entail, at least partly or occasionally, a departure from the kind of satisfaction the general public seeks in art. The public will almost always be less interested in a Mondrian exhibition or a performance of Weber's music than in a Vermeer exhibition or a Schubert concert. While we still, at least partly, feel "modern" art to be a departure from the fully accepted canons of the art tradition, "contemporary" art is a departure also from the norms of "modern" art.)

Institutions must of course respond to the changed circumstances introduced by art's contemporaneity; this means, we can say, the constant reorganization, transformation, and mutual adaptation of the elements of the system. Some of the essential aspects of these shifts are:

– *Institutional pluralism*. Contemporary art needs a network of institutions, which, precisely because of their mutual differences, are both internally flexible and heterogeneous as well as complementary. It is essential that this network be not only diversified with respect to the type and structure of its institutions, but also geographically spread out. (In recent years a number of very active and interesting centers have been established outside of Ljubljana; these institutions, which for the most part are regional or local, must be safeguarded from the whims of local politics, which views them as a needless and disturbing element.)

– *Intermediality*. The fact that today it is possible to define art primarily by its systemic context, rather than any medium-based, thematic, or formal factors, shows that art today is able to appropriate more or less any practice, space, or object and turn it into art or an element of art ("A bus ride can be art if it is perceived as art"). Art reaches across its traditional boundaries, interlacing itself in other artistic and cultural fields and bringing elements from these fields into its own system.

   – *The international aspect.* Contemporary art practices are defined essentially as international, although they can also, certainly, involve a complex play—and sometimes tension—between national and international aspects.

   If I now try to think concretely about what a new museum of contemporary art should look like, I can derive from all of this certain demands that are essential to such an institution. First and foremost, it must be flexible enough to be able to constantly respond to new circumstances as they develop and to orient itself in the new constellations. It is able to incorporate tradition into contemporaneity (through its collection and other activities), and indeed, as a museum, it must do so. But this can be a specific tradition that is constituted from contemporary practices and remains in dialogic tension with them. The museum's structure must be heterogeneous and flexible enough for it to include very different kinds of practices, serve as a producer for them, and provide them with curatorial support and critical and theoretical reflection. Such a museum must, in its essence, have a multimedia and intermedia focus. It must also be internationally focused and serve as a point of intersection and interaction between the local or national space and the world of international art. But for such an institution to have any real meaning, it must belong to a network of other institutions on both the local and international levels. Only such a network (as broad and pluralistic and as heterogeneous and flexible as possible) can truly intensify the individual institution.

   Art institutions alone cannot create artworks, and especially not great artworks. The stimulation and development of the art system, too—although these are fundamental tasks of cultural policy—are not in themselves the same as the direct production of such works. But they do ensure the conditions for the creation of these works and allow them to become accessible to the public. And this, in the end, is the ultimate and proper meaning of art institutions.

[1] Arthur C. Danto, "The Artworld," *Journal of Philosophy*, vol. 61, no. 19, 1964, pp. 571–584.

[2] The British art historian Charles Harrison wrote extensively on modernism, including the generalist study *Modernism* (London, 1997) in the Tate Gallery's *Movements in Modern Art* series.

III. AD PERSONAM

Ground and its Loss: Landscape in Slovene Modern and Contemporary Art (Four Examples)

First published in *Slovene Studies*, vol. 15, no. 1–2, 1993, pp. 35–50.

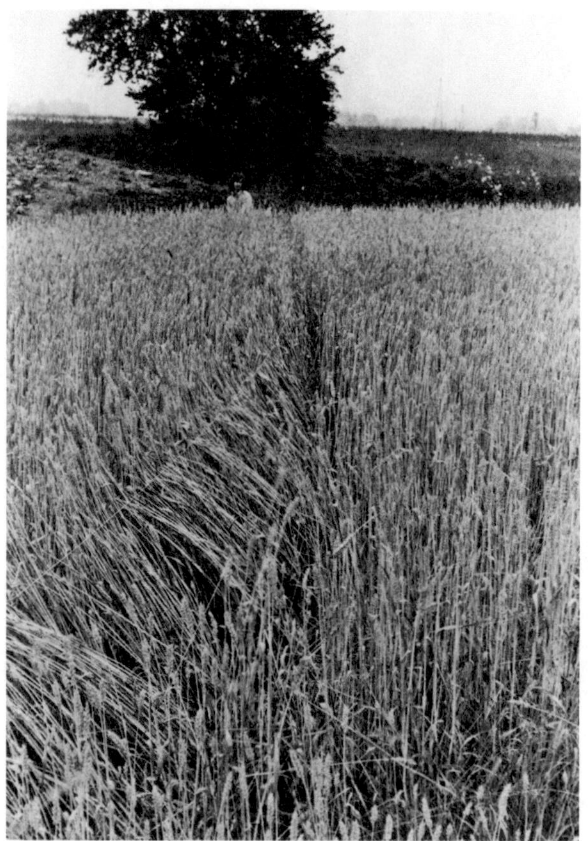

OHO, Milenko Matanović, *Wheat and Rope*, 1969

Introduction

Landscape appears relatively often as a subject in Slovene modern and contemporary art; it appears, however, in very different contexts and has thus a varying significance. Landscape is often connected with the idea of ground. I do not think here merely of a kind of *Blut und Boden* ideology (which could also be found in Slovene arts, especially in the 1930s, although it was relatively mild); in the work of some of the more important artists, this subject expresses a search for belonging, identity, for a firm base of the work. Often, however, it also speaks about a loss of ground and the impossibility to find an identity. Here, I would like to present four examples, artists belonging to four different generations from the beginning of Slovene modern art to recent art production. Each of these artists uses landscape in a specific way, and all of them connect it with themes of ground, belonging, identity, and also lack of ground, homelessness and difference.

Rihard Jakopič

One can find such dilemmas extremely clearly present at the very beginning of Slovene modern art, in the work of Rihard Jakopič. This painter was the leading figure of an extremely strong generation of artists, the so-called "Slovene Impressionists"; these artists, trained in Munich, returned to Slovenia with the idea to turn Ljubljana—which was at that time rather provincial and lethargic as regards the visual arts—into a real art center. But their aims went even further: they wanted to establish a strong national art. It is important that they understood national art not as, e.g., historic painting or folklore genre, but as truly modern art. Because of this, their works were at first rejected in Ljubljana and criticized as foreign imports. But after a successful show in an important Vienna gallery, Salon Miethke, in 1904, the importance and national character of these works began to be recognized. In fact, it was first the Viennese press which—perhaps for political reasons— stressed the particular, "Slovene" character of these works; after this show, the reception of this generation was clearly marked with the idea that their art grew from their home-ground which gave it a special authenticity and quality. Two important Slovene writers of the time, Ivan Cankar and Oton Župančič, wrote articles about the show at Miethke's, both stressing the distinct Slovene character of their works. Cankar found in them a special Slovene "mood," and Župančič wrote: "Vigor, sucked from domestic ground, endows them with freshness and makes them distinct from artists of other nations." This understanding proved to be very influential, and in the mid-1920s it was already a common theme.

As for Jakopič, such an understanding was not only an exterior interpretation of his work, but it was to a certain extent decisive for his own position and self-understanding. It was tightly connected to the project of establishing a modern national visual culture. Such a project demanded not only the production of good works, but also works that somehow belong to the national context. In a certain sense, this project was similar to the project of establishing a distinctive American modernism, as was achieved with Abstract Expressionism; of course, we must take into account not only the difference in the international importance of the two movements, but also certain differences in the understanding of the concept of "national" (which for Slovenes is more closely connected with ethnicity and territory than it is for Americans).

Despite the popular notion of "Slovene Impressionism," Jakopič's work can only in a limited sense be referred to as impressionist. It belongs much more to the Post-Impressionist context and sometimes approaches Expressionism. His position is traditionally described as a synthesis of impression and expression. His paintings are based on observing nature, but they are not a mechanical reproduction of visual sensations (as radical Impressionists' works were supposed to be). The impressions were transformed in his mind, and the depicted nature is thus loaded with expressive and emotional contents. This notion fits perfectly with the idea of "growing from the home-ground." What Jakopič eventually "expresses" is his attachment to this "ground," i.e., to the nation. (Of course he expresses his individual personality, but, as he wrote in one of his texts, a strong personality somehow synthesizes the creative powers of the whole nation, and can subsequently influence the nation.) His "impressions," therefore, necessarily became "expressions," and vice versa, the "expression" cannot be separated from "impressions," since it does not come from an autonomous source, but from the "ground."

It would be wrong to suppose that this ground can be identified with the actual Slovene landscape; but there certainly is a special connection between the two. The least we can say is that this landscape serves as a kind of symbol or metaphor for the metaphysical "national ground."

If we look at his paintings we see the importance of the paint as material and of the impulsive brushstrokes—an importance that cannot be explained just by the "expressive" aspect of his work alone. We may say that the immanent logic of Jakopič's painting lead him into abstract art where the medium itself would prevail. In such works, the expressive content of the subject would be replaced by expressive connotations of brushstrokes and color combinations. This is not a pure speculation. We know that some of Jakopič's works came very close to this kind of painting; although the motif is still present, it is totally unrecognizable and is dissolved, so to speak, in the texture of the applied paint. Most of these works, however, were small and not intended for public display and were therefore often treated as studies. This is, of course, wrong; these small works were not meant as a preparation of a final work, they were themselves the final phase of a long development.

Only later, in the 1920s, did he start to work on larger-sized landscapes where he at last approached the radicality of his small "studies," stressing the importance of the applied paint and of the brushstroke. The dualism between the motif and the medium, however, remained.

Only slowly the critics became aware that Jakopič's position, based on the idea of individual personality as an embodiment of the nation's creative powers and on the synthesis of impression and expression, not only guaranteed the special authenticity and quality of his paintings, but also obscured some very far-reaching and radical aspects of his work.

I believe it was Zoran Kržišnik who, in his book on Jakopič,[1] first drew attention to the fact that the painter's decision for the project of establishing national modern art (and also its necessary institutions, such as exhibition, art school, art museum, exhibition hall, etc.) concealed the most advanced and radical tendencies in his art—tendencies which are, in certain aspects, comparable to much later avant-garde movements, such as Abstract Expressionism in America or Art Informel in Europe. Jakopič eventually succeeded in his efforts to turn modern visual arts into an essential part of the national life, but as the price for it, as Kržišnik wrote, he had to sacrifice "some of his deepest artistic visions."

Was it only the radicality of these visions—a radicality that made such works totally unacceptable for the local public—that forced Jakopič to abandon the path he was following? I believe this is only a part of the answer. A picture based on the autonomy of its medium could not be incorporated in Jakopič's theory of artistic production, with nature and nation as its basic sources, and individual creative personality as the intermediator (a relationship which found its form in the synthesis of "impression" and "expression"). It would mean a total loss of the "ground" and there would be no excuse for it.

OHO land art

Even in the context of the radical avant-garde of the 1960s, landscape had a particular role. Of course, these artists did not depict it, but used it as the site and eventually the essential content of their works. I am thinking here of the OHO group, an extremely interesting movement active from about 1966 to 1971. The OHO artists developed a particular type of land art. They first tried to bring their works out from traditional art spaces, such as galleries, into the open public space in the city, or into landscape. Soon, they did not only install the works in the open air, but started to work with the space itself. I would particularly like to mention here a series of works made in 1969. I believe the specific character of these projects can be better understood if we compare them to American Land Art produced at about the same time.

The expression "Earthworks" very well describes the character of these American projects. Regardless of the important differences between the artists, some essential similarities in their works are also obvious. The sites of these projects are often huge deserts or industrially devastated areas. This choice stresses the idea of virtually unlimited space that is at the artist's disposal. The artist can—and usually does—build large permanent installations using heavy machinery and other advanced technical means. Often, such works function as a mark on an empty territory; i.e., the site is treated as "white paper" or *tabula rasa*, not loaded with any previous tradition or meaning, as a totally empty and neutral space, ready for artists' signs and "writings."

The connection of the Earthworks with the idea of the sublime in art was often noted. Endless space, extreme atmospheric conditions and physical efforts connected to the experiencing of such works, often even the slow process of their change and disappearance (Smithson's *Spiral Jetty* or Heizer's *Double Negative*, to mention but two examples), stress a certain heroism and imply the idea of an active individual personality vs. a huge, disposable, but extreme and powerful space. The quality of the sublime (corresponding to the original meaning of this concept as it appears in Burke's *Essay*) is also connected to the experience of the immense power of technology, which is often devastating and terrible.

The OHO land art took place in very different surroundings. Their sites were not in big cities, but in relatively small towns, not in huge deserts, but in cultivated landscape. Fields, meadows and woods demanded a totally different approach. The works could not be permanent; moreover, no trace remained after the project was completed. Therefore, OHO land art exists only as photographs and films and is, in this respect, closer to performances or actions than to the Earthworks. Further, the sites of OHO projects were not only cultivated, but also loaded with tradition and meaning. For one of his projects, Marko Pogačnik prepared a map of a valley where several OHO actions and projects were organized; on this map we can see prehistoric and old Slavic sites, a medieval church etc., as well as the sites of OHO projects, which were thus connected to history and tradition. Advanced industrial technology, of course, could not be used. OHO artists used very simple, pre-industrial tools, which demanded a close physical contact with the sites and dimensions equivalent to the artist's body. There is a film where this intimate and corporeal relationship is especially stressed. We see Marko Pogačgnik removing turf from a certain area; and he is acting as if he were skinning some large animal. The connection between the artist and the turf is indeed a close relationship of two bodies. Compare this to the character of the bodily experience in, e.g., De Maria's plan for a work where the observer would be forced to walk one mile between two parallel walls built in the desert.

For me, the very essence of OHO land art is concentrated in Milenko Matanović project *Wheat and Rope*, 1969. This work (published also in Lucy Lippard's book *Six Years: The Dematerialization of the Work of Art*) consists simply of a string drawn across a wheat-field; the string is slightly bending the wheat. It is a very gentle and temporary intervention, which functions as a kind of "scratch," constituting, so to speak, an extremely intense emotional and conceptual complex. We could perhaps think of Heidegger's descriptions of an ancient temple in his famous essay *The Origin of the Work of Art*.[2] Heidegger speaks about the power of the "temple" (i.e., a work of art) to throw light on "earth"; "Der Tempel läßt die Erde eine Erde sein" ["The temple lets the earth be an earth"], as he writes.

If we compare this piece with some works by Dennis Oppenheim from about the same time (e.g., *Surface Indentation*, 1968, or *Branded Mountain*, 1969) we notice a basically different approach. Oppenheim, too, worked in cultivated areas, but these were large, industrially tilled fields. Furthermore, many of his works include the dimension of marking a territory with the artist's sign. In *Surface Indentation*, the field is not treated as a complex synthesizing emotional contents and references, it does not call to mind the idea of a co-existence of nature and man; it is simply a material. Growing wheat is understood as a kind of industrial production, and the line cut into the even, flat surface of the field is a line cut into the material.

All these aspects are connected to a particular relationship of OHO towards nature. For them, landscape did not represent or signify the ground anymore, and, of course, they never referred to the national as their source or base. (It is worth mentioning that exactly at that time avant-garde artists and critics explicitly demanded liberation of art from the role of the constitutive force of the nation.) What they did try to achieve, however, was a harmony between their activity and the space they were working in. They developed a particular ecological approach, which tried to connect their activities and the landscape in a harmonic, although dynamic unit. For OHO, such a harmony resulted exactly from the internal differences and their supplementary relations. Consequently, their land art developed into so-called "schooling," i.e., a series of exercises and actions in nature, aiming at the development of their personalities, of the close internal relationship within the group and of the harmony between the group and its national, social and traditional context, and eventually at recognizing and accepting one's position within the cosmic order. Quite naturally, such an attitude resulted in giving up art as a separate, closed area and starting a community on a deserted farm in the village of Šempas,

where they intended to re-unite art life and the universe.
These very esoteric ideas, however, were formulated in the
very rational and precise language of land art and conceptual
art. Rationally describable concepts, even gestalts and
geometrical forms, in a certain sense form the base for this
unity and harmony and for its understanding. The emotional,
sometimes even mystical experiences of the unity of the
group and nature were, in the work of OHO, always re-
articulated and developed through highly abstract and
rational models and proceedures.

Emerik Bernard

In the art of the 1980s, i.e., in the time of New Image and
Neo-Expressionist Painting, landscape painting gained a
new importance, connected, of course, with personal
experiences, previsions, obsessions, desires and fears. The
art of Emerik Bernard was one of the highlights of that
period and is perhaps one of the highest points of recent
Slovene painting.

For Bernard, landscape offers not only a picturesque
motif, but leads into complicated questions about belonging
and separation, about identity and difference. But first he
had to solve the question how to paint a landscape at all.
For him, a landscape (or any figurative) painting could not
be taken for granted anymore. After vivid discussions in the
1970s, when phenomena like "fundamental painting"
re-actualized the modernist concepts and ideas, especially
Greenberg's analyses and demands, it indeed seemed
impossible to make a painting which would refer to anything
but its own material conditions and the process of
execution. Bernard resolved this dilemma by pointing to the
basically ambiguous character of the material used for
a painting. He questioned the idea of simple and original
presence ("presentness") of such material, and referred to
the psychology of perception to support his idea that
material presence cannot be separated from the process of
perception and therefore from interpretation. Possibilities
of double and multiple reading, therefore, essentially belong
to a painting, however "flat" and "material" it is. In the
mid-1980s, Bernard achieved a synthesis of a basically flat
painting and suggestive, deep landscape visions. The rough

material nature of the paint and other materials such as pieces of paper or cloth, old clothes, etc., is not hidden at all in these works, actually, it is even stressed. The combination and internal relationship of these materials, however, are ambiguous. They make it possible for a spectator to discover large landscapes and panoramas appearing, like a vision or a mirage, "in" the rough material surface.

The landscape (or its fragments) that appears on Bernard's painting can be precisely located. It is Istria. For over 25 years, Bernard has not only been going to Istria to work in a picturesque landscape, but he became intimately attached to this land and its people. We can therefore understand these paintings as a repeated effort to achieve not only empathy but even an identification with the land and its complex, sometimes very archaic and often contradictory culture and tradition. One might say that these works, metaphorically speaking, represent a search for home.

Bernard himself quoted a line from T.S. Eliot's *Four Quartets:* "Home is where one starts from."[3] In the context of Bernard's art, we can understand these words in the sense that a "home" becomes one only in the moment when it is abandoned or lost, when the immediate identity with it is no longer possible. Painting is thus a surrogate for belonging, or rather, for an immediate identity. Of course, "home" is really a metaphor here. Bernard is not searching for a national or regional "ground." The problem he is dealing with is connected to the problem of the relationship between art and life. Bernard recognized the importance of the avant-garde demands for re-uniting them, but he also realized that the efforts to abandon art in favor of life practice itself failed and had to fail.

In this respect we might understand his landscapes as examples or parables, speaking about the nature and destiny of art and of human existence. While looking at a landscape painting we may recognize the beauty of the represented landscape, we may even, through empathy, feel united with it, its culture, history and tradition. (Indeed we can see that Bernard is not only presenting an instantaneous view; his paintings are thick, multi-layered structures—"palimpsests," as he calls them—full of different traces and remains, half hidden or nearly lost; one could say that this complex structure itself reflects the complex structure of Istrian history and culture.) But we may suddenly become aware that we are not looking at a landscape but at a flat picture, at layers of paint and pieces of cloth. Instead of the landscape itself we are admiring its illusion, a surrogate. And as we are standing here, in front of the canvas, instead of going out to see the real landscape, "real life," it seems that this surrogate not only replaces nature but indeed prevents us from experiencing it directly. But there is another aspect to these works: while looking at them, we recognize the beauty of this landscape, of its special character, of its complexity and deep-rooted, although rapidly disappearing traditions. We thus experience a kind of unity with the depicted world; this unity has been achieved through empathy, it is an illusion, but is nevertheless emotional and genuine. We may discover that our relationship to the landscape itself and to its representation in a painting becomes strangely perverted: while we somehow enter an empathic unity with the depicted landscape, we suddenly discover that we look at the actual landscape as if it were a picture, or a text. And if it is a home, it is an abandoned one.

We could say that the whole of Bernard's artistic activity points toward one basic aim: toward a spontaneous, immediate, therefore "primary" and "original" identity with the world and with life. This is perhaps the main suggestive source of his paintings and their openness for empathy. But, as we have tried to show, he is repeatedly forced to experience how artificial art is and how this artificiality prevents him from sinking into immediate existential continuity or totality. Nevertheless, Bernard cannot simply follow the avant-garde in describing this problem through the dualism of "institution art" and "life practice" and in the attempt to revoke the separate field of art and unite it with life. Bernard supposes that the loss of this "existential continuity" (what this continuity actually is we cannot say, we are only sensing it or feeling its absence) is rooted in the very first scratch on the cave's wall, the scratch which introduced difference, definitions and signifying relations, and is thus inscribed into the very base of civilization. Being thoroughly constituted through systems of signification which introduce presence only through an absence, we can only search for such a unity, and maybe replace it with a surrogate, a "made-up," artificial work of art. Art is therefore the very space where civilization succeeds to gain in itself a balance between open experience and the forms and models of civilization (i.e., signifying structures). Bernard therefore called paintings "beings of reconciliation"; and his landscapes could well be described with these very words.

Marjetica Potrč

From the very beginning, the question of space was eminently present in the work of Marjetica Potrč, one of the leading figures of Slovene contemporary art. In the mid-1980s, she produced a series of works (some of them based on different parts of the human body, like legs, belly or eyes) that used a strong theatrical effect to deconstruct the viewer's presupposed ideas of space and their own position in it. What the artist "attacked" was the idea of a homogeneous and synchronous (or, better, timeless) Euclidian space, which is at the subject's (i.e., viewer's) disposal. She organized her sculptures in such a way that the viewer dramatically experiences the difference between the front and the backside of the work. The viewer's expectations about the back, initially unseen side are based on the pre-given spatial concepts, but the fundamental difference between the two sides radically denies these expectations. Although the two sides necessarily belong together, they can never be seen and experienced at the same time. It is thus impossible to actually experience the sculpture as a timeless whole; in our experience it always remains un-whole and essentially temporal (since we experience it as a sequence of fragments).

Such an experience has at least two far-reaching consequences. First, we become aware that we cannot understand space as a homogeneous and synchronous (or timeless) unit anymore. Second, such a concept of space includes a silent (sometimes even unconscious) supposition that the viewer remains somehow outside this space and thus has a general and complete overview of it; these sculptures, however, force us to recognize that we are ourselves in the space, "on the stage," so to speak. Therefore, we do not only see but we can also be seen; and, what is even more traumatic for us, there are certain aspects of ourselves that only another person can see but remain invisible for us.

But does this mean that the concept of space as a whole has lost all relevance? I believe not; we are repeatedly forced to refer to it to be able to orient ourselves in space and to function in it. Only now this concept cannot be taken as something "real" but as an idea, an ideal concept or ideological image. To actually experience the "wholeness" and synchronicity of space, we would have to be God.

These works treated the questions of space and the viewer's position in it in an extremely direct and personal way (the viewer was forced to take part in a certain "drama," experiencing the failure of his or her spontaneous spatial concepts), but on the other hand, they were also rather general. They dealt with some fundamental concepts of the modern (i.e., post-medieval) time, such as subject, body, space, time, etc.. In several works, begun during her stay in the USA, however, Potrč started to speak about space in a different, more explicit and specific way. For example, she introduced images into her works. Usually, these are ideal images of closed, ordered places, often loaded with symbolic significance (like a view of Rome). Very often, these places are seen from above, which underlines their utopian character. The places (cities, parks, etc.) represent, so to speak, the concept of synchronous and homogeneous space, they are manifestations of ideal concepts to which we refer while moving and acting in space. But they represent something else as well: a distinct and organized place which we can recognize. At the same time, these images (and, consequently, these concepts) are utopian; i.e., they exist as pure idea(l)s while they do not actually exist at the "place" itself. I will try to explain this with an example. If we actually enter a place that was planned and built following the ideas of utopian synchronous and homogeneous space, such as a French-style garden or an "ideal" town (e.g., Palmanova), we have to admit that we do not really experience the ideal structure but only a series of fragmented and partial aspects. To gain a view of the whole, we have to look at a map or to see the place from a distance, usually from above (e.g., from an airplane). But a place is a place only if we can be present there. With distance, we are losing the very essence of place and we are operating with intelligible ideas. There is another aspect of utopia that should not be overlooked. It can be supposed that such utopian concepts actually work as ideological images, and this means that they have their function in the distribution of power. Space, whole or un-whole, is thus not neutral anymore, the distribution of power is essential for the way it is understood and perceived.

Some of the artist's recent works introduced another dimension. In these sculptures she uses recognizable skylines of certain cities, such as Prague. These sculptures explicitly function as stage-settings. Recognizable forms, which are supposed to form an inner structure and form of space, are reduced to a mere image, a backdrop. These works reflect the ongoing process of "displacement" in our space, a process we are experiencing daily. In her sculptures, and also in her texts, Potrč stresses how the progressive displacement or de-location inflicts the space, which is now not only fragmented, un-whole and temporal, but also formless, seemingly without any strict organization and structure or indeed identity, and, in a certain sense, entropic. It does not mean that traditional points of orientation and identification have lost their function or even disappeared. But they are subject to the process of displacement and replacement; they are, so to speak, returned to their original sites, but as something "typical" and "local," as "sights," losing thereby their organic identity with their place. They become a point in the network of images that is interwoven with the amorphous and anonymous "network" of space.

It seems to me that Potrč's most recent works (the *Territory* series) somehow complete a certain way of questioning and researching space. The walls she is building now still follow the basic motif of her work—two different sides—but now she is aiming at a defining of territory. A wall thus does not only fragment, but also defines and encloses space.

[1] Zoran Kržišnik, *Rihard Jakopič*, Državna založba Slovenije, Ljubljana, 1973.

[2] Martin Heidegger, "The origin of the work of art," *The art of art history: a critical anthology*, Donald Preziosi (ed.), Oxford University Press, New York, 1998, pp. 413–426.

[3] *East Coker*, T.S. Eliot, *Four Quartets*, Harcourt, Brace, New York NY, 1943, line 192.

Art, Power and the Public: Makrolab Model

First published in *M'ars*, vol. 9, no. 3–4, Moderna galerija, Ljubljana, 1997, pp. 1–8.
Translated from Slovenian by Olga Vuković.

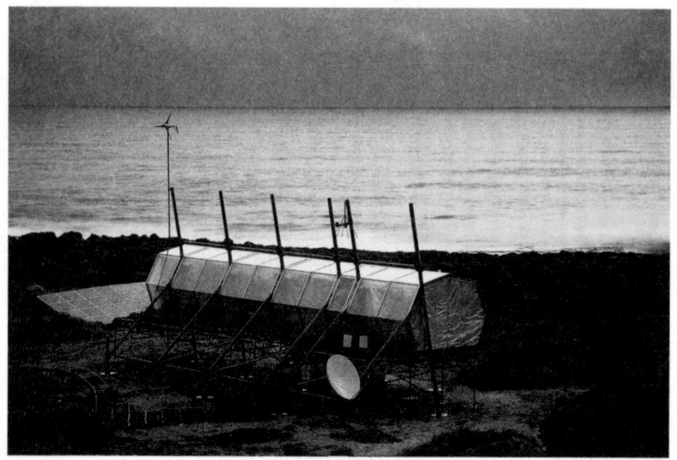

Marko Peljhan, *Makrolab mkII*, Rottnest Island, Western Australia, 2000

The work of Marko Peljhan, especially his project *Makrolab* (the project was first shown publicly at the last *Documenta* exhibition, but it is being developed further and will continue) can hardly be classified as "public art," i.e., as a work to be displayed publicly, at least not in the traditional sense of the word. Yet, a consideration of the public component of his work raises interesting and essential questions and dimensions.

What, indeed, is *Makrolab*? It is a dwelling and a working unit. In ideal circumstances, which, in fact, have not been established (yet), the Makrolab unit is completely self-sufficient. It generates electricity for its own use, and functions as a closed eco-system, which should enable its inhabitants to produce food and create an environment necessary for sustaining life. All of this should allow the crew of this station to live in complete isolation from their surroundings, to close themselves off within this separate,

self-regulated world and to function under these conditions.
Such isolation and self-sufficiency could not be realized
in Kassel, yet Makrolab was still not part of the exhibition
itself, but was located instead on a hill outside the town,
which few of the exhibition visitors (mainly those who were
familiar with the project) set out to see.

But where does the public dimension step in? Everything that has been described so far is exactly the opposite
of what we usually consider to be "public art": the project is
located external to the exhibition venue, it is not accessible
to the ordinary public, and its crew is shut away in a special
environment entirely separate from its surroundings. The
essential feature of the project, however, is that their retreat
into the isolated system does not mean the interruption of
all forms of communication. The closed *Makrolab* system
communicates with the outside world through interfaces,
or, in other words, through modern telecommunication
devices—phone, radio, TV, and, of course, the Internet.
A console placed in the *Documenta*-Halle offered information
about *Makrolab* and provided a means of communication.
Visitors could (or were supposed to be able to) keep up with
Makrolab events, get in touch with the crew over the phone,
obtain data about them on the Internet, follow their reports
and communicate with them through e-mail. The console,
therefore, was not a conventional exhibition item either, but
an information and communication point above all. Of
course, communication with *Makrolab* was not restricted to
the visitors of the *Documenta*-Halle. By isolating itself and
entering the telecommunications network at the same time,
Makrolab defined its own audience, or we could say, its own
public; and this public was not simply the artistic crowd who
came to *Documenta*. On the contrary, *Makrolab's* public is
inevitably global, because it is a public that consists of all
the people who are in a position to connect with *Makrolab*
through some global telecommunication or information
network.

Makrolab thus designates its audience and its public
as consisting of all of the users of global communication
networks, while the space inhabited by this public is the
space occupied by information and communication networks.

At this point I must make a short digression and
mention some potential doubts. The first question that

comes to mind is who, in fact, are those users that make up the global *Makrolab* public. New technologies, especially the Internet, are often described in an optimistic language, in which it is taken as self-evident that these technologies, on the one hand, provide new, global information coverage, and, on the other, create a space that allows for (inter)active participation, global connections and communication etc. We often hear that thanks to modern computer networks it does not matter whether one is sitting in New York, Kuala Lumpur or Kamnik, because one remains within the virtual world of network information in which there is no center or periphery. These assertions obscure a somewhat different reality.

1. A global "network" public can be only that public which possesses the technical means and knowledge needed to enter the global network.

2. The Croatian artist Mladen Stilinović declares: "The artist who cannot speak English is no artist." Well, the same could be applied to the users of global networks, who must speak English not only in the literal sense of the word (although this is also true) but in the metaphorical sense as well. In other words, they must accept certain conceptual and methodological premises these networks hinge on which are not necessarily as universal as it is often assumed.

3. Furthermore, it is not quite true that virtual networks have dispensed with the concept of the center and the periphery, or that actual geographical or cultural location does not play an essential role in an individual's inclusion into these networks. For example, Saskia Sassen has shown that virtual technologies do enable global production, yet this in turn leads to the centralization and concentration of control and management functions. These new key points are located geographically in developing global cities. They connect management centers (e.g. of corporations) with a developed infrastructure and other economic and cultural potentials that converge upon this framework. This means that new technologies do not eliminate but rather redefine the relationship between centers and peripheries.

4. The interrelation between an individual's entrance into the network and his/her geographical and cultural location is also crucial from another point of view. The

information that is accessible on the virtual network acquires its meaning and value in the local context, and it is this additional determination that actually defines it.

Peljhan is of course aware of this, but he is even more aware of something else: that political and economic powers continually enter the domain of the virtual networks and attempt to shape their territory and its structure in accordance with their own interests.

Despite these reservations, it is also true that the domain of the Internet and other global networks is not and cannot be completely controlled. Therefore, it provides numerous opportunities for those who are trying to problematize power systems or develop strategies of rebellion against them. Accordingly, anarchistic and critical interventions on the part of many artists cause disturbances to the system, which is, of course, also a system in which power is distributed and reproduced. They can also use these networks as platforms for the dissemination of information, communication, and strategic planning—in short, for the establishment of a critical public.

This is actually one of the essential purposes of *Makrolab*. Its crew does not isolate itself in order to run away, like some modern hermits, from the reality of the everyday world, but to create circumstances in which it will be possible to:
a) formulate certain essential problems of modern society from a distance; generate, within a closed system and in almost experimental lab conditions, discussion about these problems, and as a result
b) arrive at proposals and solutions that could be applied practically to the social context, or in other words, to develop strategic models and solutions that could be used in everyday life.

This could explain the crew's need for both isolation and a permanent connection to information networks. On the one hand, this connection allows for the input of a wide variety of information, while, on the other, it allows for the (controlled) inclusion of the global, critical public in the search for solutions, and keeps the public informed about the results achieved.

Let me recapitulate: despite all of the doubts concerning global networks, Peljhan sees opportunities in them to constitute a global, critical and active public. I could add as well that this type of public is not a self-evident premise, but actively created through projects like *Makrolab*.

Which *Makrolab* activity constitutes the actual basis for research, analyses and model development? What does the crew of this unit actually do? *Makrolab* is equipped with antennas and receivers that can catch various signals that flow, like invisible currents, above our heads. The whole project actually reveals a fascination with the fact that in addition to our material, visible territory, there exists an invisible, in one sense a non-material territory of information, messages, and communication; the latter stretches over, complements and intrudes into the material territory, yet it is a world that has its own special characteristics and laws.

I do not know what the exact line of Peljhan's reasoning was as he developed the *Makrolab* concept, but I can suppose that the project originated in a fascination with the invisible territory of signals that is created especially by invisible radio waves—this is the territory through which phone conversations, faxes, radio and TV programs, and reports transmitted over satellites and space probes flow. In short, this is a world in which ordinary phone conversations intermingle with strategic debates between corporations or military headquarters, and with atmospheric phenomena, meteorological shifts and paths of bird migrations. Peljhan was probably fascinated with the fact that it is possible, from a restricted physical location (which in his understanding remains fundamental and non-reductive), using hardware (transmitter-receiver) as an interface, to enter and connect with a remote and non-material world, and communicate with remote places, maybe even with spaceship crews. With the help of technology a person can become a researcher who travels across these territories of signals and attempts to, shall we say, make a map of them. Yet when Peljhan as a researcher actually ventured into this territory, he discovered that it was not neutral, but rather one through which power is realized.

This brings me back to the question of the public and the global relations between signals, power and the public. The territory of signals is the area in which decisions and strategies materialize that can have critical effects upon us.

In some cases, they can even decide between life and death (for example, *Makrolab* chanced upon an amazing exchange between the headquarters of large corporations that related to the fate of some African state; these corporations were literally discussing what to do with that state). In short, political and economic powers use the realm of signals for their own purposes, while, at the same time, exploiting the invisibility of these signals so that their activities can remain hidden from the eyes of the public.

There is another dimension here as well. In everyday life we do not think about what happens, for example, to our words spoken into the phone or transmitted by fax or e-mail when they enter the intermediary space between the transmitter and the receiver. We take for granted that this space is a protected private area. Usually we are not aware at all how open and accessible this area is. Thanks to modern technologies it is vulnerable to intrusions, eavesdropping, recording, interventions etc. All of this actually happens in reality at both the local and the global level.

Therefore, power plays a double game with the territory of signals: on the one hand it takes advantage of the non-public nature of this territory to establish its own communication and realize its strategic aims, while at the same time intruding into the non-public communication of others in this space, and using the data gathered to its own advantage.

Faced with the reality of this system, Peljhan realized that research and cartographic accomplishments within this space cannot remain neutral, that this space inevitably thrusts you into the game of power and forces you to begin behaving strategically. In short, as individuals and constituents of the public, we must understand our situation, define our aims within these circumstances, and try to develop strategic behavior and procedures. These are the precise aims that led to the *Makrolab* project. More specifically, the aims are:

a) to investigate the territory of signals and its relationship to power; i.e., ways in which power operates within this system;

b) based on these findings, to make an attempt to develop possible models of strategic behavior and transfer them to the public (in this sense the global public); one of the essential features of this effort is the search for concrete, practical applications and legal possibilities that enable the public to recognize the structure and content of the territory of signals.

Perhaps its is now clearer why *Makrolab* must function as an isolated and self-sufficient whole. It is not only in order to achieve conditions in which it will be possible to synthesize the data obtained and shape them into proposals, but also in order to ensure the independence and autonomy of functioning, and, in extreme circumstances, of survival.

Body Art in Slovene Art:
1960s to 1980s

First published in *Body and the East. From the 1960s to the Present*, Moderna galerija, Ljubljana, 1998, pp. 167–169. Translated from Slovenian by Igor Zabel.

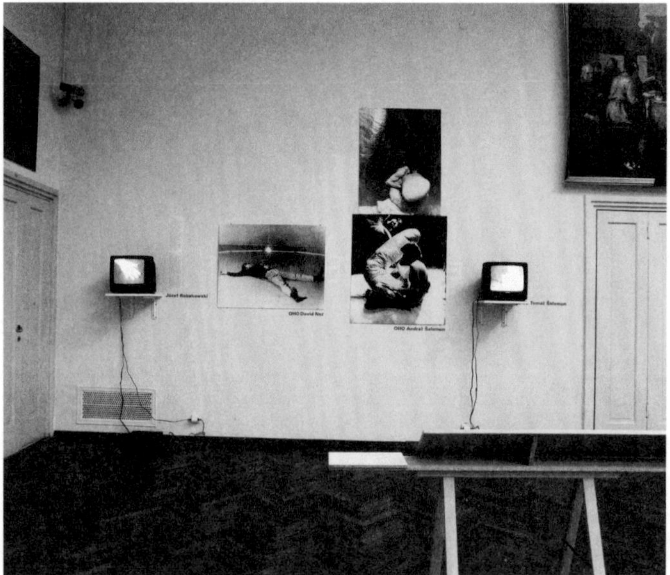

Installation view of the exhibiton *Body and the East*, Moderna galerija, Ljubljana, 1998

OHO: From the Liberated to the Cosmic Body

The beginnings of body art in Slovenia are connected with OHO, an avant-garde movement which, from the mid-1960s until it dissolved in 1971, developed an intense and varied artistic activity. Following the extension of the concept and scope of art on the one hand and tendencies to liberate the body from traditional conventions and limitations on the other, the activities of OHO in general included the body as an essential aspect. Not all the cases of the use of the body, however, could be described as body art in the narrower sense (i.e. as an artistic activity in which the artist makes use of his/her own body), there were also performances, happenings or intermediate actions (The idea of an "intermediate" position was characteristic of OHO work in general.)[1]

The problematics of OHO body art began with the action of one of the founding members, Marko Pogačnik, which occured at an exhibition of regional artists in Kranj in 1966. This was, in fact, a protest action; due to pressure from local politicians, Pogačnik's works were removed from the show. The artist therefore decided to exhibit himself, i.e., his own body. During the opening hours, he stood in the exhibition room, in the classical contraposto stance, with a board hanging from his neck on which he had written that he was exhibiting his own body since he was unable to exhibit his works.[2]

An important aspect here is that Pogačnik did not see this action merely as a protest, but explicitly also as the possibility of using his own body as a means of artistic expression.[3] And at least some of the visitors understood it in such a way.[4]

In spite of this early beginning of body art issues in the work of OHO, the following projects, which included a strong role of the body, could not be described as body art proper, but as happenings and performances (some writers[5] speak about "Fluxus actions").[6] The action by Andraž Šalamun in his environment, *Gozd* (The Wood), however, can be seen as body art. Šalamun used his environment made of soft forms filled with air as an erotic field for his body. The eroticized body was, even more emphatically, present in his *Kama Sutra* project, published as a photowork in 1970. Tomaž Šalamun's project *Sculpture 117° C*, too, is interesting in the context of body art. This work should be understood from the artist's basic idea of declaring the most diverse objects, situations and relations to be "sculptures," using photography as a means of registering and mediating these situations. The mentioned work, however, also includes a concrete physical experience of heath and coldness.[7]

In addition to this sculpture, Tomaž Šalamun involved his body in two related projects realized late in 1969 in Novi Sad and Belgrade. In the first case, he walked from the gallery in the city centre to the Petrovaradin Fortress, continuously drawing a line with chalk, and in the second case, he drew parallel lines on the floor of the gallery room. Both projects, of course, involve the idea of drawing a line, leaving a trace etc., which was strongly present in the art of the 1960s, but here, the line also has to be understood as the leftover trace of the involvement of the body.

The project that has often been often cited as the beginning of OHO body art is David Nez's *Cosmology* (1969). Originally, the work was not intended to be an environment for the artist's body, but since Nez decided to lie in it, put a stone on his stomach and breathe in a special way, he significantly supplemented his piece, and greatly expanded its connotations.[8] The posture of the recumbent body inside the circle, for example, is reminiscent of a well-known drawing by Leonardo; *Cosmology,* however, does not suggest the idea of an anthropocentric universe but rather an ecstatic experience of the body which can (through breathing and meditation) harmonize and unite with the cosmos. It should be mentioned here that Nez, in the last period of OHO and even after the group dissolved, was greatly interested in breathing and in the idea of the co-ordination of bodily processes.[9]

The 1980s: Representation, Reality and Body

The OHO project, thus, implies the idea of the liberation of the body and then (through a re-disciplinization of the body in meditation practices, rituals and esoteric "schooling") leads to its re-harmonization with the universe and eventual completion of itself in an attempt at a total community, in which art and life are not separated and which lives in harmony with itself, nature and the cosmic order. In the 1980s, however, the body was placed in a totally different context. The idea of the body as a direct, spontaneous "expression" was replaced by a division between identity and appearance, which was most obvious in the idea of the "image." So-called "hooligan" behaviour and dress in the 1960s implied the idea of expressing one's own self against the conformism of the developing consumer society; "image," on the other hand, is the deliberate acceptance of a role, i.e., a play, a (re)presentation. This shift reflects the abandonment of the utopian visions of the 1960s according to which one can get rid of social conventions and determinations and start to live an authentic, true and free life. The late 1970s and the 1980s, on the other hand, demonstrated that "authenticity" is only an illusion, or even an ideological notion; an individual cannot escape from being determined by social patterns and forms (which are, moreover, the forms through which power operates); it therefore seemed necessary to develop forms of behaviour and action which would take this insight into account. Some of Marko Kovačič's performances, e.g. *Casus Belli* (1983), demonstrated exactly how an individual and his/her body remains caught in pre-determined roles and positions; an attempt to break through this determination by accentuating the bodily experience seems an act of despair, and remains illusory.

The painter Jože Slak-Đoka has presented performances at the openings of his exhibitions since 1979. These actions were not only a parodic destruction of official opening ceremonies and a mockery of the cliches of the suffering (Slovene) artist painting "with blood from his own heart";[10] they were also a search for situations and experiences which would undermine the space of art as a space of cozy fiction: a viewer observing these actions is meant to have an unpleasant, uncanny feeling. At a group show, for example, Slak first painted graffiti on the gallery wall, and then nailed himself to the wall; he could not persuade his two collaborators to nail his other hand, too; instead, they vomited over the very formal black dress he was wearing for this occasion.

The idea of the "image" is, therefore, characteristic of an era that considered the idea of "authenticity" to be naive and which understood a deliberate game with appearances and patterns of behaviour as a way of survival, and even resistance. A subversive, revolutionary position was achieved (especially in the context of the so-called alternative culture in the 1980s) exactly through a play with the strategies of (re)presentation. These games are necessarily provocative and excessive, since they disclose the traumatic, (socially) repressed contents. This subversive presentation ranges from the disciplined body demonstrating its own submission to totalitarian patterns, to the "excessive" body that is basicaly sexualized: sado-masochistic, homoerotic, etc. The activity of Peter Mlakar can be mentioned here, who, as a philosopher (representative of the *Department of Pure and Applied Philosophy* at the artistic collective Neue Slovenische Kunst (NSK) developed the question of the body, especially in extreme situations of sexual enjoyment and suffering, as one of the centres of his thought: his speeches and lectures explaining his philosophy on different occasions (for example, at concerts of the Laibach group) often turn into performances with a strong role of the body. These oppositions were, within the alternative scene, best represented by two music groups which, as a matter of fact, both worked in the sense of a total work of art including, in addition to the music itself, also projections, performances etc. The body played an essential role for both groups. On the one hand there was Laibach, with its extreme discipline, its radical submission to the totalitarian patterns of collective behaviour, and its ceaseless persistence in a role which, maybe, isn't only a role.[11] Borghesia, on the other hand, created its rhetorics and aesthetics using imagery of the tabooed, prohibited, and repressed. In a certain sense, the strategy of Borghesia was comparable to that of Laibach: in its aim to come as close as possible to the line dividing appearance and reality, to break into reality and turn its presentational appearance into something real, changing, at the same time, reality itself into a distant image.

It is important that a presentation in which the body takes part is no arbitrary fiction, that the play stages reality, namely the traumatic, overlooked and repressed reality. So, in the 1980s, the body is caught in an endless game of distances and identifications, of realities and representations. The wish to approach border experiences here is also an attempt at disengaging oneself from the game of patterns and codes which determine every individual, making him/her "unreal," something different from him/herself. Paradoxically, this very experience can easily turn into an image or even an icon.[12]

[1] Lilijana Stepančič, in her essay "Body art in OHO" ("Body art and OHO"), published in *Konceptualna umetnost 60. in 70. let. This Art Is Recycled. (Conceptual Art of the 1960s and 1970s)*, Galerija Škuc, Ljubljana, 1997, pp. 27–31, understands the idea of body art in a broader sense; she deals with all examples of body activities in different projects, even those where the artist himself does not participate as a performer (for example, Tomaž Šalamun's project *The Sea*, 1969).

[2] Pogačnik's protest action was an exemplary act of resistance. Here, i do not think only about his use of references to the partisan struggle (he was wearing a military jacket which his father-in-law had worn as a partisan; the board hung from his neck was a reference to similar boards which hostages during the second World War had to wear before they were shot), but especially because of his precise use of legal possibilities; he did not, for example, bring his works into the exhibition room by force, but he used his right to remain in the gallery during the opening hours just as any other visitor. Unfortunately, the politicians at that time didn't behave legalistically, they began to threaten the staff of the gallery, and Pogačnik was forced to stop his action.

[3] Evidence of this is a letter by Pogačnik sent to Dr. Cene Avguštin, director of the museum, on 27 July 1966, explaining his planned action. Here, he wrote: "Second, I consider my body to be a visual means of expression. That is how I understand the depiction of the body in the Renaissance and Classical art, except that I use it for expression, and they were depicting it to express themselves." The letter is kept in the archives of the Gorenjski muzej in Kranj; I am thankful to Mr. Damir Globočnik, curator of the museum, for drawing my attention to this letter and providing me with a copy of it.

[4] *Cf.* Franci Zagoričnik, "Človek v galeriji" ("A Man in the Gallery"), in: *Glas* (Kranj), 30 July 1966. Zagoričnik described Pogačnik's action as a happening.

[5] Tomaž Brejc, *OHO 1966-1971*, Galerija Škuc, Ljubljana, 1978; Lilijana Stepančič, *op. cit.*

[6] Because of the role of physical effort, we could mention Milenko Matanović's project (from winter 1968-69); the artist walked a certain distance a thousand times, thus making a path. This work is strongly reminiscent of Richard Long's *A Line Made By Walking* (1967); the dimension added by Matanović, however, is the great effort of his own body.

[7] *Cf.* Miško Šuvaković: "Three Readings of Body Functions in Merleau-Ponty," *M'ars* (Ljubljana), no. 2, 1997.

[8] According to some witnesses (*cf.* Maja Breznik, "The Urban Theater (Happenings of the OHO Group 1966–1969)," *M'ars* (Ljubljana), no. 3–4, 1995), Nez accepted Samo Simčič's idea of including the body in the installation.

[9] *Cf.* his project *The Co-ordination of the Body Processes* (1970).

[10] In the performance *Mojo srčno kri škropite* (Sprinkle the blood of my hearth; the title is a well-known quotation from the Slovene poet Simon Gregorčič), Slak raised a sheet sprinkled with his blood out of a pile of earth.

[11] For the unclear and uncanny relationship between irony and identification in Laibach see Slavoj Žižek, "Why Are Laibach And NSK Not Fascists?," *M'ars* (Ljubljana), no. 3–4, 1993, pp. 3–4.

[12] An example of this is the photograph of the bleeding face of Tomaž Hostnik, singer of the Laibach group who was hit by a stone during a concert. Laibach and the whole NSK turned this event into a myth, and the picture (in which we can read not only a presentation of totalitarian codes, but also a personal commitment and fanaticism) into an icon.

The Field, the Map, and the Eye

Text for the exhibition *The Eye and its truth. Spectacle and Reality in Slovene Art 1984–2001*
(Moderna galerija, Ljubljana, 26. 4.–27. 5. 2001):
First published in *M'ars*, vol. 13, no. 3–4, Moderna galerija, Ljubljana, 2001, pp. 12–20.
Translated from Slovenian by Igor Zabel.

How to stage a historical show?

As I started to work on the exhibition, my intention was to provide an overview of the development in Slovene art from the mid-1980s till today. This was a time of deep change—political, social and economic, but also, perhaps no less important, in the understanding of the world and human identity within it. The two years which limit the period the exhibition is dealing with obviously refer to two works of fiction, Orwell's *1984* and Clark's *2001 Odyssey*. These two books are still essential for the self-understanding of contemporary society. Any reference to them alone turns our attention to the issues of technology, interaction with it, its social role, its functionality in the service of systems of power and control, to the transformation of human nature, etc. Tightly connected with these issues are the questions of the visual in the contemporary world. It is a time when we can speak about being overwhelmed with the visual, with a flood of images and simulacra, but also about endless struggles to achieve reality.

Soon it became clear to me that a historical presentation of the period in question should involve two essential aspects. First, it is necessary to identify the central problems, approaches, and tendencies, and secondly, it is necessary to determine a logical and connected line of historical development. Slowly I became aware that the exhibition could not be a historical presentation in a strict sense; instead, it became an attempt to draw a kind of personal map of Slovene art of the past one and a half decade.

This change was caused, I believe, by two main conditions: the essentially heterogeneous nature of the "period" and my internal observer's position.

However, if the show did not establish a clear historical picture of the period, its main issues and development, it certainly doesn't mean that such a historical approach should generally be replaced with a more personal, and therefore more arbitrary one. We could even say that the exhibition represented a "pre-historical" view of the past 16 or 17 years. It was one of the necessary steps towards a more synthetic, more complete and therefore more objective presentation of the development of art in the last quarter of the zoth century. In this sense, the exhibition was an attempt to structure the act of looking back, to identify some basic themes and issues, lines and connections, often through intuition and from an explicitly personal position. I would like to add, however, that it is exactly its pre-objective and pre-historical character, its transitional, hence more open and less strictly defined nature and the prevalence of the intuitive, metaphorical and sensual over the objective and rational that made the exhibition project especially interesting and valuable for me.

(Non)contemporaneousness

Literary history has introduced the term "non-contemporaneousness." The unusual aspect of this concept is that it derived from the realization that the creativity in any given period is never homogeneous; rather, it is a complex of different movements and approaches. In the same historical moment and space, works that one might connect with different historical periods are produced. The concept of the "non-contemporaneousness" therefore refers exactly to the contemporaneous existence of different movements. Such works are therefore "non-contemporaneous" regarding the ideal construction of historical tradition (i.e., a meaningful sequence of movements, styles, and periods, while they are contemporaneous regarding the actual time of their production. Historical studies used the concept as an attempt to harmonize the ideal image of historical development with the fact that a cross-cut through a given moment shows a heterogeneous image of different styles, approaches and directions.

Line of historical development

A historical view perhaps cannot avoid the necessity to harmonize both aspects. Regardless of the fact that we experience a given moment as a heterogeneous unity of diverse movements and approaches, we are forced to develop an ideal construction of the historical development and causal connections which is essentially linear (although this linear character can sometimes become extended and complex, as is the case, e.g., with Alfred J. Barr's famous chart of the development of modern art). Even though the museums of modern art abandon in turn the principle of a linear, historical order of their displays and arrange their collections according to other principles, the established linear scheme of development remains present, although hidden. I believe it does not make sense to denounce the idea of a historical line of development, although one should not forget that it is a construction.

The internal observer

Modern natural sciences have introduced the concept of the internal observer. The concept implies that an objective and distanced observation of a system is not possible. The observer is, with the very act of observing, within the system. Therefore, one's gaze is predetermined by one's own position within this system. Moreover, the observed object does not exist independently from the act of observing. It is affected by this act and literally created by it. My position regarding the past years of Slovene art is emphatically one of an internal observer. My gaze was formed by the developments that should now be its object. If the exhibition represents an attempt to develop a network of metaphors which should help us to identify and grasp some essential fields of interest from that time, and to place a number of works by Slovene artists into that network, then such a network is certainly constructed only through observation. In this sense, the general theme of the show, the relation between the eye and (its) truth is applicable not only to the works represented, but also the curatorial approach and the structure of the show itself.

Field

The period in question appeared as a unique (although not homogeneous) field open to every direction rather than a single movement with clear guiding lines. This field, how-ever, did not disclose itself to the eye completely and evenly; it ran back into the perspective of distance in time. The eye that tried to discern certain configurations in this field, to get an idea of its structure, was placed in one position, to one side of the field. From this point, certain things were closer and more clearly visible, others farther away and unclear, and some positively hidden. A change of the point of view would certainly change the configurations that appeared before the eye in the field. On the other hand, the point of view and the points that the eye used for orientation as it glided over the surface of the field were not accidental or neutral. They reflected the path traversed in the course of this period, meetings with artists, works, ideas and phenomena that formed the idea of the field.

The exhibition itself has also been structured as a field; not in a linear way, but multi-directionally. It was based on the possibility of bringing heterogeneous works together, to construct contrasts or an accordance of works that belong to different groups or directions. At the same time, it was intended to be a kind of map of the period in question, a topographical picture of issues and connections; it was built around certain themes that reflected certain fundamental issues and explorations of that time. It was a personal map, however; based on intuition and metaphors, on personal experiences, memories of artists and works that were orientation points for me when I was thinking of the past period. At the same time, it was strongly connected to the issues that later interested me. It was not intended to be a selection or "best of"; my view could also have traveled in a different direction, and the wish to construct a show that would be coherent in itself was no less a motivation of my work than the need to identify the crucial thematic issues of the past years. The older and the recent works appeared all on the same level, in contemporaneity, and did not speak as documents from an archive but as an immediate and living actuality.

The eye and the truth

The title of the show was taken from a 1985 print by Bojan Gorenec. My use of the title certainly extended its implications, although I believe that this is not in contradiction with its original intention. I believe that the concepts of visuality and of truth or the real have been essential not only for art in the last fifteen years and for the understanding of the social, everyday life, but also for the relationship between art and society (in the present time, art simply cannot escape dealing with this relationship). In this sense, the relationship of the visuality and reality represented the basis and the horizon for all the works in the show and their confrontations and connections.

If I now had to describe the basic questions that the show tried to address, I would mention the following ones:

Image, identity, body

The late 1970s and early 1980s brought a new concept with them: that of "image." If it was a moral imperative in the 1960s and early 1970s that one's appearance should express one's real essence as directly as possible, the idea of the "image" implies a difference, a gap between a person and his/her appearance. One can put on an image deliberately to make an intended impression, but also to reach, through irony, an outward identification with the desired role and thus a kind of fulfilment of one's desires. The voluntary subjection to an image, a role, should also be understood in relation to the systems of power that operate on different levels and force one into different roles. The image is an attempt to pervert and avoid this subordination to the social roles, or a deliberate, ironical and cool acceptance of them. Image is something that belongs essentially to the world of images—of exterior, distanced and manipulated images that overflow the everyday life, of fascinating (and therefore functional) images. Somewhere in the flickering world of images, their truth is dispersed—the power that produces, directs and uses them. This power is perhaps not based in only one center, heterogeneity and discontinuity may be characteristic of it, but it is nevertheless effective and methodical.

What could be a firm point in a world where everything seems to be changing into a spectacle of images that do not assure the reality anymore, although they claim to be reality itself? The obsessive recurrence to the body, its immediate experience, shows a wild wish to break through to the reality beyond the appearance, to the irreducible reality which discloses itself in the moments of enjoyment or pain, even of approaching the edge of death. Today, however, we do not own our bodies anymore, and not even our minds. Technologies, programming and managing procedures, power relations have penetrated us so deeply that even the Cartesian *cogito*, that pure and absolute certainty, becomes uncertain. The certainty offered by the body is elusive, it ceaselessly turns into spectacle, image. In the mid-1980s, there was much talk of the so-called "auto-poetics," i.e. about strong, individual positions that can, in a time when there is no single dominant artistic language anymore, establish their own creative systems and models. In the late 1980s and in the 1990s however, it seems that the self can only be established in the tense and dangerous play with the multiple systems that endanger and absorb it. The position of the self is a fragile one, permanently in danger, controversial, paradoxical, always forced to search for spaces in between or on the margin where it can still, ephemerally, exist.

The crisis of the visual

One of the essential suppositions of the show was that there is an essential parallelism between research of the visuality, the body and identity as it has developed within the tradition of abstract art, and the processes in the world outside art where we can also witness a hypertrophy of the visual and a strong crisis of the personal (or social) identities. The artists who deal with the issues based on the modernist abstract tradition (i.e., the "formal" relations within the pictorial field) speak about the "problematic" character of visuality and about being "overwhelmed" by it, as well as about the mechanisms of blinding and directing the gaze. They speak, in an "abstract" way, exactly about the experiences characteristic for the transformed every-day world. These artists, therefore, can be connected to those who, working in a very different way, using different conceptual starting points and formal language, touch upon similar experiences.

New concepts of space

Not only visual art but architecture and even urban planning today show a concept of space which differs essentialy from the traditional understanding of space as a neutral continuum in which we can place architectural forms and which could be functionally divided into areas connected with transport and communication networks. Space is perceived as an essentially flexible and interactive reality. It is not fixed and stable, but establishes itself as a changeable relationship of different functions, demands, directions, and traditions. It is interesting and important that, in the recent years, there has been a strong and active intermediate space between art and architecture. While artists tend to enter actual space with its formal, traditional, and social dimensions, architects often make use of art forms, such as installations and video works, to research space as an essentialy relational category and to establish models for understanding it and operating within it. It seems that, in today's architecture, we could hardly determine a strict dividing line between such "artistic" projects, utopian visions, and projects for actual buildings.

Cityscape

It seems as if the city has become the natural environment of today's experience. Nature, on the other hand, is perceived as distant or lost, but also as turned into spectacle or subject to contemporary technologies. The experience of the city, however, has also changed deeply in the past decades. The idea of a well-organised and designed organism, a closed area which, through its organisation and clear network of monuments, representative public spaces and other accents, represents a synthesis of a balanced social organisation, tradition and aesthetics, has given way to a different vision of the city. The historical city centers have lost their organic function, they are now "de-localized" into tourist sights, or, as Marjetica Potrč once put it, they function as "Disneyland." The contemporary city seems to be really living in marginal, disorganised, amorphous and seemingly impersonal areas, which slowly dissolve into suburbia.

Due to the amorphousness of these city areas, we are in fact only rarely aware of them. Contemporary art uses the possibilities offered by contemporary technology for the production of images to sharpen and concentrate our view. Industrial suburbs, residential areas, inter-spaces and voids, passers-by and marginal situations—it is through the image that these spaces, people and relations become visible and filled with meaning, albeit distant. The explosion of the visual is connected to the new technological means, which make possible the production of images, of spectacle. But they also enable us to see more sharply, more focused, and to notice and register the spaces and systems that lay in between and on the margin of the patterns of our established perception. An artist equipped with the technical means for the registration of images can become an explorer of the labyrinths of the everyday world in front of us. But the images are not necessarily merely a cold record of such a reality; nostalgia, memory, beauty, the glow of aura can suddenly re-appear in them. The world of images swings constantly between the loss of the aura and its re-appearance, between nostalgia and the banality of reality, between spectacle and truth. The truth is revealed in the spectacular nature of the images, and is again lost in it.

Perhaps we should go one step further: the contemporary city, and indeed the contemporary world as a whole, does not permit us to differentiate the reality from the image. The spectacle of the media images has penetrated reality and is now completely mixed with it. This synthesis is now the artist's immediate "natural" environment.

Systems, territories, nets

The development of technology and systems of management, production and distribution caused new models of understanding the world. The concepts of the system, territory and net became basic paradigms also in understanding art. A work is not necessarily an object anymore, it extends itself into dynamic relations, it is a territory or its map, it moves through the net, etc. These territories and nets, however, are not innocent; they are the systems through which power controls the world. The world of art, being itself part of societal relationships, is actually deeply involved with them. It cannot escape the consciousness that it is itself one of the systems through which power operates. Art is able to use its particular means, image, presentation, staging etc., to throw light on the functioning of these systems and its own role in them. However, the questions remain. Can art, in such a way, distance itself from being used by the systems of domination? Can it free itself from its functional role in the ideological, political and economical mechanisms and develop a utopian vision of spaces beyond that power, or even practically applicable models and methods of resistance?

The sub-cultural *Gesamtkunstwerk*

Art of the past century, or century and a half, has often made use of popular and sub-cultural forms. For today's art practice, too, the non-institutional and sub-cultural production is understood as a possible source for a new directness and sincerity, for a different, more engaging and interactive relationship with the audience, for formal innovation etc. Also, the non-institutional groups and organizations can be more open, more daring and experimental, which is essential for the whole field of art. In

Slovenia, the particular tension between "established" and "alternative" art proved to be particularly strong, and also productive, during the 1980s. It seems that this tension has indeed transformed the internal relations of contemporary art production. Today, it seems that a strict opposition between "established culture" and "subculture" is not so strong anymore. It does not mean, of course, that there is no difference between the national institutions and the groups of artists who, partly by necessity and partly by their own decision, work in the non-institutional or sometimes even marginal areas. The fact is, however, that contemporary art practice now functions as a connected field, with constant exchange between its different areas.

Icons by Irwin

First published in *IRWIN. Retroprincip 1983–2003*, Künstlerhaus Bethanien, Berlin; Karl Ernst Osthaus-Museum, Hagen; Museum of Contemporary Art, Belgrade; Revolver–Archiv für Aktuelle Kunst, Frankfurt am Main, 2003, pp. 77–83. Translated from Slovenian by Rawley Grau.

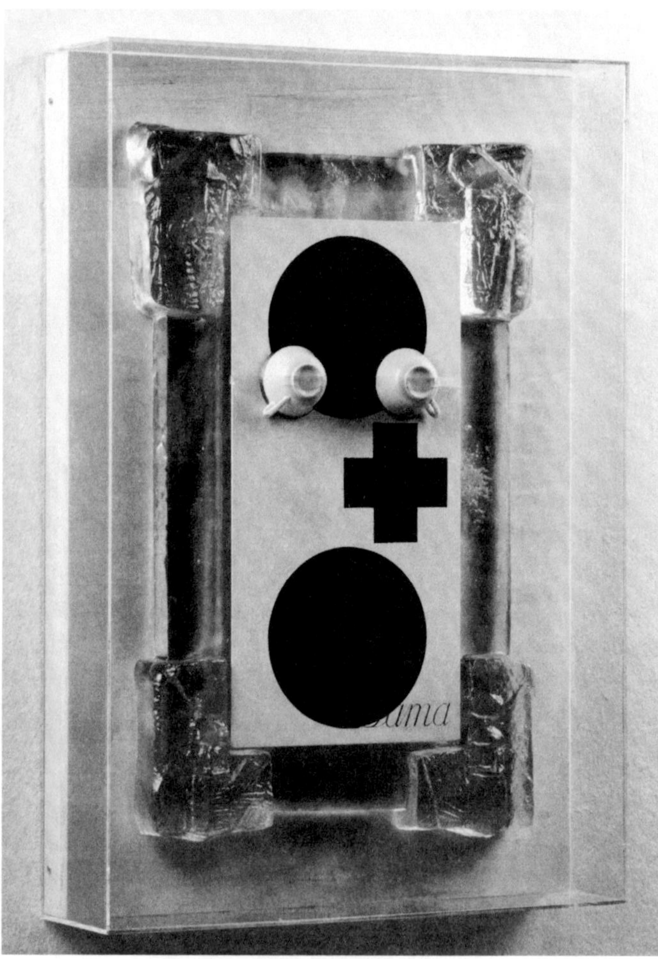

Irwin (Dušan Mandič), *Malevich Between Two Wars*, 1984

Right from the start, Irwin established three main criteria for its work (especially in the series *Was ist Kunst* [What is art]): programmatic eclecticism, the primacy of the group identity over personal identity, and affirmation of the local and the national. These criteria may be understood as strategic measures that enabled Irwin to create a frame for its work and, in so doing, to clear a space for creativity. What may at first seem to be the renunciation of originality and personality is, in fact, liberation from the pressure that requires the artist to be always producing original, innovative, and profound statements and formal solutions. Paradoxically, as soon as the artists freed themselves from such pressure, a space opened up for unfettered creativity. This creativity now found expression in the free use of motifs, techniques, and styles (rather than in the effort it took to think these things up) and in the interaction of the group (which compensated for the menacing weight of personal decisions). This does not mean that the Irwin group considers this fundamental eclecticism to be entirely without obligation, an irresponsible game, so to speak; indeed, the artists like to stress the extreme responsibility of their eclecticism. It is regulated by what they call the "retroprincip" [the "retroprinciple"], which is the basic principle of their work or, as they termed it in *The Program of the Irwin Group* (1984), the "regulatory matrix" of their working process. If we were to define the retroprinciple in a nutshell, we might say it refers to eclecticism and a utilization of works by other artists as a way of reinterpreting and, at the same time, reactualizing them. Each time, however, the process reestablishes itself on the basis of a concrete task and new reflection. The retroprinciple is, then, the endless process of reestablishing one's own position by reinterpreting, rejuvenating, and transforming both the tradition and one's own work.

Malevich Between Two Wars, one of Irwin's key paintings, presents a direct analysis of Malevich's suprematism and is a typical example of Irwin's retroprinciple. The picture brings together traditional academic portraiture, a Malevich suprematist painting (one of the variations on the cross motif), and Nazi sculpture. The suprematist painting, as "pure abstraction," is placed in a context that compels us to read it in an entirely new way. This placement is not as arbitrary or forced as it might seem at first glance.

Malevich's paintings are all painted on a white background, from which first a black square emerges, which then splits into other shapes (and colors) and their various combinations, until the whole process eventually returns, in a white suprematism (white images on a white background), to the whiteness from which it came. But somewhere the Irwins say, conversely, "There exists a foundation on which concepts and objects are constituted; there is no empty square." But this also means that Malevich's painting, its white background included, is itself constituted against a certain background. Irwin's painting demonstrates this by means of the tension between traditional bourgeois painting, modernism, and totalitarian art. In the series *Was ist Kunst*, one can, from the very beginning, find a number of references that link the series to the concept of the icon.

Thus, the manner of hanging these pictures (which, to be sure, alludes also to the traditional way of hanging pictures in private, as well as semiprivate and public rooms) is a direct allusion to the way suprematist paintings were presented at *The Last Futurist Exhibition 0.10* in 1915. There, the placement of the suprematist paintings suggested the way icons were hung; this was especially true for Malevich's *Black Square*, which was, with total explicitness, presented as an icon, or rather, in the position of an icon. Various explanations have been offered for why Malevich did this, and perhaps it was, in truth, an act of ambivalence. One possible explanation is that the artist intended for *Black Square* to take the place of the icon and thus use suprematist radicalism to demolish the authority of religion. Another view, however, points to the possibility of an actual parallelism between icon painting and Malevich's suprematism, arguing that *Black Square* did not supplant the icon but is itself, in essence, a modern icon. An important aspect of such parallelism between Malevich's painting and the traditional icon is that *Black Square* signifies a rejection of the post-medieval principle of the picture as a gaze onto an apparent reality; instead, Malevich's work returns truth to the picture itself (as Malevich explicitly stressed). In *Black Square*, this is achieved by the total reduction of the painting to its fundamental stipulations, to that which is actually given in the picture and therefore is true. Precisely because the black square in the picture is only that, and not a representation, symbol, or anything else, with this painting Malevich has achieved, as he said, "zero image." But this zero is, at the same time, the unmediated givenness of truth. In this, the parallelism between *Black Square* and the icon is clear. Just like icon painting, suprematism, too, constitutes itself as an unbroken line that runs from *Black Square* to other basic shapes (the circle, the cross) and then to more complex suprematist structures.

Of course, there are also interpretations that link Malevich with the tradition of Russian mysticism (which, perhaps, is not altogether unfounded) and ascribe a religious, or at least a spiritual, content to *Black Square*. Such interpretations are only a step away from the notion of icon painting as a typical expression of the Russian (or Eastern European) artistic, spiritual, and cultural traditions and of Malevich as a representative of such traditions. Such notions, for example, surrounded the fashionable interest in Eastern European—and especially Russian—art in the 1980s, an interest that, in particular, looked for such exotic aspects of this art and culture as those represented by the mixing of socialist-realist iconography (an expression of the exotic world on the other side of the Berlin Wall) and references to icon painting (the most characteristic expression of the specific tradition of the East—its archaism, wisdom, and metaphysical spirituality). One could, in fact, demonstrate that a number of artists tried to take advantage of this curiosity and adapt themselves to it by starting to produce just the sort of mish-mash the western market expected of them. I think there is something of this, too, covertly present in Irwin's work, namely, as an ironic response to the expectations of the western public. It is as though the series *Was ist Kunst* is saying, among other things, something like: "You expect, and require, us Eastern European artists to give you Eastern European motifs and forms; so here you have them." But what is much more important, perhaps, is for us to link the process by which the *Was ist Kunst* series transforms into the idea of the icon with Irwin's strategic procedures—and particularly, the retroprinciple—and to understand this as a new level of "framing." But this is something that takes shape only retroactively, over the many years of the entire production of *Was ist Kunst* (and thus, to be sure, defines a new point of departure for Irwin's painting practice). The reconstitution of the notion of the icon represents, then, a reflection of the group's own practice and development as painters, a redefinition of the icon, and the establishment of a frame that delineates in a new way the territory of the icon.

The essential question, of course, is, how do we understand the notion of the icon? Analyses of icon painting have revealed a very specific semantic structure, which is in essential ways very different from the post-medieval concept of a painting as a gaze onto a particular scene. In post-medieval painting, this gaze is defined by the spectator's point of view, while the painting itself is understood (often literally) as a kind of window through which the spectator views a person or event. The icon, on the other hand, is not the construction of an appearance of reality for the sake of the spectator's gaze, but rather a semantic whole constructed according to strict precepts. Compliance with these rules ensures the actual presence of something holy in the icon. That is to say, these rules guarantee an unbroken linkage between the icon as figural image and the original, since they repeat the structure of the first icon, which is itself the transferal of the original (the saint) into the image. Of course, transformations and alterations do occur, just as an original text (the text of the holy presence) might, in its essence, be preserved unchanged through a succession of translations and slightly varying repetitions. Indeed, the fact that the original text remains essentially intact is ensured precisely because of this unbroken chain of copying and recopying.

Analyses have also shown that certain typical features of icon painting, such as, in particular, reverse perspective, do not indicate any sort of incompetence on the part of the painters—as if they "did not know how" to paint perspectivally correct pictures—but rather are based on a special understanding of the relations between the image, that which is represented, and the viewer. To look at an icon does not, then, mean to look through a "window" at an apparent reality, but rather to look at a holy presence as such. Representational systems are thus adapted to this presence; reverse perspective shows that the picture is structured not from the viewer toward the scene, but from the picture outward.

The *Was ist Kunst* pictures always dealt with questions of the image as a semantic structure. In its use of images from various levels of the cultural and artistic tradition, Irwin's programmatic eclecticism is inherently linked to semantic transformations brought about by the displacement of the image, symbol, or fragment from one context to another and their combination with other similarly displaced images or signs. Irwin continually operates on the basis that no figure, image, or sign conveys meaning in and of itself; rather, its meaning can be determined only when there is a context in which it is placed and in which we view it. For Irwin's work it is, after all, essential that semantic questions be presented as questions about power and strategies of power. In saying this, we should note that, for Irwin, the discussion of the relationship between (political, economic, military, ideological) authority and image systems has never been merely academic but, rather, has affected their own position, among other things. Just as with icons, the *Was ist Kunst* pictures are in no way merely a representation of the subjective gaze or an illusion of appearance; instead, the objects that appear in the pictures are always able to acquire their own autonomous power as well. But this power is no longer linked to the presence of something holy but rather to systems of social power, which themselves take on certain attributes of the sacred. The reverse perspective of icons well suits the power of these images, which can have a strong impact on the viewer, inviting, provoking, threatening, and, as Althusser says, "interpellating" him "into the subject."[1] The *Was ist Kunst* series may also, in this way, be considered an ongoing experimental analysis of the migration of signs and symbols as they move from one system to another and, in doing so, change their meaning and function, even while retaining their original referential context (sometimes covertly, sometimes overtly). Pure forms can, if they are politically instrumentalized, acquire not only a direct political function; they can also receive a new semantic structure (for example, an abstract form can suddenly be read as a symbol or metaphor for such ideological values as freedom, zeal, power, etc.). Ideological works, conversely, when "purified" of their original context, are transformed into purely aesthetic phenomena, or even into pure form. *Was ist Kunst*, then, demonstrates the endless oscillation of various forms and discourses, back and forth, between an ideological semantic content and an entirely formal, "emptied" manifestation. At the same time, the elements from these various systems and discourses are interwoven, fragmented, redirected, and so on. This dialectic between meaning and form, functionality and emptiness, remains in ceaseless motion, even in a single work. This can be considered one of the fundamental characteristics of the *Was ist Kunst* series. This ceaseless motion is, of course, inherently connected with the process of circulating individual elements among a group, as group members appropriate elements from their colleagues, transform them, give them an additional semantic charge, and return them to the circulation process. It is this same process that also forms a foundation for introducing the notion of the icon. Irwin understands the circulation and reinterpretation of individual motifs as equivalent to the chain of copying and recopying that imbues the icon with the immediate presence of the original.

The way in which Irwin's pictures developed into icons is, however—at least in one perspective—essentially different from the traditional concept based on the notion of an uninterrupted chain stretching all the way back to an original source. With Irwin's icons, the initial original source simply does not exist. The series of images does, of course, have a beginning, but this is, in itself, of no real importance and is often merely incidental. For a motif, to be sure, obtains meaning not from its linkage to that beginning but rather from the long process of group work, in which the starting impulse has affirmed its vitality only insofar as it began to circulate among the members of the group, who took it up, modified it, added to it, and returned it to the circular flow. In this way, the motif develops an ever more complex meaning and function within the entire group process. What is more, as a certain motif gains an ever-greater conceptual and semantic charge, this exerts an influence on older works, which then, retrospectively, acquire additional semantic layers and connections. Developed in such a way, the motif's meaning is, therefore, the result of a certain process or work that could be described in psychoanalytic terms as the work of condensation, transference, and symbolization.

This does not mean, however, that Irwin's icons are devoid of the kind of original, ideal presence that inhabits the traditional icon as the result of an uninterrupted sequence of copies. Each one of Irwin's icons is, in fact, the manifestation of a general or even ideal motif that exceeds the individual realization and is itself an entity of a higher degree. (Here we might point out a direct parallelism with the relationship between the identity of the individual artist—the group member—and the identity of the group.

The group identity is something more than the sum or average of the individual identities and energies; it originates in their interactions as a new being of a different order. This is not merely one of the fundamental principles behind the functioning of the Irwin group and the NSK movement; it is also, at the same time, a primary principle of their political theory, which we could, of course, link to the role of the notion of the state in Irwin's work and in the activities of the NSK as a whole.) There does exist, then, an "original" for Irwin's icons or, better yet, their ideal archetypal image, which is present in individual realizations. This archetypal image, however, does not stand at the beginning of the line, but rather at its end, as an ideal form that derives from all of the given realizations and variations.

Each new realization, of course, must now necessarily reference the archetypal image and, at the same time, change and establish it anew. As an interesting analogy to this process, we might mention a certain musical work based on the form of the variation, namely, Gian Francesco Malipiero's *Variations Without a Theme*, composed in 1924. As the title states, no theme can be heard in this work; one can only assess the variations in terms of other variations, and only then can one imagine (but only imagine) the theme, as well. For here the theme does not exist as a relatively simple basic motif that is then developed in a series of variations exploiting its musical and emotional potential; instead, it exists as a form of a higher degree, as an idea that is constituted only in the mutual referentiality of all the individual variations in the series.

In Irwin's project, his two-directional process of developing a motif and, conversely, (re)interpreting it generated the visible image of a classification grid in which works from the *Was ist Kunst* series were placed and, through such emplacement, gained the status of icons. This grid exhibits six basic motifs, that is, six primary iconic lines. We can understand the grid as a direct reference to structuralism; thus, we can read it as the establishment of a system of differences, which are arranged in such a way that they themselves constitute a common, generic concept—which is, in fact, the ideal archetypal image. In such a scheme, there are two simultaneous lines of difference. The variations along the vertical axis are differences within the common generic concept; in other words, in their mutual relationships and differences, they constitute an ideal fundamental pattern, while the variations along the horizontal axis are differences among the generic concepts.

[1]   Louis Althusser, *On Ideology*, Verso, London and New York, 2008.

The Case

First published in *Alenka Pirman—Biserka Debeljak. The Case. Art and Crime: A Methodological Exhibition*, Moderna galerija, Ljubljana, 2005, *s. p.* Translated from Slovenian by Tamara Soban.

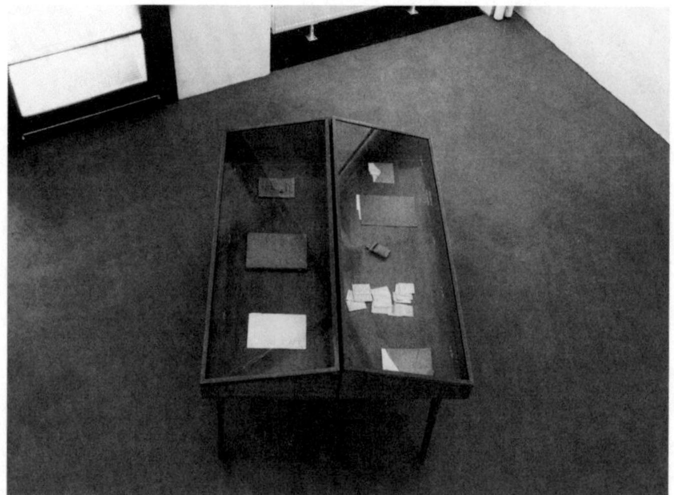

Alenka Pirman & Biserka Debeljak, *The Case*, installation view,
Mala galerija, Ljubljana, 2005

Objects

What happens to objects from different social and historical contexts once they are isolated from their original surroundings and placed in a gallery space? They are inevitably understood within the range of art conventions and systems that have developed in the last century. These conventions, however, are not completely homogeneous or in harmony with one another, so the perception of objects is also riddled with ambiguities. They can be understood as ready-mades, as importations of concrete objects into the world of representation. Or one can focus one's attention on their physical appearance, or try to guess what past stories and events they embody or indicate. By the same token, exhibited objects cannot escape becoming immediately involved in the relations between representation and the represented, between fiction and reality, between physical presence and meaning, etc. If, however, we know that the exhibited objects are documents and pieces of evidence from a trial, exhibited unchanged, just as they were, our understanding necessarily changes. If we take them for ready-mades we are aware of their concreteness. But if we are told that they are actual materials that have been used and produced in a trial, we suddenly see them as originals.

This, however, also brings a sense of frustration. The outer, physical appearance of such documents is suddenly no longer sufficient, and their ready-made nature hides more than it discloses. To get at their real meaning we need to connect them to the narrative about the trial, which is, in fact, a story about the detection, investigation and prosecution of a case and thus a story about searching for and finding the truth. Only in the context of this narrative do the documents have a role and meaning; only in this context do they become truly concrete and original.

The Back

All the exhibited materials are illegible and indeterminable, because we only see the backside of them. The thought that these are original documents and pieces of evidence can certainly be fascinating, the observer feels frustrated nevertheless because he or she is denied access to their most essential aspect, to what they tell.

But if by turning the documents around and showing merely their blank backs their real contents is hidden, what does displaying them show at all? We could say that it makes very obvious the specific form of arranging and categorizing them. Once the contents have been erased or repressed, what remains are the general categories that structure the materials: court records, pieces of evidence, photographs of the crime scene. It is essential for the various objects and documents to be categorized and arranged in this particular way, because only thus categorized could they become the foundation for a trial and the basis for an evidencing discourse about truth.

The Criteria of Truth

A closer inspection of the records, documents and other materials related to a given criminal case, and of the circumstances of the crime and the trial would reveal that every case is entangled in a complicated and virtually endless web of issues, questions, and dilemmas. Even for someone not directly involved in a case, the scrutiny of records and other documents can be a rather traumatic experience. On the other hand, every trial, and especially a major one, becomes a kind of juncture of very diverse questions and problems, ranging from legal and social issues to the way in which the information systems, and especially the mass media, function, or to the reactions of popular culture (e.g. the cases of vulgar—from the Latin word "vulgus," people— black humor). All these aspects are connected, in one way or another, to the question of truth. But because of the complexity, plurality and incompleteness of the truth it is socially mandatory to use clear and precise criteria by which to establish the truth. The concept of truth, being the basis of a court trial and thus one of the most essential aspects of the social order, demands a precise definition, a system that clearly determines the criteria for establishing it. And if the exhibited materials, which are displayed face down, only expose the general categories they belong to, then they exhibit exactly this system of defining the truth.

The Front

It is not unimportant that the exhibited materials belong to the collections of the Police Museum. The task of this museum is, so to speak, to show their front side, to present the actual story of the case, the truth about it as has been established through the principles and methods of the criminal procedure. It is, of course, possible to arrange and present such materials in a museum in different ways; an installation, for example, could emphasize the spectacular, emotional or ideological effects. But one might say say that in order to better understand the mutual relationship of criminal and social repression, and to grasp the criteria of truth that play such an important role in this relation, it is much more important to clearly expose these criteria and procedures than to arrange and install the materials in a spectacular (or, to use a current catchword, "visitor-friendly") way. This is possible if the materials are arranged strictly in accordance with the so-called seven basic questions.

The Trauma and the System

Once again, what does it mean to show the flip side of materials from a trial? I imagine that by rendering them unreadable, by confronting their silent material nature with their most general framework of categories, art has the power to re-introduce in a strange way all that it had previously excluded. Is the blank reverse side not a screen onto which our fantasies and fears are projected? Doesn't the monumentalized but dead presence of objects in the gallery space open gaps in the system of the social construction of truth, gaps through which the hidden, the repressed and the excluded escape? Is it not the short glimpse of the unbearable trauma of the real that forms the real reverse side of these documents?

Dabernig's Buildings

First published in *Dabernig, Josef. Film, Foto, Text, Objekt, Bau*, Stiftung Galerie für Zeitgenössische Kunst Leipzig für Experimentale e. V., Leipzig; Verlag der Buchhandlung Walther König, Köln, 2005, pp. 205–211.

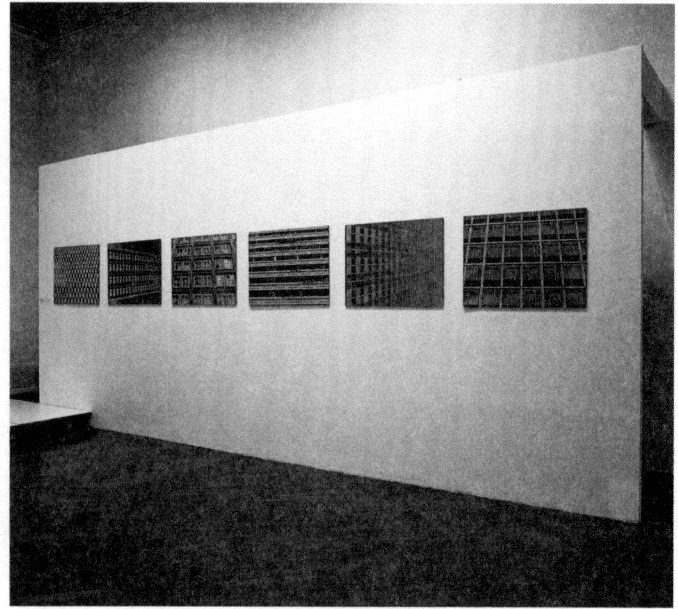

Josef Dabernig, *Untitled (*from the project *Berlinführer)*, 1996
Arteast 2000+23, Moderna galerija, Ljubljana, 2006

Architecture is certainly one of the most essential aspects of Dabernig's work. To understand the role it plays in his art we should be aware that we cannot consider it an isolated and closed field. The issue of architecture (and urban planning) transverses most, if not all the different fields he is interested in, from objects and drawings to photography, film and the books he copied. Therefore, if we speak about his actual architectural projects, we have to take into account other fields of his art, too. I believe that we cannot properly understand his architectural projects if we don't realize that his proposals and solutions are based on his multi-directional reflections about form and space and their functions.

One thing we can notice immediately is that Dabernig is not interested in architecture in general. His works indicate a taste for rational, formally minimal, and precisely ordered structures.

In general one could say that modern architecture represents the center of his interest. He doesn't seem to be interested in learning from Las Vegas. Nevertheless, it might seem a paradox that the issues of complexity and contradictions in architecture remain central for his dealing with it. He is somehow able to discover them even in the most strict and rational architectural concepts and forms, such as the modernist grid-like facades. These complexities and contradictions are not merely formal (although they are often formal as well); in fact, he has never been interested in buildings and other spatial structures only from the formal point of view. In his works, architecture indicates social and political history, different ideas and ideals of social order, different ways of understanding and interpretation, diverse understandings and reactions, and this network of meanings and interpretations creates the complexity.

Let us take his work *Berlinführer* (1996) as an example. It consists of a series of strictly frontal photographs of modernist facades in Berlin, and of several manuscript pages copied from Berlin architectural guidebooks. The work very clearly displays his interest in modernist architecture and its most fundamental forms, such as the grid. The grid-like facades evoke particular associations; as we see them, we can think of offices, social housing, corporate buildings, perhaps industry. Thus, they are not mere forms, but rather visual equivalents to social forms and orders. In a sense it seems that the work refers to the very spirit of modernity that makes itself visible with the facade grids. And yet, what he also displays is the actual diversity of this fundamental form. There is another important aspect: the photographs present architecture from both East and West Berlin, and if one doesn't actually know the buildings it is hard to say which are from the West and which from the East. The photographs are mirrored in the different descriptions copied from the guidebooks, in the diversity of understanding and appreciating, even of seeing, the same buildings. The form of the grid seems to be repetitive and unchangeable; and yet different grids have different meanings and values in these descriptions—depending on the writer's point of view and his/her aesthetical and ideological preferences. Rosalind Krauss in her well-known essay on *Grids* pointed at the internal contradictions of the grid as a basic form of modernity:

"Therefore, although the grid is certainly not a story, it is a structure, and one, moreover, that allows the contradiction between the values of science and those of spiritualism to maintain themselves within the consciousness of modernism, or rather its unconscious, as something repressed."[1] It is these repressed contradictions (not only contradictions of science and spiritualism, but also other inherent contradictions of modernity) that *Berlinführer* and other of Dabernig's works disclose with the seemingly distanced and impersonal practices of copying and photographing. One strategy that Dabernig uses (besides pointing at discrepancies in different objectively, scientifically written architectural guides and at the tension between such descriptions and the actual appearance of the buildings) is the introduction of small irregularities, sometimes almost invisible at first glance. For example, the two vertical facades in the *Berlin* series are presented horizontally. At first, one hardly notices this, as all other images are horizontal. This little joke can be understood as an ironic play not only with the seriousness and systematic nature of the artist's approach, but also with the weight of the modernist discourse. Presenting vertical buildings horizontally might be understood as a playful formulation of the post-modernist criticism that modernist architecture, especially with its use of the grid, lacks traditional divisions and doesn't care about fundamental spatial relations and hierarchies, such as bottom-top, left side-right side etc.

We could perhaps understand such small irregularities in a double way, as a hint both at the artist's personal involvement and at a certain ironic distance in his approach, e.g. in his dealing with grand narratives and their seriousness. Dabernig most often works with non-spectacular, even anonymous or impersonal architecture or interior design: office buildings, apartment blocks, highways. In many cases he show suburbs, peripheries or marginalized areas (such as Eastern Europe or South Italy), where modernist architecture seems to have never been fully developed and completely finished or has already failed and is now slowly decaying. Even when he presents city centers and important architecture (some of the buildings presented in the *Berlin* series are actually quite well-known), he does it in such a way that it is not essentially different from anonymous buildings. (On the

other hand, his works have exactly the contrary effect;
they are able to expose conceptual and formal strengths of
overlooked buildings and interiors. Let us just think of the
way Dabernig, in his film *WARS,* turns our attention to the
elegant modernist interior design of the restaurant car in
the train.) His use of camera in such works corresponds with
his interest in the non-spectacular, static, and formally
minimal. His images, too, are static, distanced, clearly
composed, and they clearly disclose a systematic approach.
And yet these non-spectacular, even impersonal buildings
attain a strange attractiveness in Dabernig's works. In spite
of its distant, objective and systematic nature, his approach
is not one of an impassive professional interested merely in
collecting and arranging data. Rather, it indicates a certain
personal relation. He seems to be strangely attracted to
these structures, and his works somehow have the power to
get the beholder to share this relation with the artist.

When Dabernig exhibited his films in Vilnius, an art
critic described them as boring.[2] And yet a highly interesting subsequent Internet discussion proved that several
visitors actually liked the films and found them attractive.
I believe this double relation corresponds to the double
nature of his work—the static, unspectacular nature of
his subjects and approach might give the impression that
his works are programmatically "boring"; yet the particular
intensity, the aura of strange attraction that Dabernig's
works bestow upon their subjects explains the interest
of the audience.

And yet we should not mistake this attraction for any
romantic esthetization. Recently, it has often been the case
that, for example, the post-socialist, post-industrialized
landscape[3] of Eastern Europe (but also such phenomena as
suburban areas of social housing blocks in Western capitals)
has been treated with a certain enthusiasm for its exotic
appearance and even a kind of aesthetic idealization. Even
artists from Eastern Europe are so far removed from the
experiences of the socialist societies already that they return
to their remains with a mixture of nostalgia, interest in the
exotic and a sort of ironic defiance. It has been (and not
without reason) objected to such idealizations that they are,
in fact, perverse, as they transform into purely aesthetic
experience what used to be dehumanized, depressive,

sometimes actually unbearable living circumstances for millions of people.[4] Dabernig never hides this darker side of the worn-out, non-renovated and unfashionable modernist spaces and anonymous buildings he presents. If there is a strong, almost obsessive attraction in them, it is an ambiguous one, and the artist never tries to hide this ambiguity. It is, perhaps, enough to mention his *Envisioning Bucharest*, a utopian proposal for urban development of the Rumanian capital. The whole work is based on Ceausescu's palace, which physically destroyed a large area of the city and badly damaged its balance. With his proposal Dabernig tried neither to conceal the physical (and ideological) brutality of the palace (that has sometimes been seen as a spectacular tourist attraction) nor to repress the trauma that it caused. Rather, he proposed a way of resolving the trauma by taking it as a starting point for reshaping of the urban structure.

Dabernig's interest in such spaces and structures is, of course, connected to his own work and its minimal, systematic, unspectacular nature. Sometimes it seems that he proposes such unspectacular (or, indeed, anti-spectacular) views as a sort of antidote against the processes of spectacularization of the world. His *Proposal for a New Kunsthaus*, not further developed, for example, seems to be an ironic comment directed towards the obsession with spectacular museum architectures that we have been witnessing in recent time (he replaces such museum architecture with anonymous "non-places" that nevertheless hide complex references to the history of modern architecture) as well as of the ability of architecture and art to appropriate any aspect of existing reality and incorporate it in their own structures.

Furthermore, this ambiguous attraction of (often peripheral and disused) modernist structures is certainly not only personal. Rather, it enables the artist and the viewers to reflect upon the nature of modernity, as if these structures were symptoms pointing at the intrinsic contradictions of modernity and its concepts. I once tried to describe Dabernig's work as a sort of personal archaeology of modernity, displaying an admiration for the utopian and rational, but also a certain pleasure at gaps, mismatches and failures in such ideally conceived structures. Dabernig always sees modernity as marked by contradictions and as heterogeneous

in spite of its claims for universality. Nevertheless, this
does not mean that he develops general overviews and
statements about modernism and modernity. He is interested in particularities, in actual sites (and non-sites), in
individual symptoms. Yet, through the complexity and
contradictions he invests his work with, he indicates the
epoch-making patterns and struggles that lie behind them
and make themselves manifest in a neglected apartment
block, a shabby bar from the 1970s or a football stadium.

All this should be taken into account when we speak
about Dabernig's own building projects and interior designs,
since they are not only based on his formal preferences and
taste alone, but also on his constant reflection on the issues
of architecture, space, form, meaning and function as it
appears in all areas of his work.

Dabernig's buildings combine minimal and basic
forms, clear spaces and a strictly systematic approach with
small irregularities or, rather, with small modifications of
the basic system that eventually produce quite complex
results. One particular pattern or system has been repeated
several times in different context and could therefore be
understood as a sort of paradigm for Dabernig's architectural work. But he doesn't use it for architectural projects
only. It often appears in his objects, e.g., in the grids built
with the ready-made aluminum elements. This pattern is
based on a sequence of units that grow in a precisely
determined rhythm. It is possible to apply this system to
sequences of architectural elements and to achieve even
more complex results with a repetition of the basic sequence
and with shifts or mirroring structures. For example,
Dabernig has used this principle on the facade of the
staircase he designed for the Beschäftigungswerkstäten der
Lebenshilfe in Ledenitz near Villach in 1995. The basis for
the facade is the grid, but here the grid is not understood as
simple addition and repetition of units, but as a dynamic
rhythm of such units. The main facade of the staircase
house is divided into two vertical halves. Each of the two is
divided into units that increase in size, following a precise
rhythm. This rhythm is accentuated with the alternating
use of two types of glass. What is important, however, is the
fact that the rhythm of units in the two halves doesn't run
parallel; it is shifted. The result is a facade grid that is not

only dynamic, but seems irregular, although it is also clear
that this effect is based on a very strict application of the
rules of a system. We can find the same pattern in the
entrance hall of the former KELAG Building (now a school)
in Villach (1997). Here, Dabernig used a grid and panels from
two types of glass not as a facade but as a wall element that
visually enlarges the space and makes it more dynamic.
In this case, he worked with two opposite walls, which, by
turning the opposite panel around, gave him the opportunity
to develop the complexity of the rules further.

It is perhaps not a coincidence, but rather the way
Dabernig works with space, that he actually never constructed a complete building. As a rule he intervenes in
existing structures. The principle of his work seems to be
to leave the structure essentially unchanged. He introduces
additional elements or develops spatial systems, which he
places into the existing structures. A very nice example of
such an additional element is the pedestrian bridge he
constructed for an administrative building in Hartenberg
(2000). The wooden bridge is in direct contrast to the
concrete and glass facade of he building. The sloping of the
bridge echoes the oblique forms used by the architect. The
new object is clearly a well-thought response to the existing
architecture, even a certain commentary on it, and it is
designed in such a way that it both accentuates its characteristics and somehow balances them with clearly different
ideas. And yet it hardly touches it, the building is left
essentially unchanged, giving almost the impression of
a temporary addition. But in spite of the fact that this
architectural intervention is formally minimal and rational,
non-spectacular and non-monumental, its details show a
playful approach and even humor. Let us take as an example
the pillars that hold the bridge. They are of the same height,
but since the bridge is slanted it seems that their height
is increasing. This could even be understood as a self-ironic
reference to the artist's own paradigmatic pattern of the
sequence of growing units.

Dabernig's approach in creating new spatial systems
within existing spaces is most obvious in his designs of
interiors. Two such places are particularly interesting, the
interior design of the Depot in Vienna (1997) and the
arrangement of the space for reading and rest at MUMOK -

Museum of Modern Art Stiftung Ludwig in Vienna (2002). In both cases he showed a high respect for the existing spatial situation. He obviously didn't want to transform these spaces or create a totally new environment in them. Rather, he constructed new spatial systems inside the existing space simply by placing certain elements and arranging them according to a particular order or pattern. This indicates another particular quality of Dabernig's interiors (especially obvious in his design of the Depot space). They are both strictly and precisely arranged and extremely open and flexible. He achieved this by simply placing only the necessary pieces of furniture into the space. The furniture is either designed by Dabernig himself or simply store-bought, but it is always simple, undecorated, minimal and geometrical. He uses it to create architectural structures in space, and although all the relations are precisely determined and arranged, it is always possible to rearrange space, if necessary, and then restore the order. The space for visitors is an excellent example of Dabernig's approach in designing (or rather, arranging) interiors. The artists placed the necessary elements according to a very precise plan, based on straight and diagonal lines. He mostly used industrially produced furniture (some of the pieces seem to be designed in the 1970s), available in shops. In choosing the items, he accentuated their simplicity and formal minimalism. I believe it is important for his understanding of such spaces that the pieces of furniture don't look like "designed," i.e., aestheticized, luxury objects. Quite the contrary, they might even give a slightly awkward impression, and this coincides with the strict order of their placement. On the wall, he placed two bookcases and a vending machine for drinks. Thus, he created a monumental triptych with the banal commercial machine at the center. (Dabernig knew, of course, that the museum space can effectively nobilitate this banality, especially when we take into account the works that deal with mass culture products, from Pop Art to contemporary artists dealing with consumer society. This is not an example of institutional critique in the usual sense of the word, but it is nevertheless an ironic reference to the power discourse incorporated by museums in the contemporary art system—a discourse that is often made obvious in the monumentality of the museum architecture.) The general effect of the space is not one of leisure. Because of the strictness of the relations and forms, there is a particular tension and sobriety in it. It seems to bring forth concentration rather than relaxation (although it functions very well as a place for study and rest). A visitor might not be immediately aware of the underlying system of arrangement, but there is a certain attraction in the spatial relations that invite him to discover not only the order of arrangement, but also the playful and ironic details and references that Dabernig has introduced to the space.

I think that the exhibition architecture Dabernig designed for *Individual Systems* (which I curated at the 2003 Venice Biennale) represents a kind of synthesis of his dealing with architecture and interior design. Again, he applied the pattern with growing units. The space of the Corderie where the exhibition was installed has a sort of modular or even grid-like floor plan. Furthermore, its character is strongly longitudinal. Dabernig's design accentuated this longitudinal nature by leaving the central aisle free while in the two side aisles he created the rhythm of gradually growing (actually, diminishing) units. These units were alternately closed and open spaces. So the aisle on the left side from the entrance started with a two-unit closed section, continued with a one and a half-unit open section, another one and a half-unit closed section, a one-unit open section and a one-unit closed section. In the right-hand aisle, the rhythm was the same (actually, we had to modify it to adapt the structure to the needs of the artists) but it was shifted forwards by one unit. So the right-hand aisle started with a one unit long open space and then continued with the same sequences as the left-hand one. The units were not only gradually decreasing but were also getting gradually lower. In such a way, Dabernig accentuated the longitudinal nature of the space by exaggerating the effect of the perspective. (Of course, for people entering from the other side of the space, the structure had exactly the opposite effect of defiance of perspective.) This system enabled the construction of white-cube spaces, necessary for the exhibition (it was an individual system that enabled separate spaces for other individual systems). But Dabernig wanted to keep the balance between the white rooms and the building of the Corderie. What he designed was actually a crossing of two spatial systems rather than canceling one system by imposing another one on it. He was extremely careful to leave the space of the Corderie as untouched and visible as possible. Therefore, the forms of the newly built rooms followed the forms of the existing architecture (which is not completely precise in measures) and therefore the white spaces often didn't have their walls at right angle. Furthermore, all the columns—the most important characteristics of the Corderie—remained visible; there was always a gap left between them and the newly constructed walls. The spaces were thus neither perfectly rectilinear nor completely closed, but nevertheless close enough to the white cube to work as exhibition rooms. And they were not completely isolated, but connected through gaps to the spaces around them.

With his design for the exhibition architecture, Dabernig developed a strict and precise system that was, nevertheless, always able to incorporate imperfections—not as mistakes, but as a part of the system itself. Therefore it was not impossible for him to modify the rhythm of spaces if the artists needed bigger or precisely rectilinear spaces. And yet, in spite of this flexibility and openness, the spatial system for *Individual Systems* also referred to the deep contradictions inherent in modern architecture. It showed his admiration for simple and rational modernist forms, but also his awareness of the relation of this forms to the utopian ideas of a perfectly organized world and the completely controlled societies in repressive and totalitarian regimes. The spatial rhythm thus had and ambiguous effect, combining attraction, precision, flexibility, irony, playfulness and threat. The fact that Dabernig exhibited his project *Envisioning Bucharest* at the exhibition made clear that such references were not coincidental. In the proposal for Bucharest, Dabernig uses the same system of units based on increasing distances and heights that was realized with the exhibition architecture. The basis of the system is the absurd brutality of Ceausescu's palace (brutality towards the city as an indicator of the brutality of the society itself). With this proposal, the precise and rational modernist logic of the system was turned into an exaggerated absurd (according to the project, the palace would be one of the smallest of a network of gigantic structures projected as a sort of grid upon the city). And yet, it becomes an antidote for the unbalance caused by the palace. And this, finally, indicates a certain therapeutic dimension of Dabernig's work, an effort to "work through" modernity, to disclose its contradictions and face them in order to try to solve their traumatic effects.

[1] Rosalind E. Krauss, *The Originality of the Avant-Garde and Other Modernist Myths*, MIT Press, Cambridge, MA, and London, 1986, p. 13.

[2] The German translation of the text by Renata Scerbavicute, "The World According to Dabernig," and a selection from the Internet discussion are available on Dabernig's web site.

[3] I say "post-industrialized," not "post-industrial," since the landscape in socialist countries had been programmatically "industrialized," no less for ideological than for economical reasons.

[4] I don't want to argue that dealing with modernist architecture and urban planning in Eastern Europe (or, for that matter, in other marginalized areas in Europe) and re-evaluating concepts and formal solutions is somehow unethical. On the contrary, I believe it is extremely important, also as a part of rethinking modernity and its traditions. The awareness that "socialist modernism" existed in Eastern Europe (or "fascist modernism" in Italy) as functional parts of repressive or totalitarian regimes shouldn't prevent us from discovering particular conceptual and formal qualities in them. But it is essential, too, that we don't forget their ambiguous nature, their synthesis of utopian visions and repressive reality, if we want to understand such projects correctly and if we want them to help us understand the contradictory nature of modernity.

A Short Walk Through Mladen Stilinović's Four Rooms

First published in *Mladen Stilinović. Umetnik na delu: 1973–1983*, Galerija Škuc, Ljubljana, 2005, pp. 8–25. Translated from Slovenian by Igor Zabel.

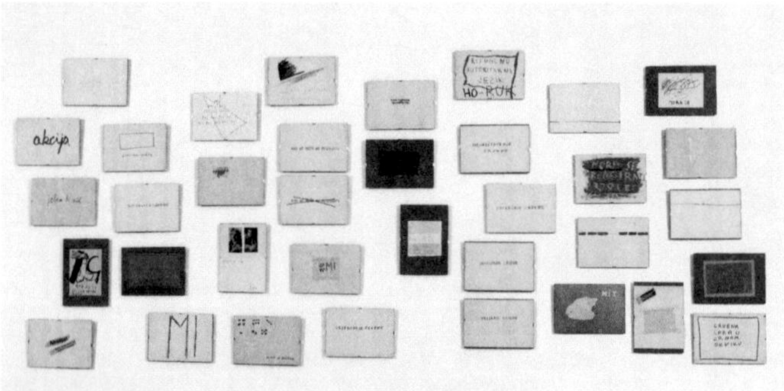

Mladen Stilinović, *Red Era*, 1973–1990

Room

A room, in the case of Mladen Stilinović, is not just an exhibition space. It is a form of organization and presentation of material.
It is, of course, connected to the tradition of conceptual and post-conceptual art, and to those tendencies in art that sought not only for new forms of artworks, but also for new forms of creating and presenting art, and for new relations with the audience. Stilinović does not take the gallery space for granted, and this is perhaps due to his experiences with the Group of Six Artists, an association of avant-garde artists active in Zagreb since 1975. The group invented a particular term that describes the way the artists presented their works. They called these events (that took place on streets, in parks, in swimming-pools, etc.) "exhibition-actions." The term indicates a particular way of thinking of production,

presentation and reception of the works of art. At an "exhibition-action," all three aspects were connected in a single interactive and collaborative creative process.

The room implies a slightly different structure. It is probably less connected to a creative process than an "exhibition-action" and more to reflection, interpretation and re-interpretation. A room is defined by a certain common theme. The theme can be a medium, a motif, a subject, etc. As he compiles and arranges such rooms, the artist builds a sort of taxonomy of his own art, thus defining the basic dictionary for understanding it. In spite of the broad variety of approaches, media and subjects in his art, we can also find in it a particular systematic approach, visible both in his works and in the way he re-arranges and re-interprets his own pieces. A dictionary would be indeed a very appropriate way of presenting his work (after all, Stilinović has used a dictionary several times); such a dictionary would necessarily be a highly complex network of cross-references.

A room is a space where works of art of different types and from different periods can be arranged together in a single pattern. The artist does not arrange them in the usual linear sequence. Rather, he covers walls with his works, constructing patterns and building new connections. Since Stilinović's work is closely related to literature and visual poetry, we could, perhaps, find a relation to the way Mallarmé dispersed the usual linear structure of the poetical text in his book *One Toss of the Dice*, producing new meanings with the spatial structure of the text and with the position and size of the printed words, and incorporating empty space into the text. In a similar way, Stilinović's works— which are, of course, individual pieces—gain new meanings from their location and relations to other pieces, developing and weaving complex micro-relations that eventually produce the main theme of the room.

Finally, the room indicates a position of the beholder that is different from the usual position of a museum or gallery visitor. Stilinović often organizes small exhibitions in his own apartment, and the way the works are presented in a gallery space can be directly related to the way they are presented in his study. This is a reason why the relation of the visitors to the exhibited works can be more intimate and immediate. Indeed, such a relation is important since the works are usually not what we call "museum pieces." Rather, they are mostly small-sized works that often demonstrate how a thought or idea has been developed, and not monumental statements. This, again, is closely connected to Stilinović's artistic strategies. His artistic work is actually a tightly knit network of micro-strategies, of very different ideas and approaches, which nevertheless form clearly recognizable patterns and taxonomies.

The Red (and Pink) Room

Soon after the death of Pope John Paul II, a Slovenian newspaper (that could be described as both "yellow" and "black") published several articles that attacked the journalists of TV Slovenia. They were accused of disrespectful behavior during the Pope's last days. And what exactly was the disrespectful behavior? The host of the main evening news wore a red tie, and the journalist reporting from Rome wore a red dress. Not only were they disrespectful towards the Pope and the mourning believers, claimed the newspaper, but they also defiantly declared that their disrespect was based on their political stance. The red tie of the TV journalist was, in the eyes of the newspaper's editor, a red flag that declared that the television house was still a "red fortress." The true content of this attack is, of course, quite obvious and directly connected to the attempts of the right-wing government to gain full control over public television. What is interesting for us here is its "exterior" form. The red pieces of clothing worn by the journalists of TV Slovenia were considered a disrespectful political provocation. At the very same time, the Vatican was literally crowded with people in red garments. But in this case red was not considered to be either disrespectful or a sign that the Vatican was, in fact, a "red fortress."

     The case of the red tie, absurd as it is, demonstrates at least two important issues. First, the use of color is not innocent and unburdened by possible meanings. Such meanings are not even necessarily intended by the person using the color. (Personally, I do not believe that even the newspaper's editor actually thought that the correspondent reporting from Rome chose her fashionable red dress—

quite similar to the dress in which the American secretary of state appeared on some of her recent official visits—in order to demonstrate her leftist political preferences.) And second, such meanings are not fixed and stable, they can change according to the situation in which they appear, they can actually be constructed according to the context. Slavoj Žižek once demonstrated the way ideology operates in every-day life by describing different concepts that achieve a tangible form in different types of toilets. His point was that it was enough for one to sit on the toilet to find oneself deep in ideology. On the other hand, one cannot avoid ideology since one has to use a certain type of toilet, and even a decision of not using it would take an ideological form. In a similar sense, wearing a tie of a particular color (or not wearing a tie at all), places one in a fluid network of political and ideological meanings.

Colors are very important in Stilinović's art. One could attempt to present a system of colors he uses. White, for example, indicates emptiness and nothingness, black is the color of death, red is the color of ideology and political power, pink could perhaps be connected to consumerism. Furthermore, the meaning of colors in Stilinović's works is directly connected to the use of colors in modernist and avant-garde traditions, and particularly in Malevich's Suprematism. However, it would be wrong to assume that Stilinović has been developing a kind of defined symbolic or even esoteric system of colors. Quite the opposite, colors seem to be always ambiguous for him, indicating certain contents, but not clearly signifying them, speaking with their material immediacy and appeal, and yet unable to get completely rid of their possible meanings.

The color red has a particular role in Stilinović's work. This is connected not only to its significance to the public life of socialist Yugoslavia in the 1970s and 1980s, but its huge importance for the global history and culture in the last century or century and a half. Red has become extremely burdened by meanings. As we saw, merely wearing a red dress can become a source of complex political and ideological hermeneutics. On the other hand, such meanings are far from being simple and clear. The Russian artist Alexander Kosolapov, to name just one example, used the color red in his work *Lenin—Coca-Cola (1980-2000)* both as

the color of the socialist revolution and of the registered
trade mark of Coca Cola, thus dialectically bringing together
the two opposing political and economic systems and
disclosing their parallelisms. And even if we identify it with
the communist revolution, the color red again implies very
different contents, from the protest against a non-egalitarian
and exploitative society to the idea of totalitarian and
repressive communist societies.

In a short text, Stilinović very precisely and concisely
describes his "use" (as he says) of the color red (and pink).
He emphasizes the plurality of meanings that are necessarily
connected to it. His strategy is to exaggerate this plurality,
so that any attempt of meaningful interpretation would
eventually lead into an absurd situation. In such a way
he tries to deconstruct the meanings and, as he says,
"de-symbolize" the color that can eventually be understood
just as color. On the other hand, however, it is simply
impossible to forget the different symbolic networks that
determine it. Therefore, says the artist, "one reads these
works both as symbols and as de-symbols."

The Room of Words, Slogans, and Proverbs

Words have always been a central part of Stilinović's art.
His works have rarely been "purely" visual. Even pieces that
do not actually include written words are often connected
to the structure of language; either their own structure is
based on linguistic structures, or they are visual representations of such structures (e.g. works that are based on a play
with words). However, the visual side of such works is not
unimportant, either. Stilinović's works point at the fact that
the way a text is physically represented (and this includes
such details as the lettering, the material on which the text
is written, the colors used in writing, the context in which
the written words appear, etc.) strongly affects its meaning.

This is, perhaps, particularly visible where the text
refers to the work itself. For the Group of Six, the aspect
of self-reflection in art has always been essential. In their
work they have used approaches that stem from
such different sources as the so-called "fundamental" or
"primary" abstract art, or concrete and visual poetry.
The common aspect of such diverse practices is, however,

the self-referential and self-descriptive character of the work. It is, however, typical for Stilinović that he often used such approaches in an ironic and playful way, so that the results can be humorous and even absurd. One of his works, for example, consists of a hand-written statement that declares, "*I have been working on this work since 11 June 1976.*" The content of this piece (or, better, this work) is, quite in accordance with the fundamental demands of "primary" art, a presentation (even a direct description) of its own conditions and the process of its production. And yet, here this approach is rendered absurd. A similar, even more exaggerated effect of absurdity can be found in Stilinović's handwritten booklet called *I Have No Time*; the pages of the booklet are completely filled with endless repetitions of the sentence "I have no time." Both works clearly demonstrate the complexity of Stilinović's approach, hidden behind what at first simply seems a witty idea. They deal with the issues of work and time, of "having" and "using" time, of empty time, etc.

The self-referential character of Stilinović's work, however, cannot be limited to those works that describe the actual material and temporal conditions and processes of their own making. It is no coincidence that Stilinović uses the word "works" rather than, for example, "pieces." A "piece" is an autonomous entity, a "work," on the other hand, is an element in the social network of work and production. For "primary" and "fundamental" art the production of a work consists of its material characteristics and the actual, physical process of making. Stilinović, however, shows that this process of making is not self-sufficient. Rather, it is included in the network of the social exchange. A "work" is produced in order to be consumed, moreover, it is produced to be sold. One of Stilinović's works announces this in a rather direct way: "*I sell works, I buy hard currency.*"

We should understand this sentence not only as a metaphorical description of the position of artistic production, but also as a direct and simple description of the situation it refers to. It is a good example of Stilinović's statements and slogans that seem to be witty paradoxes or exaggerations, but should be, nevertheless, often taken literally. The best known of these statements

are, perhaps, "*An artist who cannot speak English is no artist,*"
and "*Work is illness,*" a fake quotation from Karl Marx. At first,
the statement, "An artist who cannot speak English is no
artist" seems absurd—why should knowledge of English be
a condition for being an artist? And yet, we should take
the statement quite seriously. One cannot simply decide to
be an artist. One can only be considered an artist if one is
accepted by the system of art. Not every practice that could
be, in one way or another, described as art is acknowledged
by the system of contemporary art. Therefore, to be an artist,
one should follow the demands of the system and accept the
practices that it approves; one has to speak the language
accepted by the system. The system of contemporary art is
declaredly international or global. Artists and curators
often do not want to be described as a representative of a
particular state or nation and prefer to be designated as
"international." English, so it seems, is consensually
accepted as the language of this global system. We often see
how artists use English in their works not only to be able to
communicate internationally, but also to emphasize that
they belong to the world of contemporary art. And yet, the
generally accepted use of English as the dominant language
of the system indicates that there are more or less hidden
inequalities, relations of dominance and subordination, of
centers and peripheral areas. In short, to be acknowledged
as an artist one has to speak the language of contemporary
art, i.e., English, and thus tacitly accept the relations of
power and dominance that govern it.

Stilinović's statements often deliberately imitate the
form of political slogans. (Let us just think of his declaration, "An attack on my art is an attack on socialism and
progress!") His interest in this literary form is certainly
connected to the experience of such slogans and other
forms of political propaganda in socialist society (we should
mention the series of photographs of such slogans as they
appeared in display windows and other public places). In
Yugoslavia, the 1970s were a period of strong ideological
pressure, which was visibly displayed in ideological propaganda. It is thus no coincidence that Stilinović and several
other members of the Group of Six Artists referred to this
form in their work and adapted it to their practice. For
them, it was interesting not only because of its immanent

contradictions and absurdities, which they often revealed in their works, but also as an example of a very close connection of language and power. Political slogans can be considered a rudimentary poetic form and are, at the same time, a very direct mechanism of ideological and political power. It comes as no surprise that Stilinović and other members of the Group of Six Artists, who have always been deeply interested in the relations of the poetic and the political, found them so interesting.

One could perhaps say that Stilinović's textual works address, in the most explicit way, a tightly connected group of issues that are essential for his art in general. These issues include work, time, money (and poverty), food (and hunger), and power. We could say that he shows how political power uses different ideological mechanisms (from political slogans to media representations and moral norms) to construct and maintain social relations in which it could be sustained and reproduced. Such relations are, of course, relations of inequality and exploitation. Power can reproduce and increase itself only through keeping a majority of people in relative poverty through exploitation of their work and by persuading them that such social relations are natural. The artist, however, is not interested primarily in developing a general theory on power and work. Such general ideas are, rather, a background of a sort, while he actually works on the micro-level, building a network of references and their combination, and constructing a multi-layered reflection on the issues of dominance, production and reproduction, and their relations.

The forms of slogans, proverbs and sayings are particularly interesting in this context. They are directly involved in the way power reproduces itself through organizing social relations. They are short formulations of such relations in the form of "naturally valid" ethical norms and moral claims (e.g., "Who does not work shall not eat"). On the other hand, they are often clear and pointed descriptions of the nature of such social relations (e.g., "A poor man has no friends").

The Newspaper Room

They say that nothing is older (and more old-fashioned)
than yesterday's newspaper. And yet Stilinović's approach to
newspapers indicates that they have a more general and
more permanent value. The way he uses them indicates that
he discovers in them particular structures and mechanisms
that are firm and permanent in spite of newspapers' highly
transient value.

A newspaper is some kind of a map of time. A map
is always reductive and schematic, and it no less constructs
than represents its territory. In a similar way, newspapers
function as mechanisms of selection and combination
that, in endless repetition, reflect and by the same token
construct time, i.e. the historical moment. To be able to
function they need to have certain permanent structures,
which select and organize the endless flow of different
information, present it as news and thus continue to
construct the map of time. Such structures are primarily
formal. They are not contents, but a way of organizing it.
They are perhaps most visible in different permanent
graphic forms, in the newspaper's layout etc., as well as in
the system of editing that makes it possible for us to learn
about news quickly and effectively. Less obvious, but no less
important, are the typical textual forms used by journalists
in their texts. We often feel how empty such forms actually
are, but it is exactly this formal aspect that is effective
and functional. Images, too, show a similar tendency to
schematization. Photographs representing congresses
and sessions have a certain general quality. They are almost
interchangeable. The same is true even of portrait photographs. Individual features often disappear in favor of
a generalized image of a representative of power (who can
be a communist leader, a western politician or the director
of a big company).

Stilinović seems to be particularly interested in such
schematic forms—i.e., in the forms that construct historical
time and its relations. Often, he even emphasizes their
formal nature by taking them out of their original context
and presenting them as autonomous structures. Another
approach that he regularly uses is re-contextualization. This
doesn't just mean that he moves fragments of newspapers

into new contexts; often, he determines such a new context by writing short textual comments or adding drawings or other elements. In one series he combined small fragments from newspapers with fragments of small everyday conversations. In such a combination both seemingly unimportant types of text gain a certain weight. They now seem to be loaded with particular, albeit unclear meaning and emotional importance. In a similar work, Stilinović took schematic political statements from article titles and added to them obscene comments, such as people often make as they read newspapers.

Such re-contextualization can also be achieved by crossing two different series of works, i.e. two different taxonomies. An example of such a crossing of systems is a series of works that combines political slogans with article titles that refer to workers' strikes. Simply by systematically opposing two schematic textual forms from two different times, i.e. slogans and references, with workers' protests, Stilinović develops a complex discourse about actual social tensions and conflicts. The slogans, of course, serve as a tool to discipline society and especially the labor process; they also function as a screen that hides the actual relations of power, dominance and exploitation that govern the labor process and society in general. On the other hand, workers' strikes clearly disclose the unbearable conditions of working and living, and thus the exploitative system of social inequality.

What is also interesting for Stilinović's approach to newspapers is the way he finds little details in them that—taken out of their original context and isolated or placed in a new, unusual context—speak with incredible richness, complexity or even poetic power. This, however, is possible because of a particular way of reading. Only in such a way can results of sport matches or statistics be transformed into a poetic reflection on numbers and zero (nothingness).

The Photography Room

The photography room is different from the other rooms, as it is not based on any particular subject or issue, but on a specific medium. If we can say that the rooms indicate a particular taxonomy that is a basis of Stilinović's art, then we might also say that they no less show how closely and

essentially these different issues are connected. We could
show numerous examples of works that could be part of
two, maybe even three or four rooms. The photography
room, which is not based on any particular subject, makes
the fact that different issues and subjects actually exist as
a tightly knit, interconnected network even more obvious.
Each of them is related to and determined by the others.

It is, nevertheless, no coincidence that photography,
of all media, is to be represented in a room of its own. In
Stilinović's work, as well as in the work of other members
of the Group of Six Artists, photography has held a particular position. Stilinović and other artists of the group not
only used photography in their work, but also systematically
and critically analyzed its structure, role, and position.
(This critical and deconstructive tendency reached one of
its most extreme results in the project by Željko Jerman,
who wrote "Drop dead, photography!" with photo chemicals
on photographic paper.)

Photography as a medium has been deeply transformed
in the context of the conceptual and post-conceptual currents
in art, to which Stilinović's work is, of course, closely related.
It is well known that conceptual artists have renounced the
idea of the photographic image as an aesthetic, perfectly
executed object and replaced the concern for composition,
strong subject and skillful execution with simple, unsophis-
ticated shots that simply registered certain situations,
functioning, as it has been said, as a "copying machine."
(It should perhaps be noted that conceptual art, in spite of
its aspirations, did actually not cancel the aesthetic dimension
of photography, but defined new aesthetic criteria for it,
based on values different from those that have traditionally
distinguished a well executed photographic print.)

We might say that Stilinović uses photography in a
number of ways. It can, for example, serve as documentation
of ephemeral actions or projects that would otherwise be
inaccessible to the wider public. On the other hand, photography has the ability to register a certain situation and thus,
merely by framing and recording it, to transform it into an
artistic context. It can be used as a tool for research,
documentation and classification of reality. This is, perhaps,
particularly important for Stilinović's work. Photography is
ideal for the long-term, systematic work of recording and

analytically categorizing details of every-day reality. He
has been working on several such series. One of them
presents hairdressers' shop signs. (Two further series
represent mechanics' shop signs and signboards advertising
restaurants with barbecue.) The series represents a collection
of details of everyday reality that we often overlook. And yet,
thanks to Stilinović's systematic approach, they not
only prove to be interesting by themselves in many cases,
but they represent a cultural segment that offers a particular
insight into cultural and social history. One could say that
fundamental historical and social structures function
through the most marginal and seemingly irrelevant aspects
of everyday life. It is exactly this crossing of everyday reality
and socio-historical structures that is revealed in Stilinović's
series. The visual style of the boards, the type of the letters,
the quality of the execution, the look of the haircuts etc.
construct a truly panoramic view of ideas and ideals, and
their transformations.

In another series, the artist registered elements of
ideological propaganda in the public space that used to
be an unavoidable part of everyday life in socialist society,
especially at the time of public holidays. Stilinović systematically documented flags and slogans decorating the streets
and the banners, communist symbols and Tito's portraits
in the display windows of shops and offices. The series has
several layers. For example, it clearly shows one of the ways
in which a particular type of ideology functioned in society,
how it entered the public space and everyday life. It also
shows how schematic such slogans and symbols actually
were, and how they could be effective in spite of their
schematic, purely formal nature. They indicate one of the
essential paradoxes of the way socialist societies functioned.

Nobody, including the ruling elites, seemed to
actually believe in the slogans and rituals that governed the
life of such societies; they considered them to be pure forms
without any actual meaningful content. However, this was
enough for the social order to be able to function as usual.
It was not necessary for people to believe in rituals, it was
enough that they formally complied with them.

On the other hand, Stilinović not only uses photography, he is also interested in its properties and structure.
For example, he demonstrates that photography can be an

excellent means to study principles and possibilities of representation; furthermore, he is interested in the structure and nature of the medium, in the wide range of its attributes, from the illusion and reality effects it produces, and the symbolic structures it incorporates into its material basis. One should also notice his interest in the relation between photography and the poetic, or, more generally, linguistic structures.

Re-Thinking the Past, Re-Discovering the Present

Many of Stilinović's works that are included in such rooms go back to the 1970s and 1980s. This means that they were produced in a very different political, social and cultural context. Many things that used to be taken for granted are not common anymore. These works, therefore, often do not speak to us in the same way they used to 20 or 30 years ago. This is something we should take into account, since these works are so directly related to social and political issues and circumstances. And yet, they are certainly not mere documents about a past society. If they only showed us interesting details from past decades they would simply be a source of information, or perhaps a source of nostalgia. Their actual subject, however, are patterns of power and dominance, the ways meanings are constructed and the self-evident is determined. They also speak about art's own relation to power, its possibilities and impotence, its distance towards the structures of dominance and its collaboration with them.

Such patterns are no less functional in the new context of contemporary society as they used to be in their original context. Past forms and structures of power, as they are presented and critically reflected in Stilinović's works, hold a mirror up to the present ones.

Stilinović's art, however, is not sociology. It is primarily art, but art that is aware of its own conditions and determinants. The artist does not close his eyes on the reality around him—on his own reality. And it is by responding to this reality, to its multiple contradictions and dilemmas, that he is able to recover the poetic, the beautiful, even the sublime.

Another Speedy Day

First published in *Vadim Fiškin. Another Speedy Day, The Slovenian Pavilion,
51. International Art Exhibition. La Biennale di Venezia*, Moderna galerija, Ljubljana, 2005, pp. 3–7.
Translated from Slovenian by Tamara Soban.

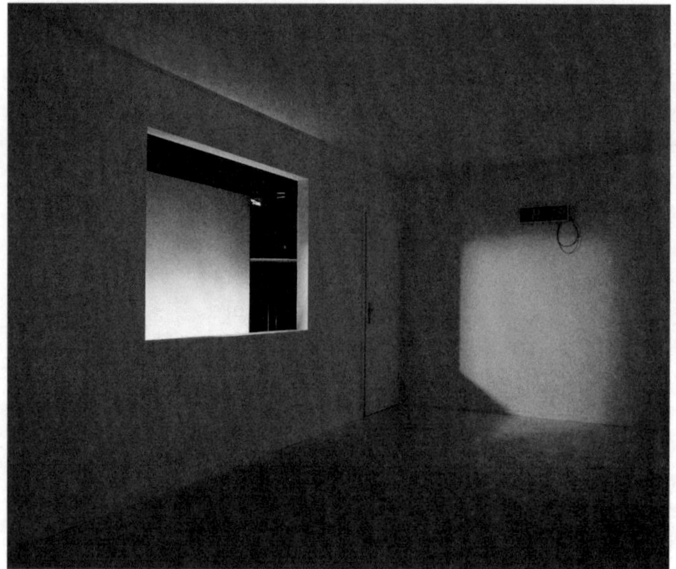

Vadim Fiškin, *Another Speedy Day*, Venice Biennale, Slovene Pavilion, 2005

Prima facie, as mounted in the gallery, Vadim Fiškin's project *Another Speedy Day* might be reminiscent of stage equipment. But what is staged on this set is just the fluctuation of light, increasing and fading at a steady pace. All the physical equipment is merely the support of something that seems to hover—though it is not immaterial—on the verge of material presence. Moreover, light is a precondition for the possibility of seeing, and at the same time, something that is in itself on the edge of visibility. Fiškin has here used the possibilities afforded by contemporary media and theater technology to stage something intangible and, as it were, barely visible. The fluctuation of light also determines the duration: the cycle of the light growing brighter and dimming lasts twelve minutes, thus demanding prolonged attention from the viewer and, consequently, producing an increased awareness of time. (Empirical analyses of audience behavior in large museums have shown that viewers in general tend to stop for a maximum of ten seconds even in front of major, visually saturated works; Fiškin's work, however, requires twelve minutes of contemplation of nothing but light.) But although the emphasis laid on the duration seems great, the work's temporal nature also makes the work ephemeral, or even momentary, as it incessantly escapes and disappears into nothingness.

The cycle of light is actually the enactment of a day, 24 hours compressed into 12 minutes. We might also say it is the enactment of one of the most fundamental human fantasies, of controlling the course of time. It can, for example, remind us of the very vivid descriptions of time travel in H. G. Wells' *The Time Machine*. The time traveler, who sits in his machine, initially sees the world as a fast running film, but soon, as the speed of his travel accelerates, he perceives only the ever quicker changes of light and darkness. This description is perhaps one of the most beautiful presentations of the fantasy of flying through time, of moving freely along the axis of the fourth dimension. Wells' time traveler speaks very explicitly about this fantasy (although he disguises it as a scientific discourse). Since technology has enabled man to defy the forces of gravity and move freely—e.g. by plane—in all three dimensions of three-dimensional space, the time traveler now wants to employ technology to conquer also the dimension of time. We could say that man wants to extend the age-old fantasy of flying to encompass the fourth dimension, which perhaps makes Fiškin's machine a time plane of sorts.

Overcoming gravity and overcoming the restrictions that prevent man from moving at will in any direction of four-dimensional space-time are closely connected. Overcoming gravity also means breaking free of the human body, of being physically bound by the parameters of space and time. The artist has described his project thus: "The light in the room changes according to a 'fast clock.' On an electronic display, the hours tick by at an accelerated pace. Daylight and nighttime light follow one another to the rhythm of the electronic clock. In the exhibition room, following the theory of relativity, an entire earth day (24 hours) is reduced to a total of 2.5 minutes, which can also be the result of traveling through space at a velocity of slightly less than the speed of light."[1] The rhythm of light pulsating in Fiškin's installation would thus be experienced by someone a mere 10 km/s from reaching the speed of light, i.e. from overcoming one of the most fundamental and absolute limitations of our universe.

H.G. Wells' time traveler (and many time travelers after him) considered time to be a dimension comparable to the three dimensions of Euclidian space. Such a fourth dimension is supposed to make movement along its axis possible, i.e., both forth and back in time, just as the three spatial dimensions enable movement both up and down or forward and backward in space. Fiškin's project, however, while enabling us to share the experience of accelerated time with the time traveler, also implicitly questions this fantasy, indicating the conflict between the flight of our desires and fantasies and the traumatic experience of the unsurpassable limitations of space-time.

Fiškin's installation is, in fact, a direct reference to Einstein's theory of relativity. The deeply troubling hidden contents of Fiškin's light spectacle are, I believe, connected to some of Einstein's fundamental statements. The first is the very idea of the relativity of time. Only at first glance does it support the time traveler's ideas of moving along the time axis. As Einstein demonstrated, there is no such generally valid time axis. There is no meta-time, just as there is (as Lacan demonstrated) no meta-language. The second aspect is that Einstein, with his theory of relativity, determined certain absolute values. His paradox of the twins demonstrates that twins, after a period spent in different systems (e.g., one on Earth and the other in a hypothetical rocket moving at a speed only 10 km/s slower than the speed of light), would be a different age. And yet, neither would be younger. It is, as Einstein demonstrated, absolutely impossible to reverse the direction of time.

Inke Arns has described Fiškin's works as "machines (media) that produce the metaphysical."[2] Indeed, they are machines, technological aggregates, but machines that work in a "poetic" manner since they are not subject only to production pragmatics but underscore in their work the complexity and contradictoriness of their own fundamental premises. Generally speaking, Fiškin's art can be regarded as closely related to the world of modern science and technology. But this does not make it rationalistic or naively technicist. On the contrary, it emphasizes that crucial line in the development of modern sciences and technology in which strict scientific positivism has intertwined or literally fused with metaphysical reflections, and technological innovations have acquired poetic or even esoteric aspects. Fiškin's work could also be related to the tradition of technological utopias. By "technological utopias" I do not mean only visions of perfectly ordered societies, based on the principles of science and progressive technological solutions. Tatlin's flying device *Letatlin* is a completely different type of utopia from, say, the vision of a world of the future as seen by Jules Verne. *Letatlin* is beyond merely searching for a new technological paradigm for the airplane (although it is that, too); it is a technological object that has acquired a metaphorical, even a metaphysical role. It can be seen as a sign of the utopian aspirations to liberate the body of its physical restrictions. The light spectacle in Fiškin's *Another Speedy Day* could also be seen as a technological aggregate based on precise mathematical calculations and technical solutions and as an enactment of a utopian fantasy. This fantasy, however, is confronted with the absolute limitations that make it impossible. And these are, actually, the limitations of our own temporal essence and our ephemeral existence. This is the trauma hidden behind Fiškin's spectacle.

[1] www.vadimfishkin.si
[2] Inke Arns, "Vadim Fiškin—Of Angels and Dreamers, Machines and Metaphysics," www.vadimfishkin.si

IV. EXTRAS

Depth on the Surface

First published as "Globina na zunanjosti" in *Delo*, 12. 2. 2001, p. 6.
Translated from Slovenian by Rawley Grau.

One of the more interesting recent miniseries has been the angry letters to the editor by readers unhappy with the television miniseries about France Prešeren. In their opinion, the series presented the great poet in an ideologically inappropriate way. The problem, I think, goes beyond the depiction of drinking bouts and obscene joke-telling. The more fundamental issue, certainly, was that the series did not confirm these viewers' preconceptions of what Slovenia's greatest poet and his destiny ought to look like. Consequently, the televised Prešeren cannot be our poet, cannot be that profound, brilliant genius who is at the foundation of the Slovene identity and, as it were, the ideal of the nation's self. All those viewers enraged by the miniseries were hardly interested in the fact that the series itself was clearly based on presuppositions about Prešeren's poetic greatness and genius, and his national importance, only it wanted to present these things in a somewhat more intelligent, less one-sided way. It was essential, then, that this Prešeren did not conform to the external attributes and models viewers expected in a depiction of the greatest Slovene poet.

As I read these letters, I often thought of another miniseries—the series of short interviews about *Manifesta 3*. This survey, too, provides some very interesting material. Notably, the interviewees' statements relate not only to the actual exhibition; rather, the exhibition was understood as a model for "contemporary art" in general (this, indeed, is how the survey questions were posed). The attitudes toward this kind of art were mostly negative (the views of the interviewees did, of course, differ, but here I will permit myself to simplify things and speak mainly about the predominant tone of these opinions). The negative feeling, however, was in fact quite similar to the reactions to the Prešeren miniseries: in the works at *Manifesta 3*, the exhibition visitors did not see the attributes they thought were essential for great art and thus concluded that these works were not great art.

In many cases these statements mainly revealed a lack of knowledge, not only about the latest art, but also more generally about the creative work of recent decades, even among people who really should know something about the subject—respected intellectuals, people who work in the cultural field, and so on. As a result, when they viewed the works on display (which for the most part were nothing terribly radical but straightforward, clear, and understand-able), they felt confused: How was it possible to tell the difference between an artwork and non-artistic reality? How was it possible to read and comprehend such works? In other words, they had no frame of reference by which to orient themselves. This might seem surprising when we consider that it is so easy to get information these days, that the general public's interest in contemporary art has greatly increased in recent decades (and not only in Western Europe and the USA—where as far back as the 1980s it was noted that the number of visitors of modern art museums had reached and sometimes even surpassed the number of those who viewed classical art—but also in South America, Asia, etc., where large contemporary art exhibitions attract hundreds of thousands of visitors), and that today intellectuals around the world feel embarrassed if they are not (at least to all appearances) knowledgeable about contemporary artistic creativity.

What, then, was the basis for the arrogant self-assurance with which a certain university professor made assertions that, more than anything, revealed a terrible ignorance of what has been happening in art since about 1925 (statements that were even more entertaining than the angry demands that the Prešeren miniseries be given a public burning, if possible along with the screenwriter and director)? The professor's confidence, I think, came from an a priori value system to which, of course, contemporary art does not conform; this system allows him to reject such art and even declare that it has no depth, that it is not based in subjective feeling, that it is superficial and of the moment, that it has no genuine humanistic vision and therefore, it would seem, no (genuine) value. It might be more precise to call this a system of signification, of external signs, by which a work declares its adoption of a certain set of values and thus places itself in the category of high (and deep) art. The depth is on the surface.

In the debates over the Prešeren miniseries, the issue was not about historical authenticity or the intentions of the creators, but about the series' conformity to an ideal image as the basis for an identity (perhaps that very identity which today is felt to be so threatened by all kinds of foreign elements, from asylum-seekers to recovering drug addicts, from children "with special needs" to waste recycling). Similarly, in the discussions about what is and isn't genuine art, the issue was not about quality in itself, but about the establishment of a dominant model that would give a certain kind of practice (as "genuine") a dominant position while excluding or marginalizing as "not genuine" any approach that does not conform to this practice. But for this kind of control, of course, you need something else as well: the relative closedness and insulation of the space.

The Soil in Which Art Grows

First published as "Humus, iz katerega raste umetnost" in *Delo*, 11. 6. 2001, p. 5.
Translated from Slovenian by Rawley Grau.

Every other year (more or less), around the time when the International Exhibition of Contemporary Art, better known as the Venice Biennale, opens in Venice, that city is flooded with a particular type of people, a multitude who almost completely overshadow the usual Venetian population—the female Japanese tourists in their Miyake dresses and their spouses with the latest technological advances in digital image reproduction, the Americans in shorts and sneakers who tell the (slightly sneering) waiter, "Seenyoray, praygo oono cappucheeno," the German newlyweds being serenaded with "O, sole mio" by a raspy tenor in a gondola beneath the Bridge of Sighs, and last but not least those useless Slovenes and Poles, who do little more than add to the size of the crowd, leave trash around the city, and upset the mayor of Venice, who also happens to be a well-known philosopher [i.e. Massimo Cacciari, mayor of Venice from

1993 to 2000 and again from 2005 to 2010—*Editor's note*].
It would be hard to describe this particular group, but they
are unmistakable: you can tell them from their walk,
their attitude, their conversation, and their clothes. They
are a kind of closed world unto themselves, which has
converged from around the globe and for a short time
settled in the city.

For a few days they occupy hotels, bars, and
restaurants, wander the streets or rush to appointments they
are already late for, carry bags filled with catalogues, greet
each other exuberantly with hugs and kisses in every
direction, pronounce their impressions loudly and preten-
tiously or, in muffled conversation, concoct various plans,
exchange information on social events, and try to come up
with an effective strategy for crashing the somewhat more
exclusive parties. This is the world of contemporary art:
artists, curators, gallerists, museum directors, exhibition
organizers, critics, collectors, and everyone else who would
like to become a part of this world as well as a whole group
of people who have some (more or less vague) connection
with contemporary art.

Venice is not just an exhibition of contemporary
artworks; it is also, especially, an exhibition, or presentation,
of the art system itself, which, condensed into a few days
in the limited space of its picturesque and theatrical venue,
displays itself in its multilayered and contradictory nature,
in its most unpalatable aspects and loftiest achievements.
Here you can get a clear idea about the workings of
the complex system we call the contemporary art world.
At every step it seems that you are confronted with a new
and different perspective on it. You see the convulsive
attempts of those who want to break out of anonymity; you
witness the ruthlessness and colossal ambition of those who,
to succeed, are willing to destroy anyone who gets in their
way; you encounter mediocrity, stupidity, and affectation,
but also, next to it, astonishing intelligence, articulateness,
openness, and human warmth. Here are the new stars of the
art world, exhausted by the attention they are getting and by
the countless tasks they have to perform, while next to them
are the disappointed stars of yesterday, whom only a few still
notice. If you are a bit more attentive, you can see how
certain countries have developed a successful strategy for

gaining recognition for their artists and thus a dominant position for their culture. (Quite obviously, this is most clear to the powerful countries, who are therefore trying to preserve their influential position in world culture at a time when globalization has caused considerable shifts in the established structures. Their presentations show a clear cultural-political vision, strategy, and awareness. Some countries try, more or less successfully, to imitate them, while the presentations of others create an impression that is more negative than positive, demonstrating unfamiliarity with the contemporary art field and the total absence of a coherent cultural policy.) You can physically feel the dividing lines and hierarchies that crisscross this world; you can see how, besides that which is public and open to everyone, there is also something hidden and closed; you can feel the centers of power and the conflicts between them, but also the peripheral regions and their petty scheming.

Sometimes, observing all the commotion and discord of the art world, which seems at times to hover somewhere in its own illusory reality, remote from ordinary real life, I ask myself if it makes any sense at all to be part of it. And I always tell myself that it does. This entire jumble is the soil from which art sprouts up. Everything in it that is bad or unpalatable is, perhaps, the price that must be paid for everything extraordinary and brilliant this world is able to give and produce. Because I work in a museum of modern and contemporary art, I see every day, as it were, that our work is not something discrete and autonomous; rather it is tightly and directly intertwined in this dense dynamic web, which crystallizes in artistic and critical achievements. As this multitude of "art professionals" pours through the exhibition halls and pavilions, now one, now another of them will suddenly stop before an artwork, forget their plans, appointments, and schemes, and, captivated, take time to concentrate on nothing but the work. And these "epiphanies," these moments of revelation and sudden captivation may, perhaps, ultimately excuse even all the political strategizing and power games, all the shallowness, pretentiousness, and ruthlessness.

Professionals, Dilettantes, and Amateurs

First published as "Profesionalci, diletanti, amaterji" in *Delo*, 16. 7. 2001, p. 5. Translated from Slovenian by Rawley Grau.

It is said that (in ordinary circumstances) one of the worst things
you can do to your fellow creatures
is to force them to listen to old
jokes. Murder is a dangerous
business, Oscar Wilde might say:
a person begins with murder, then
steals or even lies, and in the end is
killing the dinner company with
old quips. Still, I can't help recalling
just such an old joke—an anecdote,
in fact—for the plain and simple
reason that this little story is
one of the cornerstones in my
understanding of my work in
contemporary art and how this
world functions. Once upon a time
in America, they say, Arturo
Toscanini was guest-conducting a
certain symphony orchestra when
he noticed in particular, among the
other musicians, one of the cellists:
although the man was playing
brilliantly, the conductor's attention
was drawn to the glum, almost
tortured expression on his face.
After the rehearsal he went over to
him, congratulated him on his

fine playing, and asked what was troubling him. "I just hate music," the cellist answered sourly.

More and more, in recent years, people everywhere, including institutions that deal with art, have been stressing the need for greater professionalism. These are not accidental or arbitrary demands, but are "socially" necessary. The field of culture, in its various systems, must adapt itself to the profound changes taking place throughout the structure of society. Here there is no real choice; cultural work must conform to the principles that define and direct today's economic and social production if it is to operate with any success at all. The art system too, then, must become better organized, more rational and deliberate, more purposeful and more effective; in short, it must become more professional and less dilettantish.

Toscanini's cellist was certainly not a dilettante— neither in today's sense of the word, as a kind of dabbler (he obviously performed his job regularly and well), nor in the original sense of the word, which comes from the Italian *dilettare*, "to delight," and refers to someone who pursues a certain activity (especially in art and culture) seriously but for his own pleasure. Music annoyed the cellist, but he nonetheless played it well enough on the job to satisfy even the great Toscanini. He was, therefore, a true professional.

I particularly like the model this cellist presents of the true professional because, in its absurdity (can you imagine anything more absurd than a professional musician who hates music?), it is so very realistic and clear. Ultimately, this is merely the extreme expression of one of the basic demands required of every true professional: you do what you have to do whether you like it or not. The cellist was a professional because he did not allow his personal mood or opinion to influence the performance of his work. If he had done only things he enjoyed, things that made him happy, he would have been a dilettante. The difference, then, between the professional and the dilettante is that the professional performs, correctly and successfully, even things that weary him, even things he hates. Real-life experience seems to confirm this paradox. We might easily think that people usually choose their professional career in fields that, in one way or another, attract them and make them happy. But it seems to be a rule, nevertheless, that

once they are entangled in a web of more or less pleasant
but always necessary tasks, they gradually become less
excited about their field, less responsive and more indifferent. And finally, inevitably, the day arrives when the true
professional, on hearing someone mention this field,
exclaims, "Oh, I just hate it!"

But our cellist is doubly absurd—not only because he
hates his work (who doesn't, at least now and then?) but also
because this work is so closely connected to art, or rather, it
is itself art. The factory worker who packs canned goods
into boxes on a conveyor belt wouldn't be at all ridiculous or
absurd if, at the end of the work day, he exclaimed, "Oh,
I just hate these …-ing cans!" But art, it seems, is something
different, as if the only true and genuine relationship toward
it must, in fact, be *amateurism*, that is, literally, the relationship of one who loves. If you are involved with art in order
to earn money (hmm…), acquire social status, promote a
company, etc., then obviously you do not have a genuine
relationship with art. The only right answer to the question,
"Why are you involved with art?" is: for the sake of art itself,
from a love for art. "Love" here is no accidental word. In one
of his writings, Slavoj Žižek talks about how a lover, in reply
to the beloved's question, "Why do you love me?" may, indeed,
answer by listing her qualities (which, certainly, are not
insignificant), but this is not the right answer; it is not the
answer of one who loves. The right answer, of course, is this:
what is in this person is something more, some indefinable
x, which fills her whole appearance and makes her beloved
despite whatever flaws or imperfections she may have.

The true professional in the field of art is no less
absurd a phenomenon today than he is a (socially) necessary
one. He has decided on his vocation (one's profession as a
calling) for the sake of art itself—that is, out of a love for art.
Then, as a true professional, he naturally begins to hate it
(otherwise, he would be a dilettante and not a professional).
But, in his unconditional love for it, he overlooks and
forgives all its shortcomings, even his own hatred.

Greetings from the Provinces

First published as "Pozdrav iz province" in *Delo*, 13. 8. 2001, p. 6.
Translated from Slovenian by Rawley Grau.

There was once a time when people knew exactly where the center of the art world was located and where the provinces were. The center was Paris, and the provinces were more or less everywhere else. Paris eventually lost its role as the center, but it was still quite clear where the center was. New York, of course. In recent times, however, things are no longer that clear. Today, traveling through the cultural centers of Europe, you get the curious feeling that you are going from province to province. Not because there is nothing exciting or important happening in these cities, but because none of them feels like a self-sufficient center. There is always the sense that the really important changes are happening elsewhere, that the exhibition program is a reflection of other centers, and so on. If, conscious of the fact that you hail from a province, you get excited about all the different things happening in Vienna, it won't be long before someone who lives there tells you that, yes, Vienna is certainly trying to develop into a strong center but all the same it's not a real metropolis. The past few years there has been a lot of talk about the great developments in Scandinavian art, but Scandinavian artists and critics continue to say that they work on the periphery of Europe, far from the heart of the action. I remember how surprised I was a few years ago, at a time when British art had truly become a global phenomenon, to hear artists, curators, and others in London talk about feeling relegated to the margins. In Paris, you can hear people complaining about how their city, once the world capital of new art, has been downgraded to a local center. In Berlin you will hear people say that Berlin's okay but it's still not New York. And in New York, they say that the New York art scene has lost its real energy and that the most interesting stuff is happening in other cities, in Chicago and Los Angeles. But the people in those cities also have the feeling that, nevertheless, they are being somewhat pushed aside.

Such feelings are, possibly, something more than just random subjective illusions; they may well be connected with all those processes that are gradually, and at a very deep level, transforming the global economy and political power relations, as well as relations in culture. We often hear that the processes of globalization are simply a front for the West, and especially for the USA, so it can assume a new colonial control over the entire world. But the fact that, for example, it is no longer possible to say with unshakable certainty which cities are the global centers of art and culture and that even in the biggest centers people feel they are dealing with local issues and that the truly interesting, truly new things are happening elsewhere tells us there might be a different way to understand globalization processes. Slavoj Žižek has somewhere stated the thesis that in the processes of globalization multinational capital, freed from territorial localization and ties to a national base, acts as a force that subordinates the entire world to itself, so the issue is no longer the relationship between the colonial metropolis and the colony (the provinces), but rather that the flexible and unattached multi- and transnational centers of power are colonizing, as it were, the entire world.
Of course, these are not questions I myself can talk about

with competence. I mention them because, in my own experience in the contemporary art field, I have seen shifts that correspond with these ideas. The network of contemporary global art seems less and less localized, more and more dispersed throughout the world, and more and more flexible. New power centers are appearing that also act as a kind of interface between the local scene and the global network. The international art system influences local systems and languages and changes them, but we should not forget that in the process it too gradually changes. While artistic languages around the world are becoming more and more similar, they are also gradually becoming less specifically western or American. As a result of this ever greater dispersion, the role of the former cultural metropolises is changing and the distance between the periphery and the center is gradually diminishing. While today the centers remain only points—albeit critical ones—in a broader network, and are no longer the nucleus of the universe, the smaller active centers have suddenly become closer to the network of global art. Our own immediate experience confirms this. Even ten years ago it was significantly harder for artists from Eastern Europe, Asia, or South America to achieve international recognition unless they moved to one of the great centers. Today, individual artists, institutions, and cultural spaces have a much shorter and easier road to being included in the fluid global network. (This does not mean that the systems that had been dismissing a large segment of global cultural production from the central domain of art and ascribing it only a kind of ethnographic value, all the while proclaiming western principles as the self-evident norm—this does not mean that these systems have simply vanished; rather, there is today, perhaps, a mix of various relationships and powers that is slowly and gradually changing.)

In our country, it seems, the most frequent response to the question of the globalizing processes in culture is to detect a threat—to our language, culture, independence, identity—and to feel, therefore, that we have to put in place strong protective mechanisms. I think it would be more useful, however, if we could also be more conscious of the great possibilities and advantages these processes offer us.

Picasso or a Beer?

First published as "Na Picassa ali na pivo?" in *Delo*, 10. 9. 2001, p. 6.
Translated from Slovenian by Rawley Grau.

In my day, I thought of myself as a fanatical visitor to museums and galleries. Whenever I went to a city, I would spend the whole day, morning to evening, visiting exhibition venues and artistic monuments, without stopping for lunch or taking any real break.
In fact, I sometimes still do this. That's why the incident I want to write about surprised even me.
A few years ago I took part in an excursion to Munich. One of the main goals of the trip was to visit a rather large exhibition of Picasso's later works, which was then on display there. But when we got off the bus, I didn't head for the exhibition site but instead, almost automatically, went in a completely different direction. Something had suddenly become more important to me than seeing the works of art for which I had joined the excursion in the first place.

There is a tavern in Munich I have been to many times (and I still go there whenever I'm in the city).

There's really nothing especially remarkable about it: no famous history, no brilliant or quaint decor, no particularly splendid menu. It's just an ordinary Munich tavern, not unlike many others in the town. But for me, ever since my first accidental visit, it has been a special place. I simply feel incredibly comfortable there. I feel like I can completely relax in this atmosphere and forget all my worries, that I somehow become lighter.

So, without thinking it over too much, I went there, sat there for an hour or so, and enjoyed this extraordinary atmosphere once more. Later, as I was going toward the city center—now, finally, truly on my way to the Picasso show— I wondered at myself. How was it possible that, in deciding whether to go to a tavern or an important exhibition, I had given priority to the former? How could something that was essentially banal win out over something that carried such intellectual, spiritual, and aesthetic weight? I then asked myself the question: If I knew that I could only do one of these two things, which would I choose? I have to admit that even now it's hard for me to answer this. Maybe my sense of the importance of the exhibition would prevail, or maybe it would be my desire to return to a place where I feel truly comfortable.

But how is it possible that such a dilemma arises at all? How is it possible that, for the sake of an hour in a pleasant tavern, I could give up the joy of looking at art? I often revisit these questions in my mind and try to answer them. For now, matters seem to me to be more or less like this: Because I have the feeling that this particular tavern possesses the kind of pleasing and relaxing atmosphere I enjoy, I think of going there as a special experience. Going to an exhibition or looking at works of art individually is also a special experience. So I am not comparing a tavern to Picasso but, rather, two personal experiences in which I find almost equally great enjoyment.

This does not mean that sitting in a tavern is equivalent to a work of art. I experience the seemingly special atmosphere of the tavern as something immediate and irrational, as something sensual, so to speak. Certain artworks, too, can offer the viewer the possibility of a uniquely intense, sensual experience. But it is far from being true that the important artworks necessarily have this effect on the viewer, or that a work that does have such a pronounced immediate effect is genuinely good. Quite the reverse: some critics were once extremely skeptical of the immediate effect of the work and the possibility of unreflected pleasure in it, since these were considered features of kitsch. A great work was supposed to impede and avert immediate pleasure, so that, when the viewer had pondered and studied the work, the pleasure would be even greater.

The good mood I feel in the tavern is purely subjective and accidental. It is important only for me. Most people, perhaps, are indifferent to this place or might even find its atmosphere annoying. If we were to rate the tavern "objectively," by established criteria (which would also include "atmosphere"), it would very likely get only a passing grade. But this has little or nothing to do with my experience of it. The effect of a work of art, however, is not accidental; rather, the work has been constructed to achieve this effect. But what is even more important is that I cannot reduce an artwork solely to my experience of it (even if I experience it very intensely). Precisely because it is art, it is possible, and necessary, to distance ourselves from such immediacy, place the work in a certain tradition and field, compare it with other works, and make judgments about its goals, structure, and methods, including those that create its immediate effect. Thus, our idea about the artwork is created through a kind of moving back and forth between immediate experience and reflection, and this moving back and forth is what gives us our idea about the work and, with it, genuine pleasure as well.

So it's not that visiting the tavern was "objectively" equal to looking at Picasso's paintings. But in a world defined by such objective values, the individual person forms his own scale of importance, which does not always match the generally recognized value relationships. Everyone knows that Picasso was a great artist, but even so, not everyone feels like standing in front of his paintings for a long time or enjoys looking at them and analyzing them. In fact, an artist has achieved something great if you go to his show with a pleasure similar to that of going for a beer with a good friend.

APPENDIX

About the Author

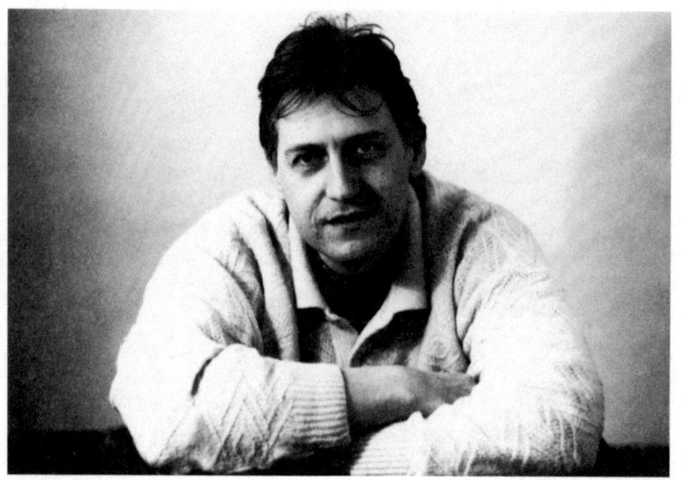

Igor Zabel, 1997

IGOR ZABEL (1958–2005) was born in Ljubljana, Slovenia. After graduating in comparative literature, art history and philosophy from the University of Ljubljana in 1982, he was for two years assistant lecturer at the Department for Comparative Literature of the Faculty of Arts, University of Ljubljana. In 1989, he received his MA from the same university. Between 1984 and 1986, he worked as a freelance writer. Starting in 1986, Igor Zabel worked as curator at the Ljubljana Museum of Modern Art, where he gained the title of senior curator and prepared a number of anthology exhibitions of Slovenian art, solo as well as thematic exhibitions: *Aspects of the Minimal. Minimal Art in Slovenia 1968–1980*, 1990; *Per Kirkeby*, 1994; *OHO–A Retrospective*, 1994; *Inexplicable Presence. The Curator's Place of Work*, 1997; *Tank! Slovene Historical Avant-Garde*, 1998 (co-curator); *2000+ Arteast Collection*, 2000 (co-curator); *The Eye and Its Truth*, 2001; *Safety and Peace! Order and Freedom!*, 2004; *Seven Sins: Ljubljana– Moscow*, 2004 (co-curator).

His curatorial work outside Slovenia includes, among others, *Disclosed Images. Selected Works of Slovenian Art of the Eighties* at the Palace of Exhibitions, Budapest, 1989; *33rd Zagreb Salon* at the Museum and Gallery Centre Zagreb, 1998; *Aspects/Positions*, Museum moderner Kunst–Stiftung Ludwig, Vienna, 1999 (member of the curatorial team); *Individual Systems* at the 50th Venice Biennale, 2003; *The Future Is Not What It Used To Be*, Galerie für Zeitgenössische Kunst, Leipzig, 2004 (co-curator).

Zabel was coordinator of *Manifesta 3*, European Biennial of Contemporary Art, in Ljubljana in 2000 and a member of the International Board of *Manifesta*. He was co-editor of *MJ–Manifesta Journal: Journal of Contemporary Curatorship* and for several years editor of the magazine of Moderna galerija Ljubljana, *M'ars*.

He is the author of two books of essays on contemporary art, and a number of essays and articles published in Slovenian and international anthologies, collected editions, catalogues and magazines. He wrote short stories and translated (into and from the Slovene language) numerous books (by Edward W. Saïd, Oscar Wilde, Amartya Kumar Sen, Immanuel Maurice Wallerstein, etc.) and texts from the field of humanities and literature.

For several years, he engaged in passing on his broad knowledge and experiences in writing and curating contemporary art to younger generations within the *World of Art–Curatorial Course for Contemporary Art* in Ljubljana.

SELECTED BIBLIOGRAPHY
1985–2005

This bibliography invites readers to additional reading of texts by Igor Zabel that are dealing with topics represented by four chapters of this book. Included are texts that were either originally written in English or later translated into English or other languages.
    This is a selection of the complete bibliography published in the Slovene collection of Igor Zabel's *Esseys II* (2008), compiled by Zoja Skušek and Jana Intihar Ferjan.

Essays in Anthologies/Collected Editions

"The Function of Subject in the Constitution of Picture after Modernism," *The Subject in Postmodernism*, international colloquium 1989, Slovenian Society of Aesthetic, Ljubljana, 1989–1990, pp. 229–244.
"The tragic playfulness of Art," *Ljubljana—mesto kulture [Ljubljana –City of Culture]*, Mestna občina Ljubljana, Evropski mesec kulture, Ljubljana, 1997, pp. 114–119.
"Vladimir Dubossarsky & Aleksander Vinogradov," p. 96; "IRWIN," p. 154; "Žiga Kariž," p. 166; "Wilhelm Sasnal," p. 288; "Miha Štrukelj," p. 314, *Vitamin P. New Perspectives in Painting*, Phaidon Press, London, 2002.
"Stane Kregar, Janez Bernik, Gabrijel Stupica; Marij Pregelj, Zoran Mušić, OHO, Tugo šušnik; Marko Peljhan, VSSD; Marjetica Potrč, IRWIN, NSK," *East Art Map– A (Re)Construction of the History of Art in Eastern Europe*, New Moment, 2002, pp. 16; 34; 60; 62.
"10 Curators in Conversation," *Cream 3. Contemporary Art in Culture. 10 Curators. 100 Contemporary Artists. 10 Source Artists, Contemporary Art in Culture*, Phaidon Press, London, 2003, pp. 9; 14–15; 16–17.
100 Contemporary Artists: "Pavel Althamer," pp. 36–38; "Valery Koshljakov," pp. 168–171; "Katarzyna Kozyra," pp. 172–175; "Luisa Lambri," pp. 176–179; "Dorit Margreiter," pp. 216–219; "Olaf Nicolai," pp. 252–255; "Roman Ondák," pp. 264–267; "Tadej Pogačar," pp. 296–300; "Ene-Liis Semper," pp. 352–355; "Slaven Tolj," pp. 376–379, *ibid.*
"10 Source Artists: OHO Group," *ibid.*, pp. 434–435.
"Like to Like: IRWIN and OHO," *45. Oktobarski salon– International Conference Continental Breakfast–Symbolic and Personal Geographies of Contemporary Art*, Kulturni centar, Belgrade, 2004.
"Safety and Peace! Order and Freedom / Episode 5," *Who if not we should at least try to imagine the future of all this? 7 Episodes on (ex)changing Europe*, Artimo/Gijs Stork, Amsterdam, 2004, pp. 92–109.
"The former East and Its Identity," *ibid.*, pp. 283–288.
"Intimität und Gesellschaft. Die slowenische Kunst und der Osten," *Zurück aus der Zukunft. Osteuropäische Kulturen im Zeitalter des Postkommunismus*, Suhrkamp, Frankfurt am Main, 2005, pp. 472–507.
"Individual Systems. A transcript of the lecture," *Ready 2 Change*, Maska; Zavod P.A.R.A.S.I.T.E., Ljubljana, 2005, pp. 173–194.

Articles in Exhibition Catalogs

1985–1990

"Collage and Palimpsest in the Work of Emerik Bernard," *Emerik Bernard: dela [Works] 1968–1988*, Moderna galerija, Ljubljana; Obalne galerije, Piran, 1988, pp. 9–42.
"The Disappointed Look. Some Thoughts on 'Trebuh' (Belly), a sculpture by Marjetica Potrč," *Marjetica Potrč: Sculptures*, Moderna galerija, Ljubljana, 1988, *s. p.*

"Zwischen 'Realismus' und Modernismus. Die Situation in der slowenischen Kunst 1945–1960. Stane Kregar–Marij Pregelj–Gabrijel Stupica," *Alpen Adria. Jenseits des Realismus. Figuration Abstraktion Informel 1945–1960*, Neue Galerie am Landesmuseum Joanneum, Graz, 1988, pp. 335–358.
"Art as Reality," *Marko Pogačnik. Landscape sculpture: 1986–1989*, Moderna galerija, Ljubljana, 1989, *s. p.*
"The Young Slovene Art of the Seventies and the Eighties. Selected Slovene Works of Art of the Eighties," *Disclosed Images*, Moderna galerija, Ljubljana, 1989, *s. p.*
"On Tadej Pogačar's painting or On cartography," *Tadej Pogačar, Slike/Paintings*, Umetnostna galerija, Maribor; Kulturna skupnost/Galerija Miklova hiša, Ribnica; ZDSLU–Zveza društev slovenskih likovnih umetnikov, Ljubljana, 1990, pp. 3–4.
"Work-in-Progress," *Rene Rusjan*, Zveza društev slovenskih likovnih umetnikov, Ljubljana, 1990, *s. p.*
"Aspects of the Minimalism in Slovene Art 1968–1980," English summary, *Aspects of the Minimalism in Slovene Art 1968–1980*, Moderna galerija, Ljubljana, 1990, pp. 47–49.

1991–1995

"Über Holografie," *Neue Tendenzen in der Deutschen Holografie*, Moderna galerija, Ljubljana; Deutsche Gesellschaft für Holografie e.v., Bergkamen, 1991, pp. 16–20.
"Opalka 1965/1–∞," *Roman Opalka*, Moderna galerija, Ljubljana, 1991, *s. p.**
"'Date paintings' in 'Détails': k vprašanju pisave in časa v slikarstvu Romana Opalke in Ona Kaware," *M'ars*, vol. 3, no. 2–3, 1991, Moderna galerija, Ljubljana, pp. 65–71.*
"The Silence of Things," *Silence: Contradictory Shapes of Truth*, Moderna galerija, Ljubljana, 1992, pp. 98–102.
"The Visual Messages of Zdravko Papič. Only a Million," *Euphonies, Zdravko Papič: Retrospective Exhibition of Graphic Design, Film Art Direction and Animated Film*, Moderna galerija, Ljubljana, 1992, pp. 4–11; 12–15.
"Konstruktivistische, minimalistische und konzeptualistische Tendenzen in der slowenischen Kunst," *Identität: Differenz. Tribüne Trigon 1940–1990. Eine Topografie der Moderne. Steirischer Herbst 92*, Böhlau Verlag, Wien, Köln, Weimar, 1992, pp. 455–464.
"Models. An Essay on Kirkeby's Art," *Per Kirkeby*, Moderna galerija, Ljubljana, 1993, pp. 9–14.*
"On Slak's Painting," *Jože Slak–Doka. I do it my way*, Moderna galerija, Ljubljana, 1993, pp. 3–7.*
"Art in Slovenia in the Eighties," *La coesistenza dell'arte. Un modelo espositivo*, La Bienale di Venezia, Venice; Museum Moderner Kunst Stiftung Ludwig, Wien, 1993, pp. 80–85; 91–93.
"Pictures and places," *Places: Lewis Baltz, Jean-Marc Bustamante, Willie Doherty, Jochen Gerz, Angela Grauerbolz*, Moderna galerija. Ljubljana, 1994, *s. p.**
"OHO–From Reism to Conceptual Art," *OHO: A Retrospective*, Moderna galerija, Ljubljana, 1994, pp. 10–28.
"Notes on Lenárdič's installation 2×2, 98280 kW; Das Bild braucht den Rollstuhl," *Zmago Lenardič*, Moderna galerija, Ljubljana, 1994, *s. p.**
"1. Die Mauer; 2. Der Garten; 3. Die Stadt," *Architektur– Skulptur. Jože Barši, Marjetica Potrč*, IFA-Institut für Auslandsbeziehungen, Stuttgart, 1995, *s. p.*
"Zur slowenischen Kunst der 80er und 90er Jahre," *Tadej Pogačar, Slowenien*, IFA-Institut für Auslandsbeziehungen, Berlin, 1995, pp. 6–11.
"Slovene Art of the Nineties–Some Remarks," *P.A.R.A.S.I.T.E. Museum*, Moderna galerija, Ljubljana, 1995, *s. p.*
"Specus spec(tac)ulorum," *V.S.S.D. Slovene Pavilion*, XLVI Esposizione Internazionale d'arte La Biennale di Venezia, Moderna galerija, Ljubljana, 1995, pp. 15–36.*
Zdenko Huzjan: A Retrospective, Moderna galerija, Ljubljana, 1995.

"On Pictures. Combinations. Interpretations and
Nothing," *John Baldessari. This not That*, Cornerhouse,
Manchester, 1995, pp. 28–34.*
"Landscapes, or A Shift of Perspective", *Jean–Marc
Bustamante*, Moderna galerija, Ljubljana, 1995, *s. p.*
"The Displaced Places," *House in Time*, Moderna galerija,
Ljubljana, 1995, pp. 9–22.*

1996–2000

"Interiors of Planit: Synopsis for a Guided Tour," *IRWIN. Interior
of the Planit*, Museum of Modern Art, Ljubljana; Ludwig
Museum, Budapest, 1996, *s. p.*
"Sets, Stories and the Unexperienced. Notes on Still
Non-Existent Sculptural Work," *Mirko Bratuša*, Obalne
galerije, Piran, 1996, *s. p.**
"A Dialectic of the Material and the Sublime," *Tugo Šušnik:
A Retrospective*, Moderna galerija, Ljubljana, 1996, pp. 23–26.
"Museum for Sarajevo. Statement," *For the Museum of Contempo-
rary Art Sarajevo 2000*, Moderna galerija, Ljubljana, 1996, *s. p.*
"Actualization of the Premodern Art in the work of
Bogoslav Kalaš," *Bogoslav Kalaš*, Mestna galerija, Ljubljana,
1996, *s. p.*
"The Gardener, or a Question With Many Answers,"
*There are Many Answers to the Question About Why to Grow
Vegetables, Jože Barši*, Biennale di Venezia, 47. Esposizione
internazionale d'arte, Slovene Pavilion, Moderna galerija,
Ljubljana, 1997, pp. 23–24; 43–45; 63–65.
"Introductory Note," *Rene Rusjan. Yesterday, for Example*, Moderna
galerija, Ljubljana, 1997, *s. p.*
"An Attempt on Music's Art," *Zoran Music Works Drawn From the
Moderna Galerija Collections*, Moderna galerija, Ljubljana,
1997, pp. 9–14.
"Signs of Divided World," *Shirin Neshat*, City of Women–Festival
of Contemporary Arts; Moderna galerija,
Ljubljana, 1997, *s. p.**
"Production of Nature. Olaf Nicolai. Nature is a Workshop,"
Annual Catalogue of the Škuc Gallery 1997, Galerija Škuc,
Ljubljana, 1997, pp. 68–74.*
"Gradski krajolik," *33. Zagrebački salon* ["City Scape,"
33rd Zagreb Salon], Zagreb, 1998, pp. 8–19.*
"Poljaki" ["Poles–People from Poland"], *Poljaki–visual communi-
cation*, IDCO–GZS, Ljubljana, 1998, pp. 18–23.*
"(Re)presenting the Difference," *Dimitry Orlac.
The Only Door*, Moderna galerija, Ljubljana, 1998, s. p.
"Dear Guest, Dear Friends of Contemporary Art!
Janja Žvegelj: Squash," *Annual Catalogue of the
Škuc Gallery 1998*, Galerija Škuc, Ljubljana, 1998, pp. 20–25.
"Found And Lost Again…," *Róza El–Hassan*, Moderna galerija,
Ljubljana, 1998, *s. p.*
"Sold Works," *Nika Špan*, Moderna galerija, Ljubljana, 1998, *s. p.*
"Slowenische Kunst seit 1945," *Aspekte/Positionen: 50 Jahre Kunst
aus Mitteleuropa 1929–1999*, Museum Moderner Kunst, Wien,
1999, vol. I, pp. 149–156.
"Marko Peljhan, 'Sky Area'. The Immaterial World of Signals,"
Connected Cities–Processes of Art in the Urban Network, Hatje
Cantz Verlag, Ostfildern, 1999, pp. 154–162.

2000–2005

"[without title]," *Dušan Kirbiš: Retrospective*, Zavod za kulturne
prireditve, Galerija sodobnih umetnosti, Celje, 2000, pp.
5–11.
L'art dans les rivalités Est-Ouest," *L'autre moitié de l'Europe*,
Galerie national du Jeu de Paume, Paris, 2000, pp. 33–47.
"[without title]," *2000+ Arteast Collection. The Art of Eastern Europe
in Dialogue with the West. From the 1960s to the Present.
Exhibition of Works for an Emerging Collection*, Moderna
galerija, Ljubljana, 2000, pp. 27–32.

"Detail und Wirklichkeit," *Vito Oražem, Fotoessay in Fünf Akten.
Erster Akt 2000-2001*, Pokrajinski muzej Kočevje, 2001,
pp. 18–21.*
"The Eye and Its Truth," *The Eye and Its Truth. Spectacle and Reality
in Slovene Art 1984–2001*, Moderna galerija, Ljubljana, 2001,
s. p.
"As If You Would Shoot a Marble," *Jože Barši. House*,
Moderna galerija, Ljubljana, 2001, *s. p.*
"The Development of Modernism after 1945," *Selected works
of Slovene Artists from the Museum of Modern Art Collections:
1950–2000. Permanent Display*, Moderna galerija, Ljubljana,
2002, pp. 12–15.
"Abstract Art, Modernist Figurative Art and Art Informel," *ibid.*,
pp. 33–38.
"From the Mid-1960s to the Mid-1980s: From the Neo Avant-
Garde to the New Image," *ibid.*, pp. 68–73.
"Contemporary Slovene Art Since the 1990s," *ibid.*,
pp. 102–105.
"Slovene Art in the 1990's," *The Art of the Balkan Countries*, State
Museum of Contemporary Art Thessaloniki, 2002, pp.
175–187.
"Tadej Pogačar," *Život umjetnosti*, no. 67–68, 2002, Zagreb, pp.
44–63.*
"Edges and Thickening of Emptyness," *Alen Ožbolt. Rob, igra solz,
dvoje še*, Moderna galerija, Ljubljana, 2002. *s. p.**
"Unclear Aspects of the Visual," *Sergej Kapus. Paintings*, Moderna
galerija, Ljubljana, 2002, pp. 4–14.
"Individual Systems," *La Biennale di Venezia: 50th International Art
Exhibition. Dreams and Conflicts. The Dictatorship of the Viewer*,
Marsilio Editori s.p.a., Edizione La Biennale di Venzia,
Venice, 2003, pp. 149–153.
"The Bomb in the Painting," *Žiga Kariž Terror=Décor. Art Now.
La bienale di Venezia: 50esima esposizione internazionale d'arte.
The Slovenian Pavilion*, Zavod K6/4, Galerija Kapelica,
Ljubljana, 2003, pp. 30–37.
"General Equivalent," *Mladen Stilinović: Pain*, Museum
of Contemporary Art, Zagreb, 2003, pp. 5–8.
"Borders and Limits," *Dušan Kirbiš. Borders and Limits*, Moderna
galerija, Ljubljana; Galerija Miklova hiša, Ribnica, 2004,
s. p.
"[untitled]," *Ivo Mršnik, 1000 & 1*, Moderna galerija,
Ljubljana, 2004, *s. p.**
"Seven Sins: Ljubljana–Moscow," Moderna galerija, Ljubljana,
2004, pp. 5–10 (with Zdenka Badovinac, Viktor Misiano).
"OHO," *Collective Creativity*, Kunsthalle Fridericianum, Kassel;
Siemens Arts Program, München; Revolver–Archiv für
aktuelle Kunst, Frankfurt, 2005, pp. 62–63.
"Towards Zero Gravity. The Meaning of Gravity and
Dematerialisation in Modern and Contemporary Slovene
Art," *Towards Zero Gravity: Gravity in Slovene Fine Art in the
20th and 21st Centuries*, Moderna galerija, Ljubljana, 2005,
pp. 50–100.

Essays, Reviews and Articles in Magazines, Journals and
Periodicals

"City panoramas. Interview with Marjetica Potrč," *M'ars*, vol. 5,
no. 3–4, 1993, Ljubljana, pp. 32–33.
"U3: 2nd Triennale of Contemporary Slovene Art," *M'ars*, vol. 9,
no. 2, 1997, Ljubljana, pp. 23–38 (with Peter Weibel).
"Those who are able to quickly change concepts survive: a
conversation with Jože Barši," *ibid.*, pp. 2–22.
"The Immaterial World of Signals," *Index*, 2.98, no. 22, 1998,
Stockholm, pp. 23–29.
"An animal which loves interpretations: interview with Oleg
Kulik," *M'ars*, vol. 10, no. 1–2, 1998, Ljubljana, pp. 3–13.
"Art and the war in Bosnia: call for papers," *M'ars*, vol. 11, no.
1–2, 1999, Ljubljana, pp. 23–28 (with Borut Vogelnik).
"Living with Genocide: Art and the War in Bosnia," panel

discussion with Igor Zabel, Marina Abramović, Zdenka
Badovinac, Dunja Blaževič, David Elliott, Jürgen Harten,
Miran Mohar, Borut Vogelnik, Tomaž Mastnak, Alexandre
Melo, Silva Mežnarić, Viktor Misiano, Edin Numankadić,
Michelangelo Pistoletto, Peter Weibel, Denys
Zacharopoulos, *M'ars*, vol. 11, no. 1–2, 1999, Ljubljana,
pp. 29–83.
"Manifesta 3," [part of: "Beyond Boundaries: Rethinking
Contemporary Exhibitions" thematic block], *Art Journal*,
vol. 59, no. 1, 2000, New York, pp. 19–21.
"Women in Black," *Art Journal*, vol. 60, no. 4, 2001,
New York, pp. 16–25.
"Marko Peljhan's theatre of resistance," *Maska*, vol. 17,
no. 3–4, Spring 2002, Ljubljana, pp. 29–32; 91–93.
"From the editors: Biennials," *MJ–Manifesta Journal*, no. 2, Winter
2003/Spring 2004, Ljubljana; Amsterdam, pp. 4–5.
"The power of proposing things, of taking risks: a
conversation with Francesco Bonami," *MJ–Manifesta
Journal*, no. 2, Winter 2003/Spring 2004, Ljubljana;
Amsterdam, pp. 88–99.
"Exhibition as a dream: from the editors," *MJ–Manifesta Journal:
journal of contemporary curatorship*, no. 3, Spring/
Summer 2004, Ljubljana; Amsterdam, pp. 4–7 (with
Viktor Misiano).
"The Strangeness of Home. Dressing and Redressing in Public
Squares. Marija Mojca Pungerčar interviewed by Igor
Zabel," *PAJ:A Journal of Performance & Art 76*, vol. 26,
no. 1, Jan 2004, pp. 40–50.

Interviews with Igor Zabel:

"Perhaps it's the destiny of utopia that they are no longer where
we expect them: an interview with Kathrin Rhomberg,"
MJ–Manifesta Journal: journal of contemporary curatorship, no. 3,
Spring/Summer 2004, Ljubljana, pp. 58–63.
"What Is to Be Done with 'Balkan Art': Interview with Igor
Zabel," *PlatformaSCCA*, no. 4, 2005, Ljubljana, pp. 26–30.

*   Texts marked with an asterisk were initially selected by
Zoja Skušek and Barbara Borčić to be included in this
book; in the end, however, due to space limitations, these
texts could not be included in this volume.

Imprint

Edited by Igor Španjol

EDITORIAL COORDINATION
Renata Catambas, Urška Jurman, Dunja Kukovec

COPY-EDITING
Karin Prätorius

DESIGN CONCEPT
Gavillet & Rust, Geneva

DESIGN
Nicolas Eigenheer, Vera Kaspar

TYPEFACE
Genath (www.optimo.ch)

PRINT AND BINDING
Musumeci S.p.A., Quart (Aosta)

ACKNOWLEGMENTS
Barbara Borčić, Jana Intihar Ferjan, Zoja Skušek

PHOTO CREDITS
pp. 20, 154, 230 Photo: Matija Pavlovec. Courtesy: Moderna galerija; pp. 32, 46, 68, 110, 126, 168, 236, 248, 262 Photo: Dejan Habicht. Courtesy: Moderna galerija; p. 60 Courtesy: NK; p. 220 Photo: Dejan Habicht. Courtesy: Moderna galerija and the artist; p. 80 Video: Siniša Lopojda. Courtesy: Moderna galerija; p. 146 Photo: Miha Škrlep. Courtesy: Tadej Pogačar; p. 178 Courtesy: Moderna galerija; p. 192 Photo: Marko Peljhan. Courtesy: Marko Peljhan; p. 200 Photo: Lado Mlekuž; Matija Pavlovec. Courtesy: Moderna galerija; p. 292 Photo: Tihomir Piner. Courtesy: Moderna galerija

PUBLISHED BY
JRP | Ringier
Limmatstrasse 270
CH–8005 Zurich
T +41 43 311 27 50
E info@jrp-ringier.com
www.jrp-ringier.com

IN CO-EDITION WITH
Les presses du réel
35, rue Colson
F–21000 Dijon
T +33 3 80 30 75 23
E info@lespressesdureel.com
www.lespressesdureel.com

AND
ERSTE Foundation
Friedrichstraße 10, 4th floor
A–1010 Vienna
T +43 50 100 15100
E office@erstestiftung.org
www.erstestiftung.org

Moderna galerija
Tomšičeva 14
SI–1000 Ljubljana
T +386 (0)1 2416 800
E info@mg-lj.si
www.mg-lj.si

Igor Zabel Association for Culture and Theory
Celovška 161
SI–1000 Ljubljana
T +386 (0) 40 654 876
E info@igorzabelassociation.org
www.igorzabelassociation.org

ISBN 978-3-03764-238-2 (JRP | Ringier)
ISBN 978-2-84066-573-1 (Les presses du réel)

Distribution

JRP|Ringier publications are available internationally
at selected bookstores and from the following distribution
partners:

GERMANY AND AUSTRIA
Vice Versa Vertrieb, Immanuelkirchstrasse 12, D-10405 Berlin,
info@vice-versa-vertrieb.de, www.vice-versa-vertrieb.de

FRANCE
Les presses du réel, 35 rue Colson, F-21000 Dijon,
info@lespressesdureel.com, www.lespressesdureel.com

SWITZERLAND
AVA Verlagsauslieferung AG, Centralweg 16,
CH-8910 Affoltern a.A., verlagsservice@ava.ch, www.ava.ch

UK AND OTHER EUROPEAN COUNTRIES
Cornerhouse Publications, 70 Oxford Street,
UK-Manchester M1 5NH, publications@cornerhouse.org,
www.cornerhouse.org/books

USA, CANADA, ASIA, AND AUSTRALIA
ARTBOOK | D.A.P. , 155 Sixth Avenue,
2nd Floor, USA-New York, NY 10013, dap@dapinc.com,
www.artbook.com

For a list of our partner bookshops or for any general
questions, please contact JRP|Ringier directly at
info@jrp-ringier.com, or visit our homepage
www.jrp-ringier.com for further information about
our program.

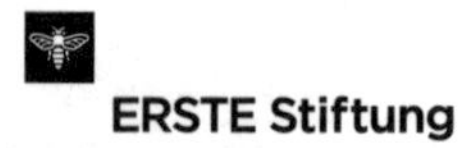
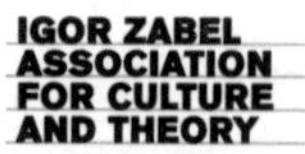
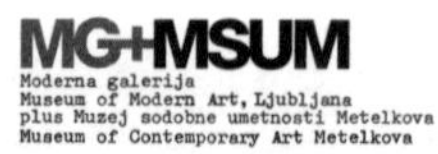

Documents Series 8: Igor Zabel

This book is the eighth volume
in the "Documents" series,
dedicated to critics' writings.

The series is directed by
Lionel Bovier and Xavier Douroux.

Also available

Documents Series (in English)

Saul Anton, *Warhol's Dream*
ISBN 978-3-905770-35-3 (JRP | Ringier)
ISBN 978-2-84066-200-6 (Les presses du réel)

Dorothea von Hantelmann, *How to Do Things with Art*
ISBN 978-3-03764-104-0 (JRP | Ringier)
ISBN 978-2-84066-361-4 (Les presses du réel)

Christian Höller, *Time Action Vision*
ISBN 978-3-03764-124-8 (JRP | Ringier)
ISBN 978-2-84066-396-6 (Les presses du réel)

Bob Nickas, *Theft Is Vision*
ISBN 978-3-905770-36-0 (JRP | Ringier)
ISBN 978-2-84066-206-8 (Les presses du réel)

Hans Ulrich Obrist, *A Brief History of Curating*
ISBN 978-3-905829-55-6 (JRP | Ringier)
ISBN 978-2-84066-287-7 (Les presses du réel)

Gabriele Detterer & Maurizio Nannucci, *Artist-Run Spaces*
ISBN 978-3-03764-191-0 (JRP | Ringier)
ISBN 978-2-84066-512-0 (Les presses du réel)

Raymond Bellour, *Between-the-Images*
ISBN 978-3-03764-144-6 (JRP | Ringier)
ISBN 978-2-84066-513-7 (Les presses du réel)